A TRUE LIKENESS

A TRUE LIKENESS

LESBIAN AND GAY WRITING TODAY

Edited and with Introduction and Prefaces
by Felice Picano

New York City

A TRUE LIKENESS

Also available from
The Sea Horse Press

The Deformity Lover and Other Poems—Felice Picano
    isbn. 0-93322-00-3 $3.95
Two Plays by Doric Wilson: The West Street Gang and A Perfect Relationship
    isbn. 0-933322-01-1 $5.95
Idols: Poems by Dennis Cooper
    isbn. 933322-02-X $4.95

Price plus $1.00 Handling to—Sea Horse Press
Box 509 Village Sta.
N.Y.C. 10014

Copyright © 1980 The Sea Horse Press
Library of Congress Cataloguing in Publication Data----
ISBN 0-933322-04-6
ISBN 0-933322-05-4

A True Likeness
    1. Homosexuality—Literary collections
    2. American Literature—20th Century
    3. Canadian Literature—20th Century
    I. Picano, Felice 1944—

PS509. H57T7 810'.8'0353   80-24894

BELEW, SUSAN: "Catalyst," "Sidewalk Cafe," "Bad Girl of the Drive-In," "Selfish Tendencies," "Flesh Monger," "Restoration," "Jungle II," "Cat Claws," and "# 1 Local" are reprinted permission of Susan Belew. BORAWSKI, WALTA: "Power of One," Live Free or Die," "Some of Us are Stretched Tighter Than Others," "Indexing Judy Garland's Life: A Found Poem, from Gerald Frank's Bio", "Perversity," "Circles Might Lead to Rectangular Beds, Straight Lines Don't," "I Am Not Billie Holiday, But I Look Good in My Dress & My Running Shoes," "Dead Languages," "Some of Us Wear Pink Triangles," "Pygmalion, L.I.," and "Surprising Kisses For Malcolm," reprinted by permission of Walta Borawski. BRACKER, JON: "The Opposites of Straight," "Love Poem," I Like That Brown One a Lot," "One Night Stand," "After Being Talked to By a Friend," "Letter to My Ex-Therapist," "Two," and "Going Home" are reprinted permission of Jon Bracker. CADY, JOSEPH: "Early Inspiration," "Graduation from the Poorhouse: In 1952," "Coming Out," "Starting 1973: What to Do Now that Peace Has Been Announced," "Destruction," "After Hearing Heterosexual Poets in October 1974: What It Seems Like to Write a Male Homosexual Love Poem Now," "Despair of Men", "Back and Forth," and "In and Out," are reprinted by permission of Joe Cady. DE LYNN, JANE: "The Designer and The Typesetter" is reprinted permission of Jane De Lynn and The Jane Rotrosen Literary Agency. DIAMOND, DAN: "True Gesture: Dreampoems" are reprinted by permission of Dan Diamond. FERRO, ROBERT: "The Aviary" is reprinted by permission of Robert Ferro and Diane Cleaver Literary Agency. GRAHN, JUDY: "In the Place Where," "If You Lose your lover," "The harvest spider," A History of Lesbianism," "The many minnows," "A Geology Lession," "The most blonde Woman," "Carol and," "Love rode," and "My name is Judith, meaning" are reprinted by grateful permission of St. Martins Press, N.Y. "Natural Lovers" is reprinted by permission from Judy Grahn © 1980. GRUMLEY, MICHAEL: "Public Monuments" is reprinted by permission of Michael Grumley and Diane Cleaver Literary Agency. HALL, RICHARD: "A Touch of Fat," is reprinted by permission of Richard Hall. HARVEY, KERRIC: "St. Valentine's Day," Birds Are the Best Things," "At the Start," "Virginia Beach Blues," "The Passion Flower," "Prom Night Was A Comedy in One Legal Act But Four Nasty Scenes," "Blind Man's Bluff," "Christmas Issue Poetry," and "Today" are reprinted by permission of Kerric Harvey. HERRON, ROBERT: "Mortiz Goes To A Garden Party" is reprinted by permission of Robert Herron. HOLLERAN, ANDREW: "Someone is Crying in the Chateau de Berne," is reprinted by permission of Eric Garber; Andrew Holleran. IOZIA, JOHN: "Fag Art" "Loneliness," "Another Version Concerning that Virgin," "The Fourth of July, 1974," "James Dean Blues," "Concerning Two Interior Decorators," "New Season," "Art Nouveau," "Pyramids," "My integrity," "Objectivity," "Something in You," "Marijuana," "My Favorite Cuban," "Last Night at Flamingo," are reprinted by permission of John Iozia, © 1976. KIKEL, RUDY: Selections from "Local Visions" are reprinted by permission of Rudy Kikel, © 1979. KRAVITZ, PHILIP: "Fisch" is reprinted by permission of Philip Kravitz. KURAS, PAT: "Hydra," "Crush," "Love Making As A Holy Woman/Live-Saving Art," "Homecoming" "This Poem is Hot," "Escapist," and "Antaeus" are reprinted by permission of Pat Kuras. LARKIN, JOAN: "Cautionary," "Housework," "Story" Work Song," "Thirds," "Direct Address," "Some Unsaid Things," and "Stop" are reprinted by permission of Joan Larkin, and The Out and Out Press, Brooklyn, N.Y. © 1975. MATHEWSON, JOSEPH: "Canned Soup" is reprinted by permission of Joseph Mathewson, © 1980. NOLL, BINK: "Signification of the Penis," is reprinted by permission of Bink Noll, © 1979. ORTLEB, CHUCK: "Gilbert and Lucien, France, 1944 or 1974," "Chaminade, An All-Male Prep School, 1965," "To All the Doctors," "Primal Liberation," "An Affair," "The Reconciliation," "Men," and "Militerotics" are reprinted by permission of Charles Ortleb. POWELL, SHIRLEY: "Solitaries," is reprinted by permission of Shirley Powell and the Jane Rotrosen Literary Agency. RILEY, BEAU: "Accidental Rennaissance," and "Cruise Ballet" are reprinted by permission of Beau Riley, © 1979, © 1980. RULE, JANE: "The Middle Children" is reprinted by permission of Jane Rule and the Georges Borchardt Literary Agency, © 1980 N.Y. SCHUYLER, JAMES: "Steaming Ties," "Watching You," and "Letter Poem #3," are reprinted by permission of James Schuyler and Maxine Groffsky Literary Agency, © 1974. SHURIN, AARON: "Recurring," "Amy Comes Out," "Avowal/Voices," "Mister Harp/Hymn," "Conversions/Winter Solstice," Raving #16" and "Raving #26:Rotations" are reprinted by permission of Aaron Shurin, © 1980. SISLEY, EMILY: "The Novel Writers" is reprinted by permission of Emily Sisley and The Mosaic Press, Tucson, Ariz. © 1980. STOCKWELL, NANCY: "An Uphill Lie" is reprinted by permission of Nancy Stockwell, © 1978. UMANS, RICHARD: "On the Door," is reprinted by permission of Richard Umans. WHITE, EDMUND: "A Man of the World" is reprinted by permission of Edmund White and Maxine Groffsky Literary Agency, N.Y.C. WHITMORE, GEORGE: "Legacy" is reprinted by permission of George Whitmore. YOUNG, IAN: "The One Time Tom Saw Bill On the Street," "A Nosegay for Jamie," "First Snow," "A Fallen Angel Answering to the Name of Joe," "Straw Man's Blues," "Dracula Dies a Thousand Deaths," "Absence Makes the Heart Grow Fonder," "A Young Poet Sits in Bed with a Cold," "Would I?" "Standing and Kneeling Figures," and "Photography" are reprinted by permission of Ian Young.

CONTENTS

Introduction: *Felice Picano* ix

FICTION
A Man of the World: *Edmund White* 1
The Middle Children: *Jane Rule* 21
Accidental Renaissance 28
Cruise Ballet: *Beau Riley* 31
An Uphill Lie: *Nancy Stockwell* 35
Margot's Novel: *Emily Sisley* 46
Someone is Crying in the Chateau De Berne:
   Andrew Holleran 65
The Designer and the Typesetter: *Jane De Lynn* 81
Moritz Goes to A Garden Party: *Robert Herron* 88
Solitaries: *Shirley Powell* 109
Fisch: *Philip Kravitz* 115
Public Monuments: *Michael Grumley* 123
On the Door: *Richard Umans* 135
The Aviary: *Robert Ferro* 148
A Touch of Fat: *Richard Hall* 160

POETRY
James Schuyler 175
Joan Larkin 179
Joe Cady 187
Chuck Ortleb 195
Judy Grahn 208
Walta Borawski 216
Jon Bracker 228
Kerric Harvey 235
Dan Diamond 242
Rudy Kikel 254
Pat Kuras 261
Bink Noll 265
Ian Young 274
Susan Belew 288
Aaron Shurin 294
John Iozia 300

DRAMA
Legacy: *George Whitmore* 309
Canned Soup: *Joseph Mathewson* 325

The Editor 356

A TRUE LIKENESS: INTRODUCTION

by Felice Picano

Not too long go, Harrison Salisbury, in a lead article in the Sunday New York Times Book Review declared that our contemporary literature was moribund and even trivial. He pointed to the current Soviet writers, Solzenitsyn, Nadezhda Mandelstam, Joseph Brodsky among others, as authors who had taken great risks to bear witness to the horrors of their time and place, and to publish what they had seen and experienced. With nothing like the granitic Soviet system to dissent from, American writers lacked the same great ethical conflict, and a shared focus of resistance. Explaining—in Salisbury's mind at least—why they weren't producing great literature.

Whether or not one could agree with Salisbury's premise, he was certainly wrong on one count—we do not lack an American dissent movement. Proponents of homosexual liberation are clearly as dissenting as Solzhenitsyn, their purpose as strong, their claim and conflict as ethical. Nor, unlike he and other Russian writers, do they lack a *Samidzat,* an underground transmission of literature. This volume is such an underground book, produced and published by a small American press devoted to the idea that people want to and should be able to read literature written by talented lesbians and gay men.

True, this book has a glossy cover, handsome jacket art, good printing, perfect binding: it could have come from a dozen or more small or university press offices in the country. It has been openly advertised in magazines and newspapers, not all of them directed at only the lesbian/gay audience. It will probably be reviewed in some of these periodicals too. How could it differ more from the ragged-edged, typescript copies of *Gulag Archipelago,* secreted in a hat box or specially installed alcove in the floorboards, against the awful possibility of the censor's or KGB's knock on the door? This is a free country. We have constitutional rights to freedom of the press. How can there be an underground dissidence movement: never mind a literary underground?

Easily. By ignoring it; by letting it happen, and allowing silence to shroud it; by belittling the movement in its size and seriousness; by adumbrating social, political, religious, and even scientific reasons for why it *can't* exist—and then saying it *doesn't* exist.

Until only a few years ago, the word "homosexual" was not printed at all in many periodicals, even in the newspapers of the largest and supposedly most sophisticated cities in the nation. The more conservative media still have not accepted the term "Gay", not to mention "Gay Liberation." This not mere playing around with semantics: it is refusing to accept our self-definition, and thus our very existence. Of course, homosexuals are reported and photographed protesting, memorializing, mourning, rioting, parading and celebrating in large (though seldom correctly reported) numbers. At times, these reports are televised, and photos are placed in the metropolitan pages of newspapers. But the reason for the riots or parades are seldom if ever alluded to. You see how easily we can be ignored.

Those media sources that have reported on us, have done so with a mixed palette, at best: and seldom in political terms; except of course when they are politically motivated against us. No, mostly we're given the psych-socio treatment. A new sex study, say, is published (always terribly prestigious, these reports, in origin), and it says that we have this or that character trait, behavioral mode, social interaction. We are not always frowned upon—for these are social scientists, remember, supposedly unbiased. So perhaps we do have more and more meaningful sex than most heterosexuals; or more alcoholism and origins in broken homes. Cover stories elaborate and announce every revelation about us. Other reports follow, dealing perhaps with urban gentrification—a strongly gay identified movement. We are perceived as a problem, a source of interest and curiosity, often a market, sometimes merely a fad, often simply as a phenomenon that produces copy and refuses to go away.

It is of course this Jekyll/Hyde presentation of gay and lesbian life in America today, which explains the common man/woman in the street's continuing mystery as to who and why we are. Closer to their lives, it also explains why they are baffled when certain cultural phenomena and events periodically sweep over and into their lives. When eleven million adolescents sing along with the song "Y.M.C.A." a hit made possibly only by the peculiar gay male sensibilities of the Villiage People, one is afraid to ask the question, do these adolescents know what they're singing, *why* they're going to have more fun at the Y? Do their parents? For that matter, do their parents know why it is that they are suddenly trying out various experimental sexual positions, couplings, and gadgets; and who made them popular, even available? When they watch a prime time TV spectacular with all-color singing dancing renditions of locker rooms and discotheques and sordid streetcorner night life, do they know what the references are being made to? When they purchase and wear much of the new chic casual clothing, do they know on which boulevard in which community on Fire Island it was first premiered, last summer?

It's safe to assume not. Yet, anyone, gay or straight, who has ever entered for even a few hours into a predominantly lesbian or gay male milieu has been immediately struck by a fully blown, variable and multi-leveled culture: from which much cultural and social patterns seen elsewhere first emanated and were developed. The semiology of this gay/lesbian milieu may be different—the iconography certainly differs—but never so far as to be alien, or in fact unapproachable. The people may be wearing different clothing, or kissing their own sex, but they still act like people—for better or worse. Institutions certainly exist similar to those they are familiar with in their own life—clubs, theaters, libraries, supermarkets, clothing stores, bars, cabarets, political groups, restaurants, neighborhoods, resorts. The fact that these are seldom different from what they previously know makes the emphasis on different coding and signs more understandable: it is a way of highlighting whatever differences really do exist.

Lesbian and gay life today is not a reflective imitation of heterosexual life: it is an entire slight shifting of perspective: and a resultant restructuring of certain social and personal relationships and ideals. Those elements most noticeable and disturbing to outsiders—say Sado-Masochism and cross dressing—are usually as noticeable and disturbing to most gays and lesbians, who have struggled to understand them. But this idea is already old-hat. *Newsweek* or some other influential journal has already moved on to new copy—the growing gay and lesbian middle class for example—mobile, financially well-heeled, so attractive and tasteful they appear to fall in love based on how beautifully they'll couple for photographers.

If it is easy to deny gay culture exists, it's a cinch to do so for one of its more important and persevering adjuncts—lesbian and gay literature. So it generally follows that there really are no lesbian poems or gay novels: there are poems written from a lesbian point of view, or novels written about male homosexual subjects.

This bizarre idea persists, despite the recent attention given to such books in the exalted pages of the New York Times Book Review Section, Chicago Tribune, and Washington Post Book World. (Although the staunchly liberal New York Review of Books still hasn't sullied its pages with even mentioning them!) In the past two years, such novels as *Ruby Fruit Jungle, Dancer From the Dance, Chamber Music, Six of One, Faggots, Cold Hands, The Lure, Nocturnes for the King of Naples* and *Just Above my Head* have recieved reviews establishing them—at least—as books of the current times, worthy of usually misconstrued critical attention. One has to consider this a real breakthrough, considering that Jonathan Katz's pathbreaking *Gay American History*, 1976, didn't receive any attention at all: and it has to be considered the basic source and text on gay history. Even so, the books mentioned above are the current "big books" of gay and lesbian literature today. And after all, let's not forget, the editors and reviewers can always claim they're only following a publishing fad.

The real world of lesbian and gay literature goes mostly unreported, except in gay, lesbian and sometimes socialist and feminist newspapers and magazines; occasionally on special cable-TV, or alternate or university radio stations. The extent to which these journals and other media reach the average lesbian/gay male in the streets is appalingly low, despite years of publication. Many lesbians and gay men—like the rest of the population—do not read. Or if they do, don't read much. Or if they do, don't only read gay books, even if they are well read in other areas. There are a variety of reasons for this, and of them, I'm prone to quote Samuel Johnson's line to Mrs. Thrale as the most basic and all-encompassing reason of all: "Ignorance, Madam. Ignorance!" Ignorance, that these books and magazines exist; ignorance often of what is to be found in them—what a variety of ideas, personalities, entertainment, etc; and often ignorance in the sense that many lesbians and gay men feel that nothing written only for them can be of more than limited interest, or of high quality.

I believe this ignorance will slowly begin to dissipate as communication between lesbian and gay authors and their audience builds. Sustained interest in authors, their works and their ideas is of the greatest importance. If you've read a book you've liked, and that author has an interview, an article, a poem, review or short story printed in some magazine or newspaper, you will be tempted to buy that magazine and to follow other writers in its pages.

It is even more pressing that non gays read this literature too. Not only for the obvious reason that by doing so they will see we are not all that different, not so threatening, and so eliminate some of the bigotry that grows out of unreasoning fear. No, I think it will help gay and lesbian readers approach their literature more easily. If you live in New York or San Francisco it's easy enough to dip into your local bookstore and ask for the new Armistead Maupin or Rita Mae Brown book. It's near impossible in Little Rock, Arkansas. This explains why the Gay Caucus at the most recent American Booksellers Association provided a listing, a sort of basic library, which each bookseller could use to build up a lesbian/gay section in each shop. It also explains why many gay and lesbian authors are seeking mass market outlets for their work. For many readers in even the largest cities, going into a bookstore to buy a gay or lesbian book can be a difficult experience. If, however, your heterosexual sister in law has ordered one from her bookclub, or picked one up at her supermarket counter, it raises the chances for gays and lesbians to purchase and read those books too.

My own awareness of the real gay/lesbian world of literature and its strength began when I began writing gay-themed poetry and short stories. Where could I publish them? *The New Yorker? Esquire? Playboy?* No way! So I went to my local gay bookstore, the venerable Oscar Wilde Memorial, and found magazines that existed in as large a selection and quantity as the glossy gay magazines I could buy on my local newstand. I brought these home, read them, followed them for several issues, and discovered a whole new area of literature—for people with interests like mine, about people like me.

I also found some terrific writing, art and editorial work. Andrew Bifrost's *Mouth of the Dragon*, Winston Leyland's *Gay Sunshine* and the Boston Co-operative's *Fag Rag*, were the first I sent my work to, and with some of these I've found a lasting association. New York's *Gaysweek* began an arts and letters section that bloomed for alas too short a time under the guidance of Byrne Fone and Richard Hall. Chuck Ortleb et al. began *Christopher Street*. Then *Blueboy* and *The Alternate* began excerpting gay books. *Mandate* added poetry to its usual format of travel, fashion, entertainment and men. Newspapers seemed to appear from out of nowhere: ditto magazines: Boston's *Gay Community News*, *The San Francisco Sentinel*, and *Bay Area Reporter*, Houston's *Upfront* and *This Week in Texas*, Atlanta's *Cruise*, Milwaukee's *GPU News*, D.C.'s *Out*, Toronto's courageous and beleaguered *Body Politic* and of course *The Advocate*. All these periodicals review and discuss gay and lesbian literature. Some have interviews with and essays by authors.

There is a reason for this much interest. What a gay man or lesbian has to say about gay life is bound to be more authentic, often more insightful and usually more conceptually challenging than most heterosexual authors on the subject, no matter how superb writers they may be. It is true that many heterosexual identified women have written excellent books about gay men and lesbians—especially historical novels: Mary Renault, Iris Murdoch and Susan Hill come to mind as those who have written most convincingly. Yet it is the lesbian writer, the gay novelist who provides the truest inner picture and the concommitant ideas and emotions: whether you agree with his/her viewpoint or not. Evidently many readers have come to this conclusion, too. The most commonly reported comments in reader's fan mail to lesbian and gay authors continues to be how much they are affected by the truthful, often unflinching portrayal of some aspect of their lives.

With all the media coverage of homosexuality in recent years, the most basic questions of our lives have scarcely been touched upon—how to deal with parents, family, and early friends; how and whether to adjust to a completely ghettoized life, or how and whether to mix in with straight society; how to love and bond without imitating repressive straight structures that don't seem to be working too well for anyone; how to be an individual without having to be a twenty-four hour a day public homosexual. These are subjects many of our current authors are addressing, and why they are being read. Especially for those readers who don't live in large urban centers where gay/lesbian communities exist, the dissemination and discussion of these ideas in print and the portrayal of different ways of leading our lives has had an educational and philosophical effect that might not be recognized for decades.

Coming out—whether it is sexual, emotional, political, spiritual or artistic—is one of the commonest themes of western literature. When Don Quixote leaves his home to fight windmills, it is not terribly different from Malone in *Dancer From the Dance* leaving his limited post-Harvard life in order to join the madcap circuit of high-flying New York-Fire Island gay society. Every new group that finds an identity for itself and produces a literature, adds to this larger theme of coming out, and to literature: whether it is the coal miner's son of D.H. Lawrence or the sassy tomboy of *Ruby Fruit Jungle*.

There simply isn't any question of whether a gay book—or woman's book, or American Indian's or Black's book—is or isn't universal. No matter what the background, what the cultural differences, if it exists, is human and recognizable, and well rendered, it is *de facto* universal. Literature is perhaps the last forum in an increasingly divided and specialized world where diversity is not only welcome, it is essential, if we are not to have our art forms decline into elitist stultification.

This theme of self-knowledge—and the critique of society that always seems to accompany it—has been forced on the lesbian and gay writer by the distance from the norm of the homosexual's perspective. To my mind, that is one of its greatest strengths. All societies need to be regularly subjected to analysis and critique, otherwise they rot in a sea of smugness and self congratulation, even when none is deserved. Critics and reviewers who constantly insist that the only difference between our literature and that of the so called mainstream lies in the erotic realm, are refusing to see this corrective aspect of gay/lesbian literature. The very representation of any other kind of sexuality, social and domestic life is a critique of the norm. If those reviewers were more honest with themselves and their readers, they would admit that successful representations of bonding and love that differ from the male-female nuclear family set-up are in fact threatening to them and their lives. As perhaps they ought to be. I would prefer to think of them not so much as a threat, but as an instruction.

A literature that only pictured the best of lesbian and gay life would be a critique of society, but would also be merely propagandistic. The best of it ought to critique gay life too. This—after communication of our differences and similarities—is the second main function of our literature: self-analysis. The publication of a book such as Larry Kramer's *Faggots*, Random House, 1978, can set off a chain reaction of shocks and aftershocks, attacks and defenses, that are ultimately of value to all gays, if only because the book's exaggeration nevertheless pinpointed absurd elements of our ideas and our lives we simply cannot deny exist. Similarly, Jane De Lynn's black comedy *Some Do*, Macmillan, 1978, received a great deal of criticism from feminists and lesbians because of the nightmare creatures her characters became once they were politically radicalized. Michael Deneny's *Lovers*, Avon 1979 implicates all gay men in the failed relationship it chronicles. Edmund White's *States of Desire* is a virtual tourguide to how geography, history, climate and politics have caused certain attitudes and institutions to develop in gay life; to become eccentric and extravagant. Its analyses, and those of the above mentioned and many other not mentioned books, have in turn been critiqued by the gay and lesbian press—and now, even by the general press and public.

Many people have asked why all of a sudden is there such a emphasis on gay and lesbian literature. The answer lies of course in the growth of consciousness following the Stonewall Riots of 1969, and the emergence of gay political and business power blocs. But is it really a *new* literature? Here, answers are less clear.

The forms that gay and lesbian books have taken seem to be more or less conventional—romance, suspense thriller, mystery, *Bildungsroman*, confession, journal, farce, picaresque, moral fable, "pillow-book," melodrama—all have been done well by lesbian and gay writers. Our verse and our drama also do not seem to be terribly new or innovative in form or structure. This may be an example of how "natural" the subject matter is—at least natural to literature as it has been practiced in the last few hundred years.

What is new, however, is the underlying assumptions behind the current generation of gay writing, which begins with the undeniable reality of homosexuality with its attendant signs, symbols, codes, mores and problems. A previous generation of writers occasionally dealt with gay life; but always as a possibility, a curiosity, as the exception rather than the rule. Not until Christopher Isherwood's three books in the Sixties, and especially *A*

Single Man, was homosexuality a fact, a *given* of a book. Yet, for every author represented in this anthology, that all-pervasive fact is inseparable from the work: warp to the woof of the story or poem or play.

It is not the only reason for the arrival of gay and lesbian literature as a force that is finding a place in even the most respected journals of books and writing. The talent of the authors in the remarkable outburst of writing in the late Seventies is one factor. People wanted to read their books, had to read them and discuss them.

Then too, we owe not a little to that oddly benevolent fact that literature does not stand still but moves on—from one group to another. In this century, in this country, it has moved from the naturalists and agrarian writers of the early years, to the expatriates of the Twenties and Thirties, to the Southern writers of the Thirties and Forties, to the urban Jewish writers of the Forties and Fifties, to the Black and women writers of the Sixties and early Seventies—to today, and the gay and lesbian writers.

When Saul Bellow published his first novels in the mid-Forties, well meaning critics advised him to drop his concern with the modern urban Jewish experience: it was far too limiting to ever reach a wide audience, to be universal, they told him. Writers like Flannery O'Connor and Eudora Welty received similar advice: their writing was seen as minor and regional. Today all three are modern classics. There is no reason to doubt that many books written by gays and lesbians today will be classics in the future. Just look some time at that annus mirabilis, 1978, in terms of published work: Edmund White's *Nocturnes for the King of Naples*, Andrew Holleran's *Dancer From the Dance*, Kramer's *Faggots*, De Lynn's *Some Do*, Bertha Harris' *Lover*, Grumley's *After Midnight*, etc.

While many different schools of writers from the past continue to write today, the only group that looks at all like a literary movement is that of homosexual authors. Within a few years they have found national—even international followings. A typical gay or lesbian author's arrival in a city on a book publicizing tour is accompanied by readings, booksignings, TV and radio interviews, fans, and also by the confluence of local authors and members of the press. Many lesbian and gay authors know many other authors personally, as well as by reputation; and very few do not wish to meet others. Given the enormous size of our country, it is one sign that the movement is still small enough and intense enough to remain a movement for a while.

Another is its power to evoke cults. Rita Mae Brown and Armistead Maupin and Fran Lebowitz have fans as devoted as any in existence. Certain other books of recent vintage have more underground followings. The literary crowd is mad about Terry Andrew's *The Story of Harold*, Avon, 1975; whereas the Drummer magazine crowd is ape over *Mr. Benson* by John Preston, a ten part serialized novel that has elicited enormous response, t-shirts, and fan clubs with monthly meetings where the members act out the s/m fantasy material in each installment. A handful of poetry books have risen to classic status almost at publication, and continue to go into printing after printing; among them Adrienne Rich's *Diving Into the Wreck*, Judy Grahn's *Work of A Common Woman*, as well as anthologies such as *The Male Muse* and *Angels of the Lyre*.

The strength of the writers' gifts and the authenticity of their experiences explain much of this popularity. But the final decision on these books has not been made in literary journals, and no critical books published by university or other prestige presses have been released on this enormous body of work. The ultimate criteria of any literature are often found at the post graduate level, and here gay and lesbian authors have been most at a disadvantage. Critics and reviewers, when they do discuss our literature, find it easier to take the publication of an important homosexual book as an excuse to critique homosexuality itself (and its cultural manifestations) rather than keep to the admittedly more difficult task of literary criticism, which requires an open mind and perceptiveness.

Nevertheless a pantheon of authors has already been established by sympathetic readers, and it is evident that writers like Edmund White, Jane Rule, Adrienne Rich and Andrew Holleran are considered among our finest writers, period; with another dozen or so moving into the haloed area. Even more important is the wide variety of experiences they are writing about, and which was one of the criteria for selection of this anthology. Since homosexuality is found in all social, racial, ethnic and financial classes in a fairly stable ratio, it should not come as a surprise that its authors would be as heterogenous in their styles and subject matter and approaches as any other gathering of thirty-odd writers.

But it is true too that the handful of books that have received the greatest attention from reviewers and readers have usually dealt with a very specific small section of gay life—the urban male experience. And for a good reason: that is where their subject matter is most pervasive and tenacious; its mores, codes and concepts the most fully developed.

The urban gay experience has almost become *the* homosexual experience. Even so there is great variety within it. Gay or lesbian life in, say, the New York City art crowd is quite different from Boston academic life, or Washington political life, or the West Hollywood film and music industries. And if we haven't yet had fine books about agricultural rural gay communes, or the industrial exurban lesbian scene, that does not mean they aren't worthy of good literature, or that good writing will not develop in those areas in the future.

Almost half of the authors represented in this book reside in or around New York City, confirming the pre-eminence of this publishing town for attracting writing talent. That is no surprise. The next best represented cities are San Francisco and Boston. Again, unsurprising, given the large gay population of the one, and the huge academic community of the other. Both cities also support a large, potent and often intense periodical media. The real surprise is the next best represented cities: Washington, D.C. and the Toronto—Montreal axis: and those least well represented: the South and the Southwest. There may well be dozens of budding authors in these areas who will soon make names for themselves from, say, Houston or Atlanta, both of which contain large, active gay and lesbian populations. I believe, however, that the next place to watch for writing is Los Angeles, currently in the midst of an astonishing growth of its homosexual community. A haven for European and East Coast writers for half a century, Southern California is beginning to produce poets, story-tellers and essayists of great talent and orginality, writers tuned to the razor edge of the present/future tense which defines gay life and which seems to be the modus operandi of that geographical area in general.

Thematically, this anthology is varied, once past the key point that the writers are gay or lesbian identified. Certain themes do stand out more than others, naturally: youth, the first personal/sexual encounter, being alone, being oneself, growing old, and how gays and lesbians are oppressed and how they in turn oppress others, often unconsciously. Yet other works here have no thematic links to these ideas. George Whitmore's *Legacy* is about growing old yes, but more about love and memory. Bob Herron's *Mortiz Goes to A Garden Party* might be about how different groups of gays look down on each other: I see it more as a farce about how easily pretensions are burst. Richard Uman's *On the Door* is not so much about being alone, as it is a clear-eyed portrait of a gay relationship unravelling.

The hundred or so poems here are even more varied—so much so that each poet seems to have her or his own thematic treasure trove that must be investigated.

I have attempted to deal with this variety, by appending separate prefaces to each author's work. Although I have tried to present what I think is a fair estimation of what each writer is up to, I hope these little prefaces will not be taken as critiques so much as "notes toward appreciation."

Naturally, as editor of this anthology, I see it as a clear refutation of Harrison Salisbury's statement that there is no important, serious American dissidence literary movement. Few of the writers represented here have work found in major magazines or literary journals. Even fewer are published by large, commercial presses. Almost all of them have had their work in the vast and growing body of small gay and lesbian presses that form the *Samidzat* of the movement.

At a recent publishing panel I moderated, I asked the panellists—some of whom worked for large publishing houses—how many authors they thought were actually earning their living writing lesbian or gay literature. The answers varied from five to ten authors. A tiny proportion: even a shameful one. Clearly gays and lesbians have not yet understood or come to appreciate how many gifted writers are going to considerable trouble and sacrifice to provide us with a literature.

There is some hope this will alter, as word on books circulates, as reviews and interviews in the general media proliferate, as gay and lesbian books get into more libraries and bookstores, and most importantly as they enter into literature classes across the country.

That is perhaps our greatest hope: that a new generation can be more fully prepared, more eager to sample the rich heritage of literature already written for them—and still to come.

A NOTE ON SELECTION

I began this anthology in the most inadvertant manner, and its evolution into its present shape and format was in part dictated by that same lack of rigidity.

When I began the Sea Horse Press in 1977, it was an experiment. Within months of the publication of Sea Horse's first book, I was receiving manuscripts, queries, letters, solicitations from all over the country. The continued success of following volumes (just to keep publishing is success in the small press world where the most promising first books are sometimes the only ones), added to that deluge of material, much of it from respected, well-known, previously published as well as new and unpublished writers. Obviously the need for quality small gay presses existed, and continues to exist. Yet, I couldn't dream of publishing a tenth of the work sent me.

I then thought of preparing a volume much like this one, consisting only of the work of new writers. In one printed announcement for another book, I even titled it: *New Voices*. When the publication of my own gay themed short stories, novels, essays and poetry brought me into the orbit of some of the best known gay writers in the country, I discovered that even they lacked adequate channels for their work: even they needed more exposure to readers. Although *A True Likeness* introduces several writers unpublished so far—Kerric Harvey, Richard Umans, John Iozia, Dan Diamond, Philip Kravitz—it also contains work by some of the best known of our authors; and reintroduces—often in different genres than they usually work in, authors who would be better known but for the financial vagaries of the publishing world.

At no time in the compilation did I feel compelled to fulfill any so called "parity" obligations. If I were a lesbian woman rather than a gay man, perhaps there would be twice as many women represented, instead of the other way around: simply through personal contacts and friendships, shared interests and reading. And, while I was extremely interested in finding more ethnic minority writing, my efforts here did not quite gel. Although I read a great deal of promising work by black gay writers, I found much other writing to be more concerned with polemics than with character, situation and language: the staples of literature. Only after the poetry section had been completed, did I discover the works of two lesbian authors I have come to admire and would have wished to include: Pat Parker and Audre Lourde. Hopefully, this will change in future anthologies. It is an area of great interest to me, and ought to be for all concerned with building a new and sane society free of past prejudices. Oriental and Hispanic gays and lesbians have already become established in other areas—social and precise sciences, as well as music and art; yet their contribution to our literature has not been striking. I look forward to reading about their experiences too.

A few authors here began as friends of mine; more become friends after I knew their work. Many more authors are not personally known to me. Of these, about half sent writing to me when they heard of the anthology, and the other half I contacted because of past admiration for their work.

In many ways this anthology is a guide, in others a stopgap before some larger, more comprehensive anthology can be more professionally prepared covering this and other ground. On the other hand I do think it fills a need for a single volume of both lesbian and gay drama, fiction and poetry. Many separate volumes of men's work or women's work, of poetry or fiction or drama already exist, and are excellent.

Although it will no doubt sound pretentious of me as an editor, I believe that *A True Likeness* for all its limitations, presents the general reader as well as the more concentrated gay or lesbian reader with some of the best writing by established and new writers of poetry, drama and fiction today.

Lastly, my selections were made on what I liked out of the enormous amount of material I've read in the last few years; on some vague but still clear to me standards of writing I have developed as reader, writer and publisher; and finally, most of all on whim.

A TRUE LIKENESS
LESBIAN AND GAY WRITING TODAY

FICTION
EDMUND WHITE

Edmund White's States of Desire: Travels in Gay America, *(Dutton, 1980) established him in the literary world and in the public's mind as being in the forefront of the new wave of gay literature today: for many, the only representative. His first novel,* Forgetting Elena, *(Random House, 1975) drew the unimaginable: a blurb from Vladimir Nabokov. White's second novel,* Nocturnes For the King of Naples, *(St. Martins, 1978) was compared to every piece of literature but* The Epic of Gilgamesh, *and still managed to elude exact definition. His important collaboration with Dr. Charles Silverstein on* The Joy of Gay Sex *(Crown, 1976) contained the wittiest and sanest writing on the subject that I've encountered, and its introduction propounded the bright idea that todays generation of lesbians and gays were not really like any of our historical forebears—explaining our dynamism and ambivalence.*

Despite all these plaudits, White's work has been more viciously attacked than that of any gay writer in decades. All the overt and hidden homophobias that are weekly administered to gay books by journalists and reviewers that has been heaped on Edmund White's head would itself make a remarkable, enlightening and frightening pamphlet.

The excerpt included here, "A Man of the World," is from White's third novel. One section was already published as "First Love" in Christopher Street Magazine. Both sections reveal a more straightforward prose style than typical of White's fiction; allied to a greater emphasis on emotion than found in his earlier books which ought to earn this book a large and devoted following.

One of White's favorite challenges is to stand the conventional on its head, and thus force you to accept his askew and delightful perspective. Only then will the pleasures of his ideas, descriptions and characterizations tumble over you. In "Man of the World" a conventional mid-western American adolescence is given the White treatment. It is a highly colored, rich and ultimately very moving story.

A MAN OF THE WORLD

My father wanted me to work every summer in high school so that I might learn the value of a dollar. I did work, I did learn, and what I learned was that my dollar could buy me hustlers. I bought my first when I was fourteen.

The downtown of that city of half a million was small, no larger than a few dozen blocks. Every morning my stepmother drove me into town from our house, a fake Norman castle that stood high and white on a hill above the steaming river valley; we'd go down into town—a rapid descent of several steep plunges into the creeping traffic, dream dissolves of black faces, the smell of hot franks filtered through the car's airconditioned interior, the muted cries of newspaper vendors speaking their own incomprehensible language, the somber look of sooted facades edging forward to squeeze out the light. Downtown excited me: so many people, some of them just possibly an invitation to adventure, escape or salvation.

As a little boy I'd thought of our house as the place God had meant us to own, but now I knew in a vague way that its seclusion and ease were artificial and that it strenuously excluded the city at the same time it depended on it for food, money, comfort, help, even pleasure. The black maids were the representatives of the city I'd grown up among. I'd never wanted anything from them— nothing except their love. To win it, or at least to ward off their silent, sighing resentment, I'd learned how to make my own bed and cook my own breakfast. But nothing I could do seemed to make up to them the terrible loss they'd endured.

In my father's office I worked an Addressograph machine (then something of a novelty) with a woman of forty who, like a restless sleeper tangled in sheets, tossed about all day in her fantasies. She was a chubby but pert woman who wore pearls to cover the pale line across her neck, the scar from some sort of surgical intervention. It was a very thin line but she could never trust her disguise and ran to the mirror in the ladies' room six or seven times a day to re-evaluate the effect.

The rest of her energy went into elaborating her fantasies. There was a man on the bus every morning who always stationed himself opposite her and arrogantly undressed her with his dark eyes. Upstairs from her apartment another man lurked, growling with desire, his ear pressed to the floor as he listened through an inverted glass for the glissando of a silk slip she might be stepping out of. "Should I put another lock on my door?" she'd ask. Later she'd ask with wide-eyed sweetness, "Should I invite him down for a cup of coffee?" I advised her not to; he might be dangerous. The voraciousness of her need for men made me act younger than usual; around her I wanted to be a boy, not a man. Her speculations would cause her to sigh, drink water and return to the mirror. My stepmother said she considered this woman to be a "ninny." Once, years ago, my stepmother had been my father's secretary—perhaps her past made her unduly critical of the women who had succeeded her. My family and their friends almost never characterized people we actually knew, certainly not dismissively. I felt a gleeful shame in thinking of my colleague as a "ninny"—sometimes I'd laugh out loud when the word popped into my head. I found it both exciting and alarming to feel superior to a grown-up.

Something about our work stimulated thoughts of sex in us. Our tasks (feeding envelopes into a trough, stamping them with addresses, stuffing them with brochures, later sealing them and running them through the postage meter) required just enough attention to prevent connected conversation but not so much as to absorb us. We were left with amoeboid desires that split or merged as we stacked and folded, as we tossed and turned. "When he looks at me," she said, "I know he wants to hurt me." As she said that, her sweet, chubby face looked as though it were emerging out of a cloud.

Once I read about a woman patient in psychoanalysis who referred to her essential identity as her "prettiness"; my companion—gray-eyed, her wrists braceleted in firm, healthy fat, hair swept up into a brioche pierced by the fork of a comb, her expression confused and sweet as she floated free of the cloud—she surrounded and kept safe her own "prettiness" as though it were a passive, intelligent child and she the mother, dazed by the sweeping lights of the world.

She was both fearful and serene—afraid of being noticed and more afraid of being ignored, thrillingly afraid of the sounds outside her bedroom window, but also serene in her conviction that this whole bewildering opera was being staged in order to penetrate the fire and get at her "prettiness." She really was pretty—perhaps I haven't made that clear: a sad blur of a smile, soft gray eyes, a defenseless availability. She was also crafty, or maybe willfully blind, in the way she concealed from herself her own sexual ambitions.

Becoming my father's employee clarified my relationship with him. It placed him at an exact distance from me that could be measured by money. The divorce agreement had spelled out what he owed my mother, my sister and me, but even so whenever my mother put us kids on the train to go visit him (one weekend out of every month and all summer every summer), she invariably told us, "Be nice to your father or he'll cut us off." And when my sister was graduated from college, he presented her with a "life bill," the itemized expenses he'd incurred in raising her over 21 years, a huge sum that was intended to discourage her from thoughtlessly spawning children of her own.

Dad slept all day. He seldom put in an appearance at the office before closing time, when he'd arrive fresh and rested, smelling of witch hazel, and scatter reluctant smiles and nods to the assembly as he made his way through us and stepped up to his desk in a large room walled off from us by soundproof glass. "My, what a fine man your father is, a real gentlemen," my colleague would sigh. "And to think your stepmother met him when she was his secretary—some women have all the luck." We sat in rows with our backs to him; he played the role of the conscience, above and behind us, a force that troubled us as we filed out soon after his arrival at the end of the work day. Had we stayed late enough? Done enough?

My stepmother usually kept my father company until midnight. Then she and I would drive back to the country and go to bed. Sometimes my father followed us in his own car and continued his desk work at home. Or sometimes he'd stay downtown till dawn. "That's when he goes out to meet other women," my real mother told me at the end of the summer, when I reported back to her what went on in Daddy's life. "He was never faithful. There was always another woman, the whole 22 years we were married. He takes them to those little flea-bag hotels downtown. I know." This hint of mystery about a man so cold and methodical fascinated me—as though he, the rounded brown stone, if only cracked open, would nip at the sky with interlocking crystal teeth, the quartz teeth of passion.

Before the midnight drive back home I was sometimes permitted to go out to dinner by myself. Sometimes I also took in a movie (I remember going to one that promised to be actual views of the "orgies at Berchtesgarden," but it turned out to be just Eva Braun's home movies, the Fuerher conferring warm smiles on pets and children). A man who smelled of Vitalis sat beside me and squeezed my thigh with his hand. I had my own spending money and my own free time.

I had little else. No one I could meet for lunch and confide in. No one who liked me. No one who wanted to talk with me about books or opera. Not even the impulse to ask for love or the belief that such things could be discussed. Had I known in any vivid or personal way of the disease, starvation and war that afflicted so much of humanity, I might have taken comfort at least in my physical well-being, but in my loneliness I worried about sickness, hunger and violence befalling me, as though these fears had been visited on me by the jealous world in revenge against so much joyless plenty.

I hypothesized a lover who'd take me away. He'd climb the fir tree outside my window, step into my room and gather me into his arms. What he said or looked like remained indistinct, just a cherishing wraith enveloping me, whose face glowed more and more brightly. His delay in coming went on so long that soon I'd passed from anticipation to nostalgia. One night I sat at my window and stared at the moon, toasting it with a champagne glass filled with grape juice. I knew the moon's cold, immense light was falling on him as well, far away and just as lonely in a distant room. I expected him to be able to divine my existence and my need, to intuit that in this darkened room in this country house a fourteen-year-old was waiting for him.

Sometimes now when I pass dozing suburban houses I wonder behind which window a boy waits for me.

After a while I realized I wouldn't meet him till years later; I wrote him a sonnet that began, "Because I loved you before I knew you." The idea, I think, was that I'd never quarrel with him nor ever rate his devotion cheap; I had had to wait too long.

Our house was a somber place. The styleless polished furniture was piled high and the pantry supplies were laid in; in the empty fullness of breakfront drawers gold flatware and silver tea things remained for six months at a time in mauve flannel bags that could not ward off a tarnish bred out of the very air. No one talked much. There was little laughter, except when my stepmother was on the phone with one of her social friends. Although my father hated most people, he had wanted my stepmother to take her place—that is, my mother's place—in society, and she had. He'd taught her how to dress and speak and entertain and by now she'd long since surpassed his instructions; she'd become at once proper and frivolous, innocent and amusing, high-spirited and reserved—the combination of wacky girl and prim matron that world so admired.

I learned my part less well. I feared the sons of her friends and made shadows among the debs. I played the piano without ever improving; to practice would have meant an acceptance of more delay, whereas I wanted instant success, the throb of plumed fans in the dark audience, the pulse of diamonds from the curve of loges. What I had instead was the ache of waiting and the fear I wasn't worthy. When I'd dress I'd stand naked before the closet mirror and wonder if my body was worthy. I can still picture that pale skin stretched over my ribs, the thin, hairless arms and sturdier legs, the puzzled, searching face—and the slow lapping of disgust and longing, disgust and longing. The disgust was hot, penetrating—nobody would want me because I was a sissy and had a mole between my shoulder blades. The longing was cooler, less substantial, more the spray off a wave than the wave itself. Perhaps the eyes were engaging, there was something about the smile. If not lovable as a boy, then maybe as a girl; I wrapped the towel into a turban on my head. Or perhaps need itself was charming or could be. Maybe my need could make me as appealing as the woman who worked the Addressograph machine with me.

I was always reading and often writing but both were passionately abstract activities. Early on I had recognized that books pictured another life, one quite foreign to mine, in which people circled one another warily and with exquisite courtesy until an individual or a couple erupted and flew out of the salon, spangling the night with fire. I had somehow stumbled on Ibsen and that's how he struck me: oblique social chatter followed by a heroic death in a snowslide or on the steeple of a church (I wondered how these scenes could be staged). Oddly enough, the "realism" of the last century seemed tinglingly farfetched: vows, betrayals, flights, fights, sacrifices, suicides. I saw literature as a fantasy, no less absorbing for all its irrelevance—a parallel life, as dreams shadow waking but never intersect it.

I thought to write of my own experiences required a translation out of the crude patois of actual slow suffering, mean, scattered thoughts and transfusion-slow boreom into the tidy couplets of brisk, beautiful sentiment, a way of at once elevating and lending momentum to what I felt. At the same time I was drawn to . . . What if I could write about my life exactly as it was? What if I could show it in all its density and tedium and its concealed passion, never divined or expressed, the dull brown geode that eats at itself with quartz teeth?

I read books with this passion, as one might beat back pages of pictures, looking for someone he could love. The library downtown had been built as an opera house in the last century. Even in grade school I had haunted the library, which was in the same block as my father's office. The library looked up like a rheumy eye at a pitched skylight over which pigeons whirred, their bodies a shuddering gray haze until one settled and its pacing black feet became as precise as cuneiform. The light seeped down through the stacks that were arranged in a horseshoe of tiers: the former family balcony, the dress circle, the boxes, on down to the orchestra, still gently raked but now cleared of stalls and furnished with massive oak card files and oak reading tables where unshaved old men read newspapers under gooseneck lamps and rearranged rags in paper sacks. The original stage had been demolished but cleats on the wall showed where ropes had once been secured.

The railings around the various balconies still described crude arabesques in bronze gone green, but the old floors of the balconies had been replaced by rectangular slabs of smoked glass that emitted pale emerald gleams along polished, bevelled edges. Walking on this glass gave me vertigo, but once I started reading I'd slump to the cold, translucent blocks and drift on ice floes into dense clouds. The smell of yellowing paper engulfed me. An unglued page slid out of a volume and a corner broke off, shattered—I was destroying public property! Downstairs someone harangued the librarian. Shadowy throngs of invisible operagoers coalesced and sat forward in their see-through finery to look and listen. I was reading the libretto of *La Bohème*. The alternating columns of incomprehensible Italian, which I could skip, made the pages speed by, as did the couple's farewell in the snow, the ecstatic reconciliation, poor little Mimi's prolonged dying. I glanced up and saw a pair of shoes cross the glass above, silently accompanied by the paling and darkening circle of the rubber end of a cane. The great eye of the library was blurred by tears.

Across the street the father of a friend of mine ran a bookstore. As

I entered it, I was almost knocked down by two men coming out. One of them touched my shoulder and drew me aside. He had a three-day's growth of beard on his cheeks, shiny wet canines, a rumpled raincoat of a fashionable cut that clung to his hips and he was saying, "Don't just rush by without saying hello."

Here he was at last but now I knew for sure I wasn't worthy—I was ugly with my glasses and my scalp white under my shorn hair. "Do I know you?" I asked. I felt I did, as if we'd traveled for a month in a train compartment knee to knee night after night via the thirty installments of a serial but plotless though highly emotional dream. I smiled, embarrassed by the way I looked.

"Sure you know me." He laughed and his friend, I think, smiled. "No, honestly, what's your name?"

I told him.

He repeated it, smile suppressed, as I'd seen men on the make condescend to women they were sizing up. "We just blew into town," he said. "I hope you can make us feel at home." He put an arm around my waist and I shrank back; the sidewalks were crowded with people staring at us curiously. His fingers fit neatly into the space between my pelvis and the lowest rib, a space that welcomed him, that had been cast from the mold of his hand. I kept thinking these two guy want my money, but how they planned to get it remained vague. And I was alarmed they'd been able to tell at a glance that I would respond to their advances so readily. I was so pleased he'd chosen me; because he was from out of town he had higher, different standards. He thought I was like him, and perhaps I was or soon would be. Now that a raffish stranger—younger and more handsome than I'd imagined, but also dirtier and more condescending—had materialized before me, I wasn't at all sure what I should do: my reveries hadn't been that detailed. Nor had I anticipated meeting someone so cross-hatched with ambiguity, a dandy who hadn't bathed, a penniless seducer, someone upon whose face passion and cruelty had cast a grille of shadows. I was alarmed; I ended up by keeping my address secret (midnight robbery) but agreeing to meet him at the pool in the amusement park tomorrow at noon (an appointment I didn't keep, though I felt the hour come and go like a king in disguise turned away at the peasant's door).

The books in the bookstore shimmered before my eyes as I worked through a pile of them with their brightly colored paper jackets bearing photographs of pensive, well-coiffed women or middle-aged men in Irish knit sweaters with pipes and profiles. Because I knew these books were by living writers I looked down on them; my head was still ringing with the full bravura performance of history in the library-opera house. Those old books either had never owned or had lost their wrappers; the likenesses of their unpictured authors had been recreated within the brown, brittle pages. But these living writers—ah! life struck me as an enfeeblement, a proof of dimmed vitality when compared to the energetic composure of the dead whose busts, all carved beards and sightless, protuberant eyes I imagined filling the empty niches in the opera lobby, a shallow antechamber, now a home to sleeping bums and stray cats, but once the splendid approach across diamonds of black-and-white marble pavement to black-and-gilt doors opening on the brilliant assembly, the fans and diamonds and the raised ebony lid of the spotlit piano.

At home I heard the muted strains of discordant music. One night my stepmother, hard and purposeful, drove back downtown unexpectedly to my father's office after midnight. Still later I could hear my stepmother shouting in her wing of the house; I hid behind a door and heard my father's patient, explaining drone. The next morning the woman who worked the Addressograph machine with me broke down, wept, locked herself in the ladies' room. When she came out her eyes, usually so lovely and unfocused, narrowed with spite and pain as she muttered a stream of filth about my stepmother and my father, who'd tried to lure her to one of those fleabag hotels. On the following morning I learned she'd been let go, though by that time I knew how to get the endless mailings out on my own. She'd been let go—into what?

That man's embrace around the waist set me spinning like a dancer across the darkened stage of the city; my turns led me to Fountain Square, the center. After nightfall the downtown was nearly empty. A cab might cruise by. One high office window might glow. The restaurants had closed by eight, but a bar door could swing open to impose on me the silhouette of a man or to expel the sound of a juke box, the smell of beer and pretzels. Shabby city of black stone whitened by starlings, poor earthly progeny of that mystic metal dove poised on the outstretched wrist of the verdigris'd lady, sad goddess of the fountain. Men from across the river sat around the low granite rim of the basin—at least I guessed they were hillbillies from their accents, a missing tooth, greased-back hair, their way of spitting, of holding a Camel cupped between the thumb and third finger, of walking with a hard, loud, stiff-legged tread across the paved park as though they hoped to ring sparks off the stone. Others sat singly along the metal fence that enclosed the park, an island around which traffic flowed. They perched on the steel rail, legs wide apart, bodies licked by headlights, and looked down into the slowly circling cars. At last a driver would pause before a young man who'd hop down and lean into the open window, listen—and then the young man would either shake his head and spit or, if a deal had been struck, swagger around to the other side and get in. Look at them: the curving windshield whispers down the reflection of a blinking neon sign on two faces, a bald man behind the wheel whose glasses are crazed by streaks of green light from the dashboard below, whose ears are fleshy, whose small mouth is pinched smaller by anxiety or anticipation. Beside him the young man, head thrown back on the seat so that we can see only the strong white parabola of his jaw and the working Adam's apple. He's slumped far down and he's already thinking his way into his job. Or maybe he's embarrassed by so much downtime between fantasy and act. They drive off, only the high notes from the car radio reaching me.

A charged space where all eyes take in every event—I'd never known anything like that till now. Maybe in the lobby of Symphony Hall, where as a child I'd gone every Friday afternoon for the kiddie matinee, but there little feudal hordes of children, attached to a mother or nurse, eyed each other across acres of marble unless ordered to greet one another, the curtest formality between hostile vassals who might as well have spoken different languages. But here, in Fountain Square, though two or three men might cluster together and drink from a paper bag and argue sports or women, each group was meant to attract attention, every gesture was meant to be observed and transgressed, and the conversation was a pretense at conversation, the typical behavior of desirable types.

That night, however, I had no comfortable assumptions about who these men were and what they were willing to do. I crossed the street to the island, ascended the two steps onto the stone platform—and sat down on a bench. No one could tell me to leave this bench. No one would even notice me. There were policemen nearby. I had a white shirt on, a tie at half-mast, seersucker pants from a suit, polished lace-up shoes, clean nails and short hair, money in my wallet. I was a polite, well-spoken teen, not a vagrant or a criminal—the law would favor me. My father was nearby, working in his office; I was hanging around, waiting for him. Years of traveling alone on trains across the country to see my father had made me fearless before strangers and had led me to assume the unknown is safe, at least reasonably safe if encountered in public places. I set great store by my tie and raised the knot to cover the still unbuttoned collar opening.

It was hot and dark. The circling cars were unnerving—so many unseen viewers looking at me. Although this was the town I'd grown up in, I'd never explored it on my own. The library, the bookstore, Symphony Hall, the office, the dry cleaners, the state liquor commission, the ball park, my school, the department stores, that glass ball of a restaurant perched high up there—these I'd been to hundreds of times with my father and stepmother, but I'd always been escorted by them, like a prisoner, through the shadowy, dangerous city.

And yet I'd known all along it was something mysterious and anguished beyond my experience if not my comprehension. We had a maid, Blanche, who inserted bits of straw into her pierced ears to keep the holes from growing shut, sneezed her snuff in a fine spray of brown dots over the sheets when she was ironing and slouched around the kitchen in her worn-down, backless slippers, once purple but now the color and sheen of a bare oak branch in the rain. She was always uncorseted under her blue cotton uniform; I pictured her rolling, black and fragrant, under that fabric and wondered what her mammoth breasts looked like.

Although she had a daughter five years older than I (illegitimate, or so my stepmother whispered significantly), when Blanche hummed to a black station only she seemed able to tune in she seemed like a girl. When she moved from one room to the next, she unplugged the little bakelite radio with the cream-colored grille over the brown speaker cloth and took it with her. That music excited me, but I thought I shouldn't listen to it too closely. It was "Negro music" and therefore forbidden—part of another culture more violent and vibrant than mine but somehow inferior yet no less exclusive.

Charles, the handyman, would emerge from the basement sweaty and pungent and, standing three steps below me, lecture me about the Bible, the Second Coming and Booker T. Washington and Marcus Garvey and Langston Hughes. Whenever I said something he'd laugh in a steady, stylized way to shut me up and then start burrowing back into his obsessions. He seemed to know everything, chapter and verse—Egyptians, Abyssinians, the Lost Tribe, Russian plots, Fair Deal and New Deal—but when I'd repeat one of his remarks at dinner, my father would laugh (this, too, was a stylized laugh) and say, "You've been listening to Charles again. That nigger just talks nonsense. Now don't you bother him, let him get on with his work." I never doubted that my father was right, but I kept wondering how Dad could *tell* it was nonsense. What mysterious ignorance leaked out of Charles's words to poison them and render them worthless, inedible? For Charles, like me, haunted the library; I watched his shelf of books in the basement rotate. And Charles was a high deacon of his church, the wizard of his tribe; when he died his splendid robes overflowed his casket. That his nonsense made perfect sense to me alarmed me—was I, like Charles, eating the tripe of knowledge while Dad sat down to the steak?

I suppose I never wondered where Blanche or Charles went at night; when it was convenient to do so I still thought of the world as a well-arranged place where people did work that suited them and lived in houses appropriate to their tastes and needs. But once Blanche called us in the middle of an August night and my father, stepmother and I rushed to her aid. In the big Cadillac we breasted our way into unknown streets through the crowds of naked children playing in the tumult of water liberated from a fire plug ("Stop that!" I shouted silently at them, outraged and frightened. "That's illegal!"). Past the stoops crowded with grown-ups playing cards and drinking wine. In one glaring doorway a woman stood, holding her diapered baby against her, a look of stoic indignation on her young face, a face one could imagine squeezing out tears without ever changing expression or softening the wide, fierce eyes, set jaw, everted lower lip. The smell of something delicious—charred meat, maybe, and maybe burning honey—filled the air. "Roll up your windows, for Chrissake, and lock the doors," my father shouted at us. "Dammit, use your heads—don't you know this place is dangerous as hell!"

A bright miner's lamp, glass globe containing a white fire devoid of blues and yellows, dangled from the roof of a vendor's cart; he was selling food of some sort to children. Even through the closed windows I could hear the babble of festive, delirious radios. A seven-foot skinny man in spats, shades, an electric green shantung suit and a flat-brimmed white beaver hat with a matching green band strolled in front of our car and patted our fender with elaborate mockery. "I'll kill the bastard," Dad shouted. "I swear I'll kill that goddam ape if he scratches my fender."

"Oh-h-h . . . ," my stepmother sang on a high note I'd never heard before. "You'll get us all killed. Honey, my heart." She grabbed for her heart; she was a natural actress, who instinctively translated feelings into gestures. The man, who my father told us was a "pimp" (whatever that might be), bowed to unheard applause, pulled his hat down over one eye like Chevalier and ambled on, letting us pass.

We hurried up five flights of dirty, broken stairs, littered with empty pint bottles, bags of garbage and two dolls (both white, I noticed, and blond and mutilated), past landings and open doors, which gave me glimpses of men playing cards and, across the hall, a grandmother alone and asleep in an armchair with antimacassars. Her radio was playing that Negro music. Her brown cotton stockings had been rolled down below her black knees.

Blanche we found wailing and shouting, "My baby, my baby!" as she hopped and danced in circles of pain around her daughter, whose hand, half lopped off, was spouting blood. My father gathered the girl up in his arms and we all rushed off to the emergency room of a hospital.

She lived. Her hand was even sewn back on, though the incident (jealous lover with an axe) had broken her mind. Afterwards, the girl didn't go back to her job and feared even leaving the building. My stepmother thought the loss of blood had somehow left her feeble-minded. My father fussed over the blood on his suit and on the strangely similar Cadillac upholstery, though I wondered if his pettiness weren't merely a way of silencing Blanche, who kept kissing his whole hand in gratitude. Or perhaps he'd found a way of reintroducing the ordinary into a night that had dipped disturbingly below the normal temperature of tedium he worked so hard to maintain. Years later, when Charles died, my father was the only white man to attend the funeral. He wasn't welcome, but he went anyway and sat in the front row. After Charles's death my father became more scattered and apprehensive. He would sit up all night with a stop-watch, counting his pulse.

That had been another city—Blanche's two rooms, scrupulously clean in contrast to the squalor of the halls, her parrot squawking under the tea towel draped over the cage, the chromo of a sad Jesus pointing to his exposed, juicy heart as though he were a free-clinic patient with a troubling symptom, the filched wedding photo of my father and stepmother in a nest of crepe-paper flowers, the bloody sheet torn into strips that had been wildly clawed off and hurled onto the flowered congoleum floor. Through a half-open door I saw the foot of a double bed draped like a veteran's grave with the flag of a tossed-back sheet.

In my naiveté I imagined all poor people, black and white, liked each other and that here, through Fountain Square, I would feel my way back to the street, that smell of burning honey, that blood as red as mine and that steady, colorless fire in the glass chimney. . . . These hillbillies on the square with their drawling and spitting, their thin arms and big raw hands, nails ragged, tattoos a fresher blue than their eyes set in long sallow Norman faces, each eye a pale blue ringed by nearly invisible lashes—I wove these men freely into the cloth of the powerful poor, a long bolt lost in the dark that I was now pulling through a line of light.

I opened a book and pretended to read under the weak street lamps, though my attention wandered away from sight to sound. "Tommy, bring back a beer!" someone shouted. Some other men laughed. No one I knew kept his nickname beyond twelve, at least not with his contemporaries, but I could hear these guys calling each other Tommy and Freddy and Bobby and I found that heartening, as though they wanted to stay, if only among themselves, as chummy as a gang of boys. While they worked to become as brutal as soon enough they would be, I tried to find them softer than they'd ever been.

Boots approached me. I heard them before I saw them. They stopped, every tan scar on the orange hide in focus beyond the page I held that was running with streaks of print. "Curiosity killed the damn pussy, you know," a man said. I look up at a face sprouting brunette sideburns that swerved inwards like cheese knives toward his mouth and stopped just below his ginger mustaches. The eyes, small and black, had been moistened genially by the beers he'd drunk and the pleasure he was taking in his own joke.

"*Mighty* curious, ain't you?" he asked. "Ain't you!" he insisted, making a great show of his leisurely, avuncular way he settled close beside me, sighing, and wrapped a bare arm—a pale, cool, sweaty, latenight August arm—around my thin shoulders. "Shit," he hissed. Then he slowly drew a breath like ornamental cigarette smoke up his nose, and chuckled again. "I'd say you got Sabbath eyes, son."

"I do?" I squeaked in a pinched soprano. "I don't know what you mean," I added, only to demonstrate my newly acquired baritone, as penetrating as an oboe, though the effect on the man seemed the right one: sociable.

"Yessir, Sabbath eyes," he said with a downshift into a rural languor and rhetorical fanciness I associated with my storytelling paternal grandfather in Texas. "I say Sabbath 'cause you done worked all week and now you's resting them eyeballs on what you done made—or might could make. The good things of the earth." Suddenly he grew stern. "Why you here, boy? I seed you here cocking your hade and spying up like a biddy hen. Why you watching, boy? *What* you watching? Tell me, what you watching?"

He had frightened me, which he could see—it made him laugh. I smiled to show him I knew how foolish I was being. "I'm just here to—"

"Read?" he demanded, taking my book away and shutting it. "Shi-i-i . . ." he hissed again, steam running out before the *t*. "You here to meet someone, boy?" He'd disengaged himself and turned to stare at me. Although his eyes were serious, militantly serious, the creasing of the wrinkles beside them suggested imminent comedy.

"No," I said, quite audibly.

He handed the book back to me.

"I'm here because I want to run away from home," I said. "I thought I might find someone to go with me."

"Whar you planning to run to?"

"New York."

There was something so cold and firm and well-spoken about me—the clipped tones of a businessman defeating the farmer's hoaxing yarn—that the man sobered, dropped his chin into his palm and thought. "What's today?" he asked at last.

"Saturday."

"I myself taking the Greyhound to New York Tuesday mawning," he said. "Wanna go?"

"Sure."

He told me that if I'd bring him forty dollars on Monday evening he'd buy me my ticket. He asked me where I lived and I told him; his willingess to help me made me trust him. Without ever explicitly being taught such things, I'd learned by studying my father that at certain crucial moments—an emergency, an opportunity—one must act first and think later. One must suppress minor inner objections and put off feelings of cowardice or confusion and turn oneself into a simple instrument of action. I'd seen my father become calm in a crisis or feel his way blindly with nods, smiles and monosyllables toward the shadowy opening of a hugely promising but still vague business deal. And with women he was ever alert to adventure: the gauzy transit of a laugh across his path, a minor whirlpool in the sluggish flow of talk, the faintest whiff of seduction . . .

I, too, wanted to be a man of the world and dared not question my new friend too closely. For instance, I knew a train ticket could be bought at the last moment, even on board, but I was willing to assume either that a bus ticket had to be secured in advance or that at least my friend thought it did. We arranged a time to meet on Monday when I could hand over the money (I had it at home squirreled away in the secret compartment of a wood tray I'd made last year in shop). Then on Tuesday morning at six a.m. he'd meet me on the corner near but not in sight of my house. He'd have his brother's car and we'd proceed quickly to the 6:45 bus bound East—a long haul to New Yawk, he said, oh, say twenty hours, no, make that twenty-one.

"And in New York?" I asked timidly, not wanting to seem helpless and scare him off but worried about my future. Would I be able to find work? I was only sixteen, I said, adding two years to my age. Could a sixteen-year-old work legally in New York? If so, doing what?

"Waiter," he said. "A whole hog heaven of resty-runts in New Yawk City."

Sunday it rained a hot drizzle all day and in the west the sky lit up a bright yellow that seemed more the smell of sulfur than a color. I played the piano with the silencer on lest I awaken my father. I was bidding the instrument farewell. If only I'd practiced I might have supported myself as a cocktail pianist; I improvised my impression of sophisticated tinkling—with disappointing results.

As I took an hour-long bath, periodically emptying an inch of cold water and replacing it with warm, I thought my way again through the routine: greeting the guests, taking their orders, serving pats of butter, beverages, calling out my requests to the chef . . . my long, flat feet under the water twitched sympathetically as I raced about the restaurant. If only I'd observed waiters all those times. Well, I'd coast on charm.

As for love that, too, I'd win through charm. Although I knew I hadn't charmed anyone since I was six or seven, I consoled myself by deciding people out here were not susceptible to the larceny (which I thought grand, they petty) of a beguiling manner. They responded only to character, accomplishments, the slow accumulations of will rather than the sudden millinery devisings of fancy. In New York I'd be the darling boy again. In that Balzac novel a penniless young man had made his fortune on luck, looks, winning ways (since I hadn't finished the book, I didn't yet know where those ways led). New Yorkers, like Parisians, I hoped and feared, would know what to make of me. I carried the plots and atmosphere of fiction about with me and tried to cram random events into those ready molds. But no, truthfully, the relationship was more reciprocal, less rigorous—art taking the noise life gave and picking it out as a tune (the cocktail pianist obliging the humming drunk).

Before it closed I walked down to a neighborhood pharmacy and bought a bottle of peroxide. I had decided to bleach my hair late Monday night; on Tuesday I'd no longer answer the description my father would put out in his frantic search for me. Perhaps I'd affect an English accent as well; I'd coached my stepmother in the part of Lady Bracknell before she performed the role with the Queen City Players and I could now say *cucumber sandwich* with scarcely a vowel after the initial fluty *u*. As an English blond I'd evade not only my family but also myself and emerge as the energetic and lovable boy I longed to be. Not exactly a boy, more a girl, or rather a sturdy, canny, lavishly devout tomboy like Joan of Arc, tough in battle if yielding before her visionary Father. I wouldn't pack winter clothes; surely by October I'd be able to buy something warm.

A new spurt of hot water as I retraced my steps to the kitchen, clipped the order to the cook's wire or flew out the swinging doors, smiling, acted courteously and won the miraculously large tip. And there, seated at a corner table by himself, is the English lord, silver-haired, recently bereaved; my hand trembles as I give him the frosted glass. In my mind I'd already betrayed the hillbilly with the sideburns who sobbed with dignity as I delivered my long farewell speech. He wasn't intelligent or rich enough to suit me.

When I met him on Monday at six beside the fountain and presented him with the four ten-dollar bills, he struck me as ominously indifferent to the details of tomorrow's adventure which I'd elaborated with such fanaticism. He reassured me about the waiter's job and my ability to pull it off, told me again where he'd pick me up in the morning—but, smiling, dissuaded me from peroxiding my hair tonight. "Just pack it—we'll bleach you white win we git whar we gohn."

We had a hamburger together at the Grasshopper, a restaurant of two rooms, one brightly lit and filled with booths and families and waitresses wearing German peasant costumes and white lace hats, the other murky and smelling of beer and smoke—a man's world, the bar. I went through the bar to the toilet. When I came out I saw the woman I'd worked with in a low-cut dress, skirt hiked high to expose her knee, hand over her pearl necklace. Her hair had been restyled. She pushed one lock back and let it fall again over her eye, the veronica a cape might pass before an outraged bull: the man beside her, who now placed a grimy hand on her knee. She let out a shriek—a coquette's shriek, I suppose, but edged with terror. (I was glad she didn't see me, since I felt ashamed at the way our family had used her.)

I'd planned not to sleep at all but had set the alarm should I doze off. For hours I lay in the dark and listened to the dogs barking down in the valley. Now that I was leaving this house forever, I was tiptoeing through it mentally and prizing its luxuries—the shelves lined with blocks of identical cans (my father ordered everything by the gross), the linen cupboard stacked high with ironed if snuff-specked sheets, my own bathroom with its cupboard full of soap, tissue, towels, hand towels, wash cloths, the elegant helix of the front staircase descending to the living room with its deep carpets, shaded lamps and the pretty mirror bordered by tiles on which someone with a nervous touch had painted the various breeds of lapdog. This house where I'd never felt I belonged no longer belonged to me and the future so clearly charted for me—college, career, wife and white house wavering behind green trees—was being exchanged for that eternal circulating through the restaurant, my path as clear to me as chalk marks on the floor, instructions for each foot in the tango, lines that flowed together, branched and joined, branched and joined . . . In my dream my father had died but I refused to kiss him though next he was pulling me onto his lap, an ungainly teen smeared with Vicks Vaporub whom everyone inexplicably treated as a sick child.

When I silenced the alarm, fear overtook me. I'd go hungry! The boarding house room with the toilet down the hall, blood on the linoleum, crepe-paper flowers—I dressed and packed my gym bag with the bottle of peroxide and two changes of clothes. Had my father gone to bed yet? Would the dog bark when I tried to slip past him? And would that man be on the corner? The boarding house room, yes, Negro music on the radio next door, the coquette's shriek. As I walked down the drive I felt conspicuous under the blank windows of my father's house and half-expected him to open the never-used front door to call me back.

I stood on the appointed corner. It began to drizzle but a water truck crept past anyway, spraying the street a darker, slicker gray. No birds were in sight but I could hear them testing the day. A dog without a collar or master trotted past. Two fat maids were climbing the hill, stopping every few steps to catch their breath. One, a shiny, blue-black fat woman wearing a flowered turban and holding a purple umbrella with a white plastic handle, was scowling and talking fast but obviously to humorous effect, for her companion couldn't stop laughing.

The bells of the Catholic school behind the dripping trees across the street marked the quarter hour, the half hour. More and more cars were passing me. I studied every driver—had he overslept? The milk man. The bread truck. Damn hillbilly. A bus went by, carrying just one passenger. A quarter to seven. He wasn't coming.

When I saw him the next evening on the square he waved at me and came over to talk. From his relaxed manner I instantaneously saw—puzzle pieces sliding then locking to fill in the pattern—that he'd duped me and I was powerless. To whom could I report him?

Like a heroin addict or a Communist, I was outside the law—outside it but with him, this man. He didn't attract me but I liked him well enough.

We sat side by side on the same bench. A bad muffler exploded in a volley and the cooing starlings perched on the fountain figure's arm flew up and away leaving behind only the metal dove. I took off my tie, rolled it up and slipped it inside my pocket. Because I didn't complain about being betrayed, my friend said, "See those men yonder?"

"Yes."

"I could git you one for eight bucks." He let that sink in; yes, I thought, I could take someone to one of those little flea-bag hotels. "Which one do you want?" he asked.

I handed him the money and said, 'The blond."

JANE RULE

So much writing about lesbians and gays continues to portray them as alienated and problem riddled that it is a pleasure to come upon a story like Jane Rule's "The Middle Children," reprinted here. In this story all is—if not sweetness and light—at least serenity and amusement, good sense and small problems solved lovingly with awareness and maturity. Few pieces of our literature show us the familial—social creatures that we really are. Even fewer do it with Rule's deceptively simple prose style and bon-mot economy.

Jane Rule is one of our most admired lesbian writers. Her first novel, Desert of the Heart, *1966, Norton, was the story of how two young women chose their own individual lives—one lesbian, one heterosexual—told without the hysteria or polemicizing of so much feminist literature that followed it. Her collection of stories,* Theme for Diverse Instruments, *Talonbooks, 1976, from which this story is taken, presents Rule's writing talents in full—her sophistication, her power of analysis, her original characters, her dry humor and her subtle ability to disturb and cut through cliche.*

Jane Rule was born in New Jersey in 1931. Her other books and novels are This is Not for You, Against the Season, *and her reader,* Lesbian Images. *She lives in British Columbia.*

MIDDLE CHILDREN

Clare and I both come from big families, a bossy, loving line of voices stretching away above us to the final authority of our parents, a chorus of squawling, needy voices beneath us coming from crib or play pen or notch in tree. We share, therefore, the middle child syndrome: we are both over earnest, independent, inclined to claustrophobia in crowds. The dreams of our adolescent friends for babies and homes of their own we privately considered nightmares. Boys were irredeemably brothers who took up more physical and psychic space than was ever fair. Clare and I, in cities across the continent from each other, had the same dream: scholarships for college where we would have single rooms, jobs after that with our own apartments. But scholarship students aren't given single rooms; and the matchmakers, following that old cliche that opposites attract, put us, east and west, into the same room.

Without needing to discuss the matter, we immediately arranged the furniture as we had arranged furniture with sisters all our lives, mine along one wall, hers along the other, an invisible line drawn down the center of the room, over which no sock or book or tennis racket should every stray. Each expected the other to be hopelessly untidy; our sisters were. By the end of the first week, ours was the only room on the corridor that looked like a military barracks. Neither of us really liked it, used to the posters and rotting corsages and dirty clothes of our siblings, but neither of us could bring herself to contribute any clutter of her own. 'Maybe a painting?' Clare suggested. I did not know where we could get one. Clare turned out to be a painter. I, a botanist, who could never grow things in my own room before where they might be watered with Coke or broken by a thrown magazine or sweater, brought in a plant stand, the first object to straddle the line because it needed to be under the window. The friends each of us made began to straddle that line, too, since we seemed to be interchangeably good listeners, attacting the same sort of flamboyant, needy first or last or only children.

'Sandra thinks she may be pregnant,' I would say about Clare's friend who had told me simply because Clare wasn't around.

'Aren't they all hopeless?' Clare would reply, and we middle children would shake our wise, cautious heads.

We attracted the same brotherly boys as well who took us to football games and fraternity drunks and sexual wrestling matches on the beach. We used the same cool defenses, gleaned not from the advice of our brothers but from observing their behaviour.

'Bobby always told me not to take the 'respect' bit too seriously if I wanted to have any fun,' Claire said, 'but I sometimes wonder why I'd want 'respect' or 'fun'. Doesn't it all seem to you too much trouble? This Saturday there's a marvelous exhibit. Then we could just go out to dinner and come home.'

We had moved our desks by then. Shoved together, they could share one set of reference books conveniently and frugally for us both. We asked to have one chest of drawers taken out of the room. Neither of us had many clothes, and, since we wore the same size, we had begun to share our underwear and blouses to keep laundry day to once a week. I can't remember what excuse we had for moving the beds. Perhaps by the time we did, we didn't need an excuse, for ourselves anyway.

I have often felt sorry for people who can't have the experience of falling in love like that, gradually, without knowing it, touching first because pearls have to be fastened or a collar straightened, then more casually because you are standing close together looking at the same assignment sheet or photograph, then more purposefully because you know that there is comfort and reassurance for an exam coming up or trouble in the family. So many people reach out to each other before there is any sympathy or affection. When Clare turned into my arms, or I into hers—neither of us knows just how it was—the surprise was like coming upon the right answer to a question we did not even know we had asked.

Through the years of college, while our friends suffered all the the uncertainties of sexual encounter, of falling into and out of love, of being too young and then perhaps too old in a matter of months, of worrying about how to finance graduate school marriages, our only problem was the clutter of theirs. We would have liked to clear all of them out earlier in order to enjoy the brief domestic sweetness of our own sexual life. But we were from large families. We knew how to maintain privacy, a space of our own, so tactfully that no one ever noticed it. Our longing for our own apartment, like the trips we would take to Europe, was an easy game. Nothing important to us had to be put off until then.

Putting off what was unimportant sometimes did take ingenuity. The boys had no objection to being given up, but our corridor friends were continually trying to arrange dates for us. We decided to come back from one Christmas holiday engaged to boys back home. That they didn't exist was never discovered. We gave each other rings and photographs of brothers. Actually I was very fond of Bobby, and Clare got on just as well with my large and boisterous family. Our first trip to Europe, between college and graduate school, taught us harder lessons. It seemed harmless enough to drink and dance with the football team traveling with us on the ship, but, when they turned up, drunken and disorderly at our London hotel, none of our own outrage would convince the night porter that we were not at fault. Only when we got to graduate school did we find the social answer: two young men as in need of protection as we were, who cared about paintings and concerts, and growing things and going home to their own bed as much as we did.

When Clare was appointed assistant professor in art history and I got a job with the parks board, we had been living together in dormitories and student digs for eight years. We could finally leave the clutter of other lives behind us for an apartment of our own. Just at a time when we saw other relationships begin to grow stale or burdened with the continual demands of children, we were discovering the new privacy of making love on our own living room carpet at five o'clock in the afternoon, too hungry then to bother with cocktails or dressing for dinner. Soon we got quite out of the habit of wearing clothes except when we went out or invited people in. We woke making love, at breakfast and made love again before we went to work, spent three or four long evenings a week in the same new delight until I saw in Clare's face that bruised, ripe look of a new, young wife, and she said at the same moment, 'You don't look safe to go out.'

In guilt we didn't really discuss, we arranged more evenings with friends, but, used to the casual interruptions of college life, we found such entertainment often too formal and contrived. Then for a week or two we would return to our honeymoon, for alone together we could find no reason not to make love. It is simply not true to say such things don't improve with practice.

'It's a good thing we never knew how bad we were at it,' Claire said, one particularly marvelous morning.

When we didn't know, however, we had had more sympathy for those around us, accommodating themselves to back seats of cars or gritty blankets on the beach. Now our friends, either newly wed in student digs where quarreling was the only acceptable—that is, unavoidable—noise, or exhausted by babies, made wry jokes about missing the privacy of drive-in movies or about the merits of longer bathtubs. They were even more avid readers of pornography than they had been in college. We were not the good listeners we had been. I heard Clare being positively high minded about what a waste of time all those dirty books were.

'You never used to be a prude,' Sandra said in surprise.

That remark, which should have made Clare laugh, kept her weeping half the night instead. I had never heard her so distressed, but then perhaps she hadn't had the freedom to be. 'We're too different,' she said, and 'We're not kind any more.'

'Maybe we should offer to baby sit for Sandra and lend them the apartment,' I suggested, not meaning it.

We are both very good with babies. It would be odd if we weren't. Any middle child knows as much about colic and croup as there is to know by the time she's eight or nine. The initial squeamishness about changing diapers is conquered at about the same age. Sandra, like all our other friends, had it all to learn at twenty-three. Sometimes we did just as I had suggested, sitting primly across from each other like maiden aunts, Clare marking papers, I thumbing through books that could help me to imagine what was going on in our apartment. Or sometimes Sandra would call late at night, saying, 'You're fond of this kid, aren't you? Well, come and get him before we kill him.' Then we'd take the baby for a midnight ride over the rough back roads that are better for gas pains than any pacing. I didn't mind that assignment, but I was increasingly restless with the evenings we spent in somebody else's house.

'You know, if we had a house of our own,' I said, 'we would take the baby for the night, and they could just stay home . . .'

I realize that there is nothing really immoral about lending your apartment to a legally married couple for the evening so that you can spend a kind and moral night out with their baby, but it seemed to me faintly and unpleasantly obscene: our bed . . . perhaps even our living room rug. I was back to the middle child syndrome. I wanted to draw invisible lines.

'They're awfully tidy and considerate,' Clare said, 'and they always leave us a bottle of Scotch.'

'Well, we leave them a bottle of Scotch as well."

'We drink more of it than they do.'

I didn't want to sound mean.

'If we had a house, we could have a garden.'

'You'd like that,' Clare decided.

Sandra's husband said we could never get a mortgage, but our combined income was simply too impressive to ignore. We didn't really need a large house, just the two of us, though I wanted a studio for Clare, and she wanted a greenhouse and work shop for me. The difficulty was that neither of us could think of a house that was our size. We weren't used to them. The large, old houses that felt like home were really no more expensive than the new, compact and efficient boxes the agent thought suitable to our career-centered lives. Once we had wandered through the snarled, old garden and up into the ample rooms of the sort of house we had grown up in, we could not think about anything else.

'Well, why not?' I asked.

'It has five bedrooms.'

'We don't have to use them all.'

'We might take a student.' Clare said.

We weren't surprised at the amount of work involved in owning an old house. Middle children aren't. Our friends, most of whom were still cooped up in apartments, liked to come out in those early days for painting and repair parties, which ended with barbecue suppers on the back lawn, fenced in and safe for toddlers. Our current couple of boys were very good at the heavy work of making drapes and curtains. They even enjoyed helping me dig out old raspberry canes. It was two years before Clare had time to paint in the studio, and my greenhouse turned out to be a very modest affair since I had so many other things to do, cooking mostly.

We have only one room left now for stray children. The rest are filled with students, boys we decided, which is probably a bit prudish, and it's quite true that they take up more physical and psychic space than is ever fair. Still, they're only kids, and, though it takes our saintly cleaning woman half a day a week just to dig out their rooms, they're not bad about the rest of the house.

Harry is a real help to me with the wine making, inclined to be more careful about the chemical details than I am. Pete doesn't leave his room except to eat unless we've got some of the children around; then he's even willing to stay with them in the evening if we have to go out. Carl, who's never slept a night alone in his life since he discovered it wasn't necessary, doesn't change girls so often that we don't get to know them, and he has a knack for finding people who fit in: take a turn at the dishes, walk the dogs, check to see that we have enough cream for breakfast.

Clare and I have drawn one very careful line across the door of our bedroom, and, though it's not as people proof as our brief apartment, it's a good deal better than a dormitory. We even occasionally have what we explain as our cocktail there before dinner when one of Carl's girls is minding the vegetables; and, if we don't get involved in too interesting a political or philosophical discussion, we sometimes go upstairs for what we call the late news. Both of us are still early to wake, and, since Pete will get up with any visiting child, the first of the day is always our own.

'Pete's a middle child,' Claire said the other morning, hearing him sing a soft song to Sandra's youngest as he carried her down the stairs to give her an early bottle. 'I hope he finds a middle child for himself one day.'

'I'd worry about him if he were mine,' I said.

'Oh, well, I'd worry about any of them if they were mine. I simply couldn't cope.'

'I just wouldn't want to.'

'There's a boy in my graduate seminar . . .' Clare began.

I was tempted to say that if we had a family of our own, we'd always be worrying and talking about them even when we had time to ourselves, but there was still an hour before we had to get up, and I've always felt generous in the early morning, even when I was a kid in a house cluttered with kids from which I dreamed that old dream of escape.

BEAU RILEY

Beau Riley is best known as a poet, and it is the poetic that most nearly describes the two small pieces of fiction included here. Each one is constructed with the associational intuition of verse rather than the relentless logic of narrative. Each contains a pair of moments tied together inexorably, and unforgettably for the narrator. Ben in "Cruise Ballet", is not the same person as the unnamed gardener in "Accidental Renaissance;" but shares an almost Proustian concern with the minutest detailing of form and how it is fulfilled. Both stages in the growth of a gay man's consciousness are revealed: the apprehension of love itself in "Accidental Renaissance," and of love's disturbing probability in "Cruise Ballet." Simultaneously, the style evolves from the turn of the century formality of the first—identity—story to the very contemporary idiom of the last tale, dealing as it does with the "trick-acquisition barter mode" of gays today.

Riley's poetry has appeared in a variety of gay peridocals most frequently in Gay Sunshine *and* Mouth of the Dragon. *I believe these selections show him to be a prose writer of rare and original talent.*

ACCIDENTAL RENAISSANCE

I was born last Tuesday at four in the afternoon.

The date was June 21, the longest day of the year, and the light at that hour filled the cavernous building with yellow, flashing occasionally in excruciating bursts, though this may have been imagination. As will be seen, there is reason to distrust my account of the events of that day.

On Tuesdays it is my custom to take the Sutter Street car to the end of the line, near the domain of the Sutro family. There on the littoral is the bathing establishment which bears their name and which is a boon to the public health. For some years its tonic effects had drawn me there on my days off. I am, or was, employed as a gardener at a private home in the City. I fear that my stay in the hospital where I write these words may cost me my livelihood, even though my illness, my collapse, is indisputably not voluntary. Also, as implied above, I consider myself reborn: I must in conscience state that a change in myself may prevent my return to that household. For how could I again take up my duties, previously so satisfying, after the events of Tuesday? And how work again in the soil of San Francisco with hands that bear the blood of a boy?

I procrastinate. It has been some hours since I began this story and, overcome with remembrance, laid down my pen, unable to continue. My thoughts ranged instead over my own boyhood, dark and undetailed for its first eight years, coming bright only on the ship *Constance*, aboard which I rounded the Horn to begin my life as a gardener's boy. I was apprenticed to my father's cousin's husband, at the very house where still my belongings lie, among which is a faded daguerreotype of parents I never knew. Still you see, I digress, not to recall though I must, the color of an afternoon.

His hair was the same hue, a yellow ennobled to white. His fair skin, translucent, was indistinguishable at the temple from the fuzz of his sideburns; and his eyes—I cannot write 'blue' and be satisfied. The lashes I can say were transparent when dry, faded russet arrows when wet. That much is easy. What I can never hope to speak of reliably is his body; for it was that, a slight thing all angles, which enmeshed me, which in memory is all event and nothing whatever of substance. So it began.

The outer band of the enclosure is an open lane reserved for free swimming. I usually exercise there vigorously on arrival. Then, as man is an habitual creature, I rest in the gallery for a quarter-hour with a chilled bottle of mineral water. Ordinarily this interval is followed by my immersion in the hot pool, then by a cold salt shower, another of cool freshwater, and my departure on a solitary walk to dinner on the Bay side of the City, always a meal of oysters with bread and wine. This agenda accounted for my day and afforded all I required of respite from duty.

But last week, on going to the changing rooms for a nickel to purchase my drink, I was caught, no other word, by the cantilevered grace of this boy's body in motion. Too eager to join his friends, he burst from his cubicle, not quite covered by his bathing costume. Do not misunderstand me: though his naked breast was indeed visible, it was not flesh which held my eye. Rather, I was haunted on the spot, still am as I write, by the tide of his limbs as they flowed into the complex black garment, he on a dead run for the exit, the blanch of his skin and the dark of the suit a slow-moving surge of entrapment.

There. Having done what I can to convey that moment, the worst is over. Nothing in the rest of this story can be as difficult to call into my mind as this, though the tragedy itself is not yet broached. Perhaps one day, if I live long, I will find a man or woman wise enough to explain; no not that, to *comprehend* for me the distortion of time, of the very fabric of perception, which that brief episode in the changing room represents. I have sometimes glimpsed a similar thing in my garden, when I see the life of a white rose complete in a moment. Fragmented among a bud here, a full blossom there, and farther on the dessicate swelling of last week's unsnapped hips, the entire cycle impresses itself of an instant on my eye. But this I understand no better than the other. And, as in my garden I shake my head and pass on, that day I fetched my nickel and my water and sat, stunned but otherwise as usual, in the gallery.

My boy, for so I call him now, was among his fellows in the children's lanes, which are ranged immediately below the gallery. The boys were a tangled mess: some posed in that pride at which only flowering youth can succeed; some raced or tagged, like the seals who sported in contiguous water not a hundred yards beyond the wall of the building; and some made use of the waterslides, again like the seals on their rocks.

It is this tableau which seems punctuated in memory with painful upwellings of sunlight. Perhaps I have confused a memory of the ear—the shrieks of daring and of laughter from the boys—with one of the eye. Perhaps neither is real and only my heart, in anticipation, was swelling in rhythmic pain. I have confessed my unreliability on this. I will confine myself to the actual, though even in this the sequence of things is impossible to specify.

My boy appeared on the top of the slide, standing, wavering between bravura and fear. I think he meant to attempt the descent while erect. In any case he slipped and his fall, another tide of black and white, was marked by my cry. It must be that my hoarse voice silenced the crowd, for in my ears I still hear the dull double whump, first of his body and then of my feet, both striking the aisle of planking which runs between the lanes. And I hear the delicate snapping of his back.

A trickle of blood from his nose ran down my caressing hand as he died. At the instant I was pierced, as I think by his departing spirit. Certainly my pain was his and certainly I think I am he, myself gone elsewhere in his place.

Of my own place in the garden I do not think, but I shall, I must, return when I am able, to the sea, and there discover my new life.

CRUISE BALLET

Ben leaned on the railing and wished again that there were fellows. There were always fellows in the old days; a well-bred man could count on it, draw support in the thin times from his fellows. Still, the quality of life had suffered worse losses; one must be grateful the race continued to hang on and occasionally to enjoy.

As he thought, he scanned the comers and goers on all three levels of the building, as they made their ways about the central court. As a matter of course he'd spotted Adonis, or at any rate an Adonis; and he followed the man's progress from point to point, not becoming excited, not interrupting the main thread of his thought; for Adonises are easily spotted when one has no fellows. And too, this Adonis was ordinary among gods: he was of medium build, tanned; his hair was sand-colored and his clothes were snug. He was like most Texas beauties.

Thinking the word Texas brought Ben up short; he remembered to be annoyed at the heat and humidity. He remembered to be amused that he only bothered about the climate if he were otherwise vexed. Sighing, smiling slightly, he sat where he could continue to watch the parade and to enjoy the ratifying, calming mood of philosophy that was descending upon him, a mood he'd taught himself to evoke.

Adonis, he now noticed, had ascended to the third, his own, level and was proceeding about the area with that intentness of purpose which disguises purposelessness from the uninitiated and which proclaims to the initiated very clearly what is going on. Adonis was seeking whom he might suck, Ben said to himself. Having so concluded, Ben considered his body, making sure he was displayed appealingly and obviously enough to attract Adonis' attention firmly in the quick glance he was sure he'd be given.

Making his way around to Ben's side of the court, Adonis flicked a glance and registered Ben. Then, as if in an over-rehearsed play, he came directly to the chaise beside Ben's and composed his own body appealingly on it. After a careful interval, he said without clearing his throat, "Nice view."

"Quite," said Ben, who at such moments, under the influence no doubt of their delicate and precise formality, thought in a vaguely British mode. "Lovely."

After another specific interval Adonis cleared his throat and said, "How'd ya like ta fuck a sissy?"

Ben reeled with the pleasurable impact of the words, not yet quite a lascivious feeling. Rather he admired the other's complete sense of style; he admired the mastery they were both displaying: first, the unerring zeroing-in, without a hitch or a nervous gesture, with a discreet hesitation; next, the directness, the maturity, the self-control they'd both shown; last, the other's dangerous but successful coup in shifting from the high-formal to the low-comedic. Careful! Here was a man he might love. All this emotion took only a beat; without missing cue, Ben shifted to informal-consultive, replied, "I think we could work it out." And he thought, how elegant, how finely tailored our dialog.

"I'm James."

"Ben." They were friends now. Another very short pause while they both shifted about for the opening of the next segment of the dance, a formal frame within which they might improvise. Ben thought of saying, 'Your place or mine?' It was a fine phrase in its own right, but, he decided, more appropriate in a wilder and more bacchic surrounding than this. He began to look for another phrase when Adonis, James, signalled his intention to utter the next remark by shifting his posture more toward Ben. Duly, Ben stopped his own thoughts as James said, "Your eyes are so very blue."

Shattering! A complete departure from the trick-acquisition-barter mode, it was a foray into the mode of heavy-emotion, or, dare Ben think it, of love. Ben could not believe his ears. He had written James off as just another pretty face, during the opening moments, when he'd first spotted him two floors below. True, there'd been a flash of something very strong between them when he'd first realized the other's command of the style was formidable; but still he'd hardly dared believe James might be really interested in himself, might care for Ben more than for the aesthetics of the cruise. He was quite unmanned by this thought and was able to make no reply whatever.

After a while, too long indeed for any thread of the previous formal tapestry to be taken up again, James said, "Listen, I have no idea how to go about this and I'm scared shitless I might ruin it, so make allowance. Five years ago, before this building was here, when everybody used to have coffee in the old union, I saw you and thought, 'Who is that fat fairy with the intense forehead and why do I give a damn, since he's obviously so unsuitable?' Since then, I've seen you, sometimes, always with irritation; and today the vibes just snapped all of a sudden when I saw you'd lost your baby fat and must have gotten your act together and I think I love you and I don't even know you. I read a lot and when people fall in love this way in books it always works out badly and maybe I've blown it all. But I'm an Aries and I just had to say what I was thinking."

Ben was overawed by James' speech. He thought the proper thing to do in this case would be to rise soundlessly, take the other's hand and walk off into the sunset; for it was now dusk, he realized. But it wasn't 'the other' sitting there by him, and it was no longer a playful dance; something inside Ben warned him that if he were to reply, this time, entirely on style, he might have nothing to show for it but the form, or the memory of a form. And he feared that result. Adonis' words, no, James' words, cutting as they did across convention, were at once the ideal and the real: Ben simply did not know what to do. He was immobilised by these thoughts and he soon felt James' discomfort at his silence. James was making the little movements which suggest impending withdrawal. "Stay," said Ben, and they sat on into the darkness.

The next morning they both realized their behavior owed something to the movies or to other mythic imagination, on the one hand, while on the other being quite prototypical; they were not masters of this insight. Ben cooked breakfast carefully. But since last night his perception of himself kept slipping into and out of the idealized, the fantastic. He was unnerved; the simplest gesture, from a kiss to the breaking of an egg, was a task. He had feared a misstep everywhere, feared to awaken and find that James wasn't real, feared to find himself alone and unloved. Only his experience of serving breakfast to strange men got him through. He wondered what he would do if this with James should work out badly, if it became yet another one-night-stand. He wondered how, if it did, he could ever overcome yet another time his secret fear that gay people could never be happy.

"Perhaps we shouldn't be gay," said James just at that moment; and it wasn't a surprising remark. "I mean, it would have been a lot less trouble along the way for me, and you too, I guess, if we hadn't had to put up with it. But I have and I'm here and I like you and I'd like to stay. If you'd like me to?"

Ben was trying not to think of earlier, lost lovers. His reply was slow in coming but firm. "Fine. Stay." He was, and he supposed James was, at a loss how to behave now, having failed always before, having for consideration no successful examples. And having, besides themselves, no fellows.

NANCY STOCKWELL

For many lesbians and gay men being out of the closet is so much an accomplished way of life, so taken for granted, that living any other way seems grotesque. Yet only ten years ago, most homosexuals were still trying to pass for straight, still leading outwardly heterosexual lives. And even today, especially outside of the large urban centers that comprise the largest portion of the gay and lesbian population of this country, many still pretty much keep to themselves, and when they do operate, do so indirectly, secretly, furtively.

Nancy Stockwell's story "An Uphill Lie," from her collection of Kansas Stories, Out Somewhere and Back Again, 1978 is a portrait of a repressed gay man, Ted Craverse, married and respected, who has taken to manipulating the lives of those around him out of frustration and revenge. Two of those lives are nineteen year old Claude and fifteen year old Nancy, the narrator, whose relationship Craverse insidiously destroys. Stockwell tells her sad story from an odd and interesting perspective; the point of view of the young girl, who more than Claude or marriage, wants to be a professional golfer. She is attracted to hard, brown, good women golf pros, and makes a choice for that life—and probably lesbianism too—as she comes to understand exactly what kind of monster Craverse really is.

"An Uphill Lie" like its double entendre title, is a subtle and intelligent rendering of one aspect of the mid-American gay experience, our past and our present burden.

AN UPHILL LIE

Ted Craverse, the manager of Jacob's Hardware, was sorting nails and bagging them in the back room of the store. He put a sack in the pan on the hanging scale and then turned around.

"Let me tell you what the deal is in a story, that way it's easier to understand," he said to Claude Jacobs, whose father owned the store. Craverse always talked. He was always going on and on about something.

Claude wore a hangdog look and slumped his narrow shoulders. He was tall and thin, except for a slight plump around the middle. In high school Claude's friends had called him "Baby Huey" after the oversized comic strip duck who wore diapers. Claude looked older than nineteen because of his shape and his almost finicky mannerisms. And often, as he did now, he rounded his shoulders like a child who feels guilty.

"See, if your sister goes and marries that punk she's got engaged to, your Dad is gonna have a heart attack!" He snapped his fingers. "Boom! Just like that. And then what? What about your plans then? You couldn't begin to think of being a salesman, having your own territory, with that kid here getting in with your father. Because that's what he'll do. He doesn't have to be a quiz kid to know a good deal when he sees one. Besides he's got no choice, see, because if you don't make friends, especially with in-laws, your life is gonna be hell from morning to night. And if I know anything at all, life isn't gonna be any bowl of cherries with your sister Peachy, either."

"You think it's that bad, huh, Ted?" Claude tried to act mature but he sounded unsure of himself. Anyone could have seen it.

"Didn't I just say so, son? What's the matter? You don't believe me, huh? Come on, did I ever steer you wrong?"

I was standing by the plumbing fixtures, the shiny, plated faucet turns just inside the opening to the back room, listening to them. Craverse looked at me, telling me to affirm what he had said, or perhaps his look meant for me to reinforce Claude's sheepishness. I could never quite tell what Craverse was up to; there was a slyness about him.

When I said nothing, Craverse frowned at me, and shook his head as if to say *hopeless, hopeless*. He had that way of standing and staring at me, making me wait while he made up his mind about something. That's the way he made it seem, but I was sure he was just seeing how self-conscious I would get before he let me off the hook. He held his head back, scrutinizing the curve of my shoulder, hip and leg. And then he scuffed away some of the nails that had fallen with the side of his shoe.

"Marriage is the hardest thing in the world," he went on. "Course it's better than bein' single too long. When your father hired me sixteen years ago, Betty and I were having a pretty hard time of it too, not making much money, wondering what to do, but see we had a partnership. She was just starting out as a beauty operator. We saved for two years before we had enough money to make the garage into a shop for her. If we hadn't been in it together, like partners, we never would have made it. Both have to agree on what they want. Know what I mean? Peachy's only sixteen. She doesn't know what she wants. And your father *does not* want Peachy to marry that kid. You don't want him to find out how Peachy and John got that diamond ring do you? Claude? Ever think about the consequences in it for you?"

I stared at the tatoo on Craverse's right forearm. It said *USS Rigger* in an embellished style of lettering. I thought it was strange for him to have chosen that style, strange for a man like Craverse who was small, wiry, plain and hard, with a thin, narrow face and hazel eyes. Though, somehow, his mouth vaguely matched the lettering. He had a wide mouth and his lips were large and fleshy, almost puffy. His upper lip always parted from the bottom as if he had been adenoidal at one time.

"So," Craverse said, "you shouldn't have gone behind your father's back and let Peachy talk you into ordering that ring out of the catalog. That's what started the whole thing, son. I think we'd better think about how to try to right the situation, don't you? I mean, that's a question your're going to have to settle in your own conscience. You come on out to the wife's beauty shop tonight and we'll have a talk about what to do about it." He slapped Claude on the seat of the pants and walked away.

Claude looked at me. "I don't know whether to shit or go blind." he said. "I guess I shouldn't have let Peachy talk me into ordering the ring for her."

"I just came in to tell you that I'm going out to play golf and I'll be home tonight," I said.

"I'll come over when I get through talking to Ted."

Golf was the main thing I thought about, particularly since last summer. I woke up every morning and thought about what I'd practice on when I got through with the babysitting job I had. I read golf magazines, while I babysat, or practiced designing my dream course.

I also read the sports section of the paper every morning to see if Delores Alsterly had won any tournaments and what her standings were. I followed the other women golfers too, but I always looked first for Alsterly. There was never much news of the women, but there was just enough to keep my imagination alive, to let me believe there was some kind of a possibility for me.

I got the idea about being a professional when I was fourteen but it became a great desire after the summer I played in the Pro-Am tournament in Kansas City in a foursome with Delores Alsterly, a pro from the Broadmoor Country Club in Colorado Springs.

After the round we went down to the women's locker room. She introduced me to all the golfers. She said, "This is my friend Nancy—we could take a lesson from her backswing." We sat around in lounge chairs down there and talked about techniques and equipment, about how to get more power out of your swing, about certain small problems with a club that had been shaved wrong and wasn't lofting like it should. I watched their faces, their hands. I wanted my hands to look like that, with long fingers and flat thumbs to guide the clubhead straight for the pin I stared at their hands, watched the muscles on the undersides of their wrists as they made gestures or touched each other. All their muscles were hidden, on the insides of their upper arms and under their beautiful, suntanned shoulder blades.

And then Delores and I sat together at the awards luncheon. She asked a friend of hers to switch seats so we could sit together. I told Delores I hadn't done as well in this tournament as I had expected or wanted to. Partly, I told her, it was because I had never played grass greens before, that we only had sand greens in Myola, and partially it was because I'd gotten so nervous when I found out I was in her foursome.

"Your qualifying round must have been pretty good," she said, "if you made it into Championship."

"I think it was more like luck," I said.

"Luck? Hey, luck is just putting two steady hands on desire," she laughed. "What'd you do in the qualifying round?"

"Well . . . par, but I didn't have a handicap to turn in because they don't figure up things like that in Myola, but anyway, they said without a handicap I was just borderline, between A Flight and Championship. They let me choose which I wanted to be in. I just chose Championship without thinking about it."

"How old are you?"

"Fifteen."

After lunch Delores walked me out to the car where my mother was waiting. Delores put her arm around my shoulder as we walked and said it was nice playing with me. I wanted to put my arm around her waist so it would be easier to walk. My golf bag kept bumping between us so I switched it to my other shoulder. She took my hand then pulled my arm around her waist so we could walk in step.

"Just keep practicing," she said. "That's what I do. Just don't stop."

"I won't," I said.

"And if you want to be a pro, never compare yourself to anyone else," she said as I put my clubs in the back seat and got into the car.

"And remember," she smiled at me and stuck her arm through the window to shake hands, "never try to shoot over a trap from an uphill lie—if you can help it."

After that tournament all I could talk about was golf, about every shot I'd made, about every shot that Delores Alsterly had made, all the ins and outs of every position.

Finally, one night at the dinner table as I was going over it again, my mother blew up. She said, "I've heard absolutely all I can stand about that golf tournament. Talk about something else." Then she put her elbows on the table and leaned forward. "You can't make a living at golf. Look at how you did in that tournament, it's just too hard. And that Alsterly or whatever her name is only won a hundred dollars. She's a pro and she didn't do so hot either. Do you realize how few people ever get anywhere trying to be professionals? Huh? Do you? It's just one heartbreak and struggle after another. It never ends. Besides you can see what those women have done to themselves. What they get to looking like," she went on. "You saw. They don't even bother wearing any make-up or lipstick. You start hanging around with that element and pretty soon you'll think it's alright to look like that!"

I played with my food and stared at the green Fiestaware plate. I jiggled my leg up and down under the table. What could I do? Was there a promise? Yes, there was so much promise. I could feel it in my leg muscles and in my wrists and hands; it ran through me like the blood in my veins.

"You better be thinking about what you're going to do with your life. You're going to graduate this spring, in case you've forgotten. You better either go to college or get married," she said.

When the idea of Claude and me getting married had come up, Claude had talked all that over with Craverse, too, out in the beauty shop. That was last year when Claude was a senior and had to make a decision about what armed service to join or whether to let himself get drafted. It seemed to him that he had to decide it all, his whole future, at that time. After his talk with Craverse, Claude told me he wanted four kids when we got married and didn't want to leave me alone with them while he was in the Navy, which was what he wanted to join since Craverse had been in the Navy. But anyway, he told me, he'd decided to join the National Guard and that way he wouldn't have to go anywhere except to summer camp for two weeks once a year. He said after we got married he thought it would be good to live out near Liberal, Hays, Colby or Goodland, some place like that, and open up a sales territory to get some experience before he came back and went into the hardware store with his father. But, he said, he and Ted hadn't quite decided yet which place was the best territory for a salesman or what might open up in the meantime . . . that you never knew, that his Dad might turn the store over to him. And Ted would be there if a problem came up.

"Have they got any golf courses out there?" I had asked Claude.

"Sure," he said. "Nice sand greens. I asked Ted about it for you. He said you won't have any trouble playing golf out there."

I thought of Claude, I'd gone with him for almost two years and we had done what we were not supposed to do. And we had done it every weekend after that, sometimes at his house, sometimes in the car on a country road, sometimes at the drive-in movie, and sometimes, in the fall, at the Boy Scout camp. I started to think seriously about marrying him out of indecision and what seemed like so many barriers to other possibilities. I knew if I married him I wanted to live near Kansas City because of the golf courses up there. Big eighteen hole courses with grass greens. Nothing like the little course in Myola which had only nine holes, sand greens and was only 3,600 yards altogether. Par 35 for men, 39 for women. I always shot off the men's tees and played their par for practice. The eight hole was the longest and hardest; I liked it best. It was an uphill dog-leg to the left and the green was across a ditch. The courses in Kansas City had great, long stretches trimmed neatly. Here at home it was hard to tell the fairway from the rough. There was nothing subtle about the way you had to play here; you had to plow through and go straight after what you wanted. It taught me that much, the first step for anything. We did have sandtraps, though, which require a change in attitude and the touch of finesse to get yourself out. I practiced playing towards them, around them and out of them so I'd know how to make almost any shot to the green when I played a bigger course. I thought I would undoubtedly land in a trap sometime, during the most important match, the one I day-dreamed about, the match I still thought I would play in a big tournament, the one I would win. I wondered how I would ever get that far. I knew in the back of my mind that I'd never play that tournament if I married Claude.

When Claude came over after his talk with Ted about Peachy and her engagement ring, he said, "Wanna go to the drive-in tomorrow night?"

"What's playing?"

"Judy Canova in *Cattle Queen of the West*. Why?"

"Yeah, OK," I said.

We sat in the black and white station wagon and watched the movie. I was always fascinated by Judy Canova's pigtails. Why would a grown woman have pigtails? During the movie Claude said, "Guess what."

"What?"

"Ted talked to Peachy today. Dad got him to talk to her at the store because, you know, Dad can't even say two words to her anymore before he ends up screaming and threatens to kill her or something like that, so Ted talked to her. He talked her into putting the ring in the safe at the store until she really makes up her mind about getting married. I agree with Ted," he said, "that John's a good-for-nothing. Ted says she'll come around."

"I don't know," I said. "Ted doesn't run the world, you know."

"Oh he knows all about this stuff. He's really knowledgable. Hey, by the way, you know he thinks we ought to have a little talk. He said we could come out to the shop tomorrow night."

"Why should we talk to Ted?"

"Well he says there's things we need to be aware of. Like talking about the future, things like that."

"I don't want to talk to Ted about the future."

"I think we should talk to him. What's it going to hurt?"

"What exactly are we supposed to talk about?"

"About personal stuff. He says there's some things we ought to discuss, like about when we get married."

"What about when we get married?" In my mind a brown hand made a gesture, pointing to my cleated shoe which was aimed at a bad angle to the pin.

'Well he says there things . . ."

"Like what? Just tell me what."

"Things about a couple's sex life," he blurted out.

"What about a couple's sex life? Why don't you tell me what you're talking about."

"Look, Ted says we might not be doing it right."

"Did you tell Ted? How could you tell Ted? How *could* you?"

"I told you I tell Ted everything.—you know, to get his advice 'cause he knows a lot . . . you know . . ."

"You promised me. You promised *me*."

"Lookit, I'm sorry," Claude said. "What'd you want me to do, talk to my father?"

He kept harping little by little through the movie. "It doesn't hurt to talk. What's the matter with you. Can't you talk about sex?" Finally he said, "It's important to me."

Ted's house was a small, one-story house with tar paper on one side where he was making an addition. When we pulled into the gravel driveway, Ted was sitting in a rusty metal lawn chair smoking a cigarette.

"There he is," Claude said, waving his arm out the window. He opened his door and got out.

Ted walked up to us. He smiled and showed his small, short teeth, brown in the spaces in between from tobacco. He put his arm around Claude's shoulder and looked over at me. "Let's all go on back to the shop," he said. I felt the distance between the two of them and me. Ted had created it by touching Claude. It was an enormous space and irreversible.

Big wires ran from the top of the house across the top of two clothesline poles in the backyard and into the shop through a big hole near the roof. Inside, there were two hair dryers. They were the type which had clear plastic bubbles for headpieces. The long counter below the mirrow on the wall was cluttered with curlers, romance magazines, Coke bottles, overflowing ashtrays, plastic flower arrangements, bobbie pins, bottles of shampoo, neutralizers, waving lotions, and hair sprays. And there was the acrid odor of chemical solutions, the kind of odor that burns your nostrils, seeps through the meatuses and leaves a chalky, bitter taste in your mouth. There was also a machine for permanents. It had black wires six inches long which dangled from it, with metal tubes on the ends, like a milking machine that had multipled its teat clamps.

"Let's see here. Clear that seat for her," Ted said to Claude. He pointed at the chair used for haircuts. It was jacked up as if a child had been the last to sit in it. Claude picked up the plastic apron from the seat and tossed it on the countertop along with all the rest of the junk. Ted pulled the chair away from the counter and turned it sideways so when I sat in it I would face the two other chairs. He swept several pink plastic rollers away with the side of his shoe. He motioned for Claude to sit down across from me in the chair beside his.

"Well I guess we've pretty much solved the problem with Peachy for the time being," he said earnestly. He lit a cigarette. Claude watched him. I read the label on a gallon bottle of something.

"Peachy'll come around." Claude put in. "She's basically scared of Dad."

"Even though a person ought to be able to do as they please," Ted said, glancing at Claude, "I think Peachy and John would be better off to wait a while, even though often times parents don't approve of things which are really OK to do. But let's see," he went on, "now let's just see. Tell me how you two have been getting along." He turned to me. Then he looked back to Claude, patting on the knee as he looked at me for an answer. I swore at him in my head.

"OK," I said. "We're OK."

"Just OK or are there any problems?"

"I don't think so," I said.

"You're getting married. Right?" His eyes were intense. Small. There was a vein in his forehead.

"Well . . ." I started to say we weren't totally sure.

"Sure," Claude said. "Probably next summer. Or maybe in the winter next year."

"That's good—to hold off a bit, I mean," Ted said, puffing on his cigarette. "Not too long though—I mean there's always the risk of children—and if I can be more personal here, you know the more you do it, the greater the risk becomes. Of course, how ever long you want to wait. It doesn't mean you can't give each other a lot of pleasure in the meantime."

I looked down and saw my white sandals dangling in mid-air, unable to touch the floor. I pulled my feet up and rearranged myself to sit crosslegged in the chair.

"I can see I've kinda embarrassed her a little," Ted said. He gripped Claude's knee again and shook it back and forth in a cajoling way.

"Look," Ted said, studying me, "I guess I should say, there's a lot to getting married. And everybody needs help . . ." he looked at Claude's face and then said, "sex is one of the most important things. If you don't like it, or if the husband has needs, that get put off, it can make a bad situation." Then he added, "Of course!" as if he really weren't telling us anything at all. "Now let me just go on here and then you can ask me any questions, nothing to be ashamed of. There's a lot can be done to remedy problems. Claude, do you have any questions you'd like to ask me?"

I could tell Claude was trying hard to think of something. I knew he had thought Ted would do all the talking and would be relieved if he could just think of some question and let Ted to the rest.

"Well is it OK to do it a lot, like several times a week?" Claude finally said lamely.

"It's just like exercise, son, the more you do it, the better it is for you. Of course, there are times when you can't have intercourse. You know what I mean?" Ted looked back and forth between us, like a teacher with that kind of simple explanatory exterior. Claude seemed convinced.

"Didn't we kind of talk about that before?" Claude said.

"Yes, I think we may have. I think we said that when a woman has a period, her cycle, you don't want to do it then."

I was trapped. As an out, I pretended to act like Claude, like a student in this. But I was nervous, shaking underneath. And mad. As angry as I'd ever been. I kept thinking just another ten or twenty minutes and it will all be over, all I had to do was wait, just wait.

"Of course, there's so many other things to do, it hardly matters," Ted said. Claude nodded studiously.

"You probably already know all about this, about what to do during those *times*, but I thought I might go over it with you in case there are any questions," Ted said to me. "I'm sure you already know about the way to massage him." He jogged Claude's knee again and then began to smooth out a wrinkle in Claude's pant leg. "It's kind of a delicate thing," he went on, "but both people can get a lot of pleasure from it. It's just a matter of doing the right things." I didn't look at him. My left eye squinted involuntarily and I gritted my teeth. "You just want to take hold fairly close to the top and squeeze just a bit, isn't that right, Claude?"

Claude sat motionless, except to nod as if he were paying attention to a long division problem on the blackboard.

Then suddenly Ted leaned back in his chair and shoved his hands into his pockets. He stretched his legs out, crossing them and pointing the toes of his shoes in the air. I almost thought he was going to stop. "It's all just a natural thing. Lots of people are hesitant about the most natural things—like oral sex, for example." He frowned and blew smoke into the air. He puffed his checks out and made a smoke ring. He eyed Claude. "Most people thinks it's a homosexual thing. You know what I mean by homosexual? Course there's nothing wrong with homos. Did either of you ever try anything homosexual, or you know, with a homosexual?" We sat there. "Nancy, I said, did you ever think about that, or know what I'm talking about?" His voice forced me to look at him.

"Well now don't be afraid to try it. Either one of you," he said. He sat up in his chair. His voice was harsh now. "You're not afraid of things are you Claude?" He put his hand on Claude's leg, squeezing his thigh. "Claude?" Claude shook his head quickly. "Good boy," Ted said. He looked back and forth between us. "But I want to get back to this other thing for a minute. About the other thing, now I don't think this is embarrassing to anyone here," he put an arm around Claude's shoulder buddy-like and continued to stroke Claude's leg with his other hand. "After all we've talked frankly with each other and heaven knows this is all going to stay just between us. It's just a delicate matter. I'd like to make sure . . . that you understand . . . uh, nature, let's say." Ted concentrated, wrinkling his forehead, studying his hand smoothing Claude's pant leg as he spoke. I shut my eyes. Ted went on talking. I tried not to listen. Words came and went. Finally I heard him say, "Whoa, whoa son, whoa there now." And then he slapped Claude's thigh. The noise was smart and sharp, startling, it must have stung horribly, and I looked up.

Ted leaned back in his chair and fished in his shirt pocket for his cigarettes. He tamped the pack of Camels against the side of his fist. After he lit the cigarette, he tossed his lighter in the air and caught it with the same hand, grabbing it in mid-air with a snap of his wrist. He stared at me for a minute. Then he said, "I hope I've been a little help for you both. You're nice kids. If you ever have any more questions, you know where I am. I'm right here." He stood up on that. We all stood up. Ted held the beauty shop door open for us. When he walked us to the car, he walked between us, one heavy arm on my shoulder, the other around Claude and he whispered to him, "I hope I didn't make you feel like . . . uh . . . an experiment or anything like that, son. Know what I mean? I'll see you Monday at the store."

When we drove towards town, Claude said cheerfully, "I don't think we'll have any trouble in our marriage, do you?"

I didn't answer him.

"Isn't Ted great?" he said.

"No he isn't, he's a dirty, double dealing bastard," I said.

"What's the goddamn hell the matter with you?"

"Nothing," I said.

"Well you still want to get married don't you?"

"No, I don't, not to you."

"OK, OK," he said condescendingly, "OK, alright, what's the big beef all of a sudden? You got a burr under your saddle blanket or what? How come? What got into *you* all of a sudden?"

He kept pounding away with questions until we rounded the corner at my house and pulled up by the spirea bushes on the side. He jerked on the emergency brake angrily and said, "You must be a prude—I can just imagine what you're gonna be like when we get married."

"I told you I wasn't getting married," I yelled at him. I got out of the car and looked at his red, baby face frowning through the open window of the station wagon. "I'd rather have to shoot over a sand trap from an uphill lie," I said and walked away, so frightened, guilty, afraid, trembling.

"What the hell is that supposed to mean?" he yelled. "Hey, come back here, what's that supposed to mean? I guess I'm supposed to know what the hell that means! Come back here," he bellowed. "Come the hell back here and translate that for the goddamn human race!"

EMILY SISLEY

Emily Sisley writes of "Margot's Novel," "Published in 1980 by the Mosaic Press, the main text of The Novel Writers is about coming out of the closet in middle-aged, professional level, upper-income gaydom."

"For more than twenty years, a tightly knit group of gay friends (men and women) have amused themselves by weaving required first sentences into "novels" that they read aloud to each other at special weekend gatherings. The crisis occurs when the least adept of them manages to sell a novel depicting all of them in such thin disguise that it threatens to blow their cover. The Novel Writers describes how through a series of events and interactions the friends individually and collectively come to grips with coming out publicly.

"Margot's Novel" is one character's version of a "dirty novel." The piece is anything but "dirty," representing as it does a sensitive (albeit humorous) account of how such an erotic encounter might realistically occur in the context of Lillian's life."

I will merely add that my particular delight in Emily Sisley's selection lies in the fact that I'm certain that such lovely, unexpected and highly charged affairs are occurring this minute among thousands of housewives across this nation who wouldn't dream of calling themselves lesbians.

MARGOT'S NOVEL

I had noticed the woman who moved next to George and me. She had been out on her terrace on afternoon when I was vainly trying to mesmerize our ratty plants into growing in Manhattan's smog. We had spoken cheerfully, but it was only last Thursday that I had discovered her name: Birgit Sondergaast. A letter for her had mistakenly been dropped into our mail slot, so I knocked on her door and she answered.

I had not remembered her being so beautiful—she was ever so tall so that I had almost to look up to her face. Since I am five-seven, this meant she must be at *least* five-ten—almost as tall as George.

Her incredibly blonde hair fell loosely in a cascade of baby-soft tresses that seemed simultaneously to caress the back of her neck, her shoulders, and her very ample bosom—the last of which stood out firm and forcefully through the tight but long tank top she was wearing, and I could see she had no bra—the nipples stood out prominently. Her bare arms were the tone faintly suntanned white marble might be, and her tight slacks flaired just slightly at the bottom—where immaculately pedicured and exceptionally long feet

47

were barely clothed in handsome sandals that I knew had to be handsewn.

But it was her face that arrested my attention so that for a single moment I forgot why I had come. She was beautiful in the way Scandinavian film stars tend to be. Carefully plucked eyebrows followed the crests above her eyes, eyes that were at once blue and green; I could not decide which, but they were like mirrors to the Mediterranean. A finely chiseled nose stood between two of the highest-arched cheeks I had ever seen—*even* in those film stars—but I found her mouth to be the most incredible feature of this striking face. Her lips were long, almost to the center of the spaces beneath the high cheek bones. The upper lip came to widely separated points, and the lower lip almost pouted in its fullness. I had never seen such a sensuous yet oddly kind and *sweet* mouth.

She was resting a bracelet-ridden arm against the doorway, and she smiled pleasantly. I knew that all I had detailed of her I had noticed in the briefest moment. Yet I suddenly felt I had looked too long and I felt myself stammer slightly when I said, "This mail was delivered to us by mistake, and I thought you'd want to have it right away."

Again I felt a little embarrassed because no one would be in a hurry to get junk mail, but I knew that wasn't it: I had already read the return address of a publishing house in Germany. But Birgit did not seem to notice my flush of embarrassment. She merely smiled, thanked me. It wasn't a big production, and I liked the way, smiling, she said, "Oh, thanks so much" as she tossed the letter over onto a desk and added, "I was just about to have some iced tea on the terrace. Would you care to join me?" There was something so pleasant and genuine about her whole presentation that I accepted.

The apartment was pleasantly ordered—almost masculine in its simplicity. The furnishings were definitely Sloane, and it crossed my mind that I should not have acceded to George's wanting to get everything *immediately*—so that now our apartment was cluttered with everything from Hammacher-Schlemmer to Aunt Grace to the defunct Grant's in Poughkeepsie.

An exceptionally fine stereo set was shelved along with the rows and rows of books. I had known about *that*, because all new apartment houses have less-than-soundproof walls—but Margot's taste in music was good, although some afternoons I found the preponderance of Schumann and early Brahms a little tiresome. On those occasions I merely turned *our* hi-fi louder and listened to Bach keyboard music, or Bellini if I was soaking in the tub.

A typewriter and some papers were on her desk, everything quite neat. The room was large—much larger than our living room—but it only had a dining alcove and small kitchen. I assumed Birgit lived alone and wondered why assuming this made me feel more comfortable about being there.

While she was getting the ice tea I spent some time "checking out" her books. I noticed a fair number of volumes in German, but I determined not to inquire whether she was German. I loathe people who ask, "Where are you from?" or "What do you do?"—although I was terribly interested in knowing the answers to both.

"Ah, here we are," she said as she returned with two large pewter tankards filled with iced tea. In them I could see sprigs of mint. She paused and stepped back, indicating that I should go first onto the terrace, then suddenly extended one tankard and asked, with a trace of accent that I found most intriguing, "Oh. Would you mind? I should see what's in this letter." Sitting down on one of the two chaise longues there, I noticed her plants were growing a lot better than ours. She sat on the other chaise, her tankards on the white metal garden-furniture table between us. "This is terribly rude of me, but would you mind terribly if I just peeked inside to see what this is about?"

"Of course not," I replied with a smile, and turned to idly inspect her plants. Did I water our too much or not enough?

Birgit *did* only "peek," and she turned to me smiling and said, "This really calls for champagne more than iced tea."

"Oh? Good news?" I asked.

"My publisher has sent a contract for a new translation of *Concluding Unscientific Postscript*. I'll be working from the original Danish."

"How wonderful," I said, meaning it. "Are you a special fan of Kierkegaard?"

I watched with interest and found, with relief, that she gave no sign of surprise I knew what she was talking about. Only three years before, George thought Kierkegaard was the name of a fiord in Norway. Not Birgit. She took a quick sip of iced tea and merely said, "No, not really. I'm afraid I'm no expert on existentialism—it's just that I seem to have a knack for translating, and it beats teaching in a University. I loathe the way women still have to scrape and bow in Germany. I'm German, you probably guessed, but my father was born in Denmark of Swedish parents. No, I guess if anything I'm something of a nihilist—but you know how caught up everyone is these days with Being and Nothingness."

I loved the way she had said "loathe;" it is one of my favorite words. But I paused only to sip some tea before I quickly said: "Wohin gehören Sein und Nichts, zwischen denen spieland der Nihilismus sein Wesen entfaltet."

Birgit threw back her head and the blonde hair went with it. She squealed with delight. She slid her hand across the table, but she did not touch mine. "You know German! Oh, God, how marvelous. You know, I simply loathe Germans, but I get so lonesome to hear the language." She leaned forward rather intently. "And you speak it so perfectly!" She paused slightly. "But I don't know that quotation—or, how stupid of me, is it yours?"

This time I threw my head back. I suddenly wondered how short-cropped black curly hair looks with your head thrown back. I know I am attractive, and that blue eyes look good with black curly hair, and I was grateful for the splendid capping job Dr. Steinschwartz has completed last winter. Suddenly I wanted to be really *beautiful*. I could not understand why I cared whether Birgit thought I was good looking or not, but I did. But I did not hesitate after my little laugh to say, "Good God, I've never said an original thing in my life. That's Heidegger—*The Question of Being.*"

Birgit smiled and tipped her head in a little salute from off the edge of her temple. "Ah, then *you're* the expert on existentialism!"

"Hardly," I responded with a smile. I returned to my tea without saying anything more. But I sat there secretely thinking how it was the first time in my whole life I was happy I had majored in philosophy. Right before flunking my comprehensives I spent hours memorizing lines from Heidegger because I thought they were so *poetic*. What a happy choice of language! "Silly old fool," I thought to myself as I remembered how Aunt Grace had begged me to concentrate on French.

"Well, I'm not surprised," Birgit commented. "Not surprised at all. I knew I would like you from when I first heard your record collection."

"Oh?" (I didn't realize I played music as loudly as Brigit.)

She smiled. "I can't seem to get off this Romantic kick. Your tastes seem to be so much more—well, more developed, more refined."

"On the contrary," "I *adore* the Romantics." It was true; I suddenly realized I *loathed* Bach. I desperately wanted to hear something Schumannesque. "It's George," I quickly lied. "He adores Bach."

Birgit sprang up quickly from the chaise longue. "What would you like to hear?"

I thought madly. "Schumann's E-flat Piano Quartet." Carl had played it for a solid week before he and Jeremy took off for Fire Island. He had told me that the quartet's *Andante cantabile* was the single most beautiful piece of music in the entire Romantic repertoire.

"My most favorite piece of music in the entire Romantic repertoire!" Birgit cried as she went in to put on the record.

She returned with a pitcher and poured more iced tea. I took the cigarette she offered—though I protested I hadn't meant to stay and *should* run home for my own pack, and we settled back into our own chaise longues and our own little worlds. Nothing, not one word was by either of us. Yet I felt that we were in the *same* chaise longue, that there was some indefinable bodily contact between us, and that the music was a vague and diffuse thing being given shape only because we, Birgit and I, were sitting hearing it together. I found myself taken over by a strange, almost *elegant* excitement, and the sensation of genital arousal soared through me. By the time the *Andante cantabile* came I thought that whatever it was, it was the most tender and exquisite sensation I had ever enjoyed. I started to weep, soundlessly. When the quartet ended I turned to Birgit and was surprised to see her cheeks, too, drenched in tears. I had a sudden urge to touch her face, but I only looked at her.

She spoke very softy, and said only two words: "Thank you."

My puzzlement must have shown in my face, because Birgit leaned forward as if to get up. "I mean, thank you *so* much for coming over. I can't tell you how much I enjoyed it—I *do* hope we'll get together again soon."

Now she was up, I rose too. I extended my hand, thinking what a marvelously German thing it was to do. "I'm *sure* we will. And"—I paused because I knew what I wanted to say, but not why or what it meant—"thank *you.*"

Birgit smiled. Her tears had dried and left little marks down her face. I thought she looked infinitely more beautiful than when I first looked at her in the doorway. She showed me out, and we shook hands again.

When I got into our apartment, I leaned my face against the door frame for the longest time. I couldn't find any Schumann, so I put on the Franck Violin-Piano Sonata—something George had picked up at Korvette's one day in what I had thought was an excess of vulgarity—and dialed the machine to keep repeating. I soaked in the tub for more than an hour, and only had time to throw on a crinkle-cotton robe before George came in.

He was in one of his horny moods and I seductively opened my robe. (While sitting in the tub I had mused on what a good body I have.) He fucked me thoroughly, and I enjoyed every moment of it. But when it was all over, I realized it was not what I wanted.

I had intended to tell him about Birgit, and what an interesting woman she was, and how I was so pleased because one *does* need friends. But when he asked how my day had been, for some reason I told him nothing had happened.

*

For some weeks Birgit and I had been seeing a lot of each other. Never planned things—we never arranged to get together, and we *never* discussed other people, or played bridge, or went shopping, or whatever. But I took greater interest in the terrace and found myself devoting hours to fiddling with the plants (which I had loathed doing before) instead of "thinking" about them. They began to flourish. I painted the chairs and bought a new little table in Macy's basement.

But I never invited Birgit into our apartment. We would run into each other in the hallway, or chat across the terrace wall, and usually it would end up by my going over to her apartment for iced tea. We once compared notes about the relative virtues of Nestea, Lipton's, and Salada as instant mixes. That was the only "domestic" thing we ever talked of—and only because I was getting embarrassed drinking all that tea, and bought her some packages which turned out to be the wrong brand.

We talked about philosophy, and music, Germany, and New Haven. More often than not we sat quietly and listened to music or chatted about trivial things that somehow seemed important when *we* talked about them.

It was becoming more and more embarrassing to me that I had never told George about Birgit. One Saturday morning he came in from the terrace and said, "Hey! Who's that broad with the gorgeous knockers?"

"Oh, you mean Birgit?" I said. "She's from Germany, an awfully nice girl."

"Ugh," George muttered. "If there's anything I can't stand it's a dame from Germany."

The subject never came up again, and tonight, for the first time, Birgit and I had *planned* to get together. It had all come about when I commented that George was going to be out of town on business. Birgit spoke up at once: "Oh, why don't you come over for dinner?"

I screwed up my face in imitation of the way she so often does, and wondered if it looked as attractive on me. "Birgit, that's *terrible*. I'm always popping over here. Why don't you come"—I broke off for a second because I somehow did not want to say "our place"—"next door?"

"Oh, don't be silly. You're always cooking, and I so rarely have the chance. I hate fussing when I'm all alone, but I'd *love* to fix dinner here if you'll come."

We set the date for 7:00.

All afternoon I played an obscure Mendelssohn Violin-Piano Sonata I had uncovered in an old record store on Sixth Avenue. After busying myself around the house I luxuriated in a prolonged bath. I spent some time inspecting my body, carefully and meticulously shaved my legs with a regular razor rather than the electric one I customarily use. I decided to wear my fake-Pucci shorts because Margot had on several occasions commented on what lovely legs I have. I do. My other very best feature is my bosom. I chose a Lady Manhattan shirt with a wide, flowing, early-19th-century-type collar and lace down the front. I left several buttons open and was pleased with the effect when I studied myself in the mirror.

Then I made up with extra care, choosing a new shade of gray for eye shadow and an irridescent pink for lipstick. I was unhappy about the mercurochrome stain where I'd been hacking at an ingrown toenail, but I wore my best Town & Country sandals anyway.

Promptly at 7:00 I rang Birgit's buzzer, and she opened the door with a smile. She ushered me in with a great wave of her arm, and immediately out to the terrace. I noticed that the table in the dining alcove was immaculately set with a damask tablecloth, real napkins, good china, stainless silverware of Danish design, two kinds of wine glasses, and a small candelabra.

She excused herself for only a second and returned with a small ice bucket in which rested a bottle of champagne (*not* George's "Chateau Adirondack") and two exquisite champagne glasses. "How delightful!" I commented.

"Hmm," Birgit smiled, "that's what I adore about you, Lillian." (The way she said my name was, the only word is *thrilling*. I have always loathed my name, and almost everyone in the whole world called me Lil, including George. I had never even thought of myself as "Lillian" until Birgit started saying it. It rolled out so beautifully, it always seemed a *compliment* the way she said it.) "Anyone else would have said, 'What's the celebration?' "

We both laughed, and as we drank more—from a second bottle—we laughed even more. Once we laughed so hard I grasped Birgit's arm. For a moment I thought she flinched. On second thought I realized it was *I* who shuddered. It was not unpleasurable, but it was a shudder. I laughed again and finished my champagne.

Dinner was sheer delight. The food was gourmet, the wines excellent; we had our coffee and a small brandy in the living room. Birgit turned the air-conditioner on, so the French doors to the terrace were closed. The skyline had never looked so beautiful, and I wondered why—our apartment had the identical view.

Birgit flopped some pillows onto the floor and sat there as she sipped her brandy. "Would you like some music?" she asked.

I nodded.

"Anything special?" she asked.

"Oh, I don't know"—I paused.

Then a curious thing happened. We suddenly and simultaneously, *together*, said, "How about 'our song'?" We laughed as hard as we had on the terrace, and Birgit uncoiled herself to go out on the E-flat Piano Quartet of Schumann. We stopped laughing, I found myself grabbing some pillows and joining Birgit on the floor.

We sat quietly, absorbed in the music, occasionally sipping a brandy or puffing on a cigarette. When the *Andante cantabile* started, I put my glass on the coffee table and—quite calmly, as if I knew what I was doing and had done it before—I reached out both hands and rested them lightly on Birgit's shoulder. She stared into my eyes for what seemed an eternity and then, quietly and easily, she crouched forward toward me, put her hands on my waist and—still staring at my eyes—kissed me full on the mouth.

I had never been kissed like this, yet I responded as if I had been practicing all my life. Birgit's wide, sensuous mouth closed over mine with complete sureness—her lips were only slighted parted so that each one moved as though with separate life.

Sometimes it seemed her whole mouth sucked mine, drawing first the lower and then the upper lip into a press that sealed the corners of my lips—which then gently reopened as the tip of her tongue encircled the inner outlines of my lips and planted curious sucking pecks at each corner of my mouth. Sometimes our lips parted more generously, and we explored each other's tongue and inner lips. It was all so strange—not the wet, "sloppy" openmouthed kisses I had known and never very much liked. These were kisses—or, better to say, one long uninterupted kiss—like waves of the sea, undulating, advancing, receding, rolling, turning, invading, consuming, yet consistently gentle. Our mouths were like impassioned spokesmen for some overwhelming question that soared through our bodies and found both answer and promise in the very way our lips clung to one another. As we kissed, our bodies drew closer until we were encircled in each other's arms, pressed together, breast to breast.

I was beside myself with excitement. I had never known the pleasure of my breasts against another woman's breasts. There is some special way the flesh yields and melts together—and it was only in then that I realized I was necking with a woman. I hadn't thought about that. I had only sensed Birgit as a *person*, another human being, someone to whom I was overwhelmingly attracted. What before I had only "sensed," I now wanted to *feel*. I wanted my whole body to become as immersed in our lovemaking as it had been in the way we shared music, the tears of undefined joy that sharing brought.

This kiss, this series of kisses, lasted until I was in a state of rapture. I clung to her fiercely as if I could not live unless our breasts were eternally fixed onto each other's. I found my lips wandering all over her mouth. I could hardly breathe, but I dared not break away even to gasp in pleasure. We kissed until the music ended. Then we reluctantly *tried* to separate a little, tentatively pulling back as if this prolonged kiss was so special no other kiss would ever be like it—that was too grave a risk.

But finally we did part. I found it extremely hard to regain my balance. I felt I might faint, and my heart was pounding wildly.

Birgit looked at me so deeply I thought her eyes would burn mine out. She said a single word, and I watched her lips (those lips that had clung to mine, and I wanted them again) move as she said the word:–"Lillian." I shivered with pleasure.

Words were forming in my throat, and I knew they were strange, perhaps a little mad. But I was oddly unafraid. I wanted to say them, and I did. I stared back into those blue-green eyes and said calmly, "I love you."

The room was still and Birgit's eyes filled with tears that dropped quietly down her cheeks. I touched those cheeks, loved their wetness and I pleaded, "Please don't cry."

She shook her head with a tiny laugh and said, "I can't help it. I'm so happy."

I drew her close to me again. I desperately wanted her mouth on mine. We kissed more, and then deftly—I knew this was no "first" for Birgit, and I was *glad*; I felt a little afraid of my own inability to proceed, even though I *wanted* to—Birgit opened my shirt. She undid my bra. Suddenly her mouth was at my breast and we sank down on top of the pillows, she on top of me.

There was no mouth in all the world but Birgit's. It circled my breast, then came to rest over the nipple while her hot tongue darted there. Those exquisite cheeks worked to suck the nipple and as much of the breast as her mouth could cover. I groaned in ecstasy and ran my fingers back and forth through her soft blonde hair. First the left, then the right breast, and back again—and then to my mouth, which responded even more than before, and then again to my breasts and stomach, while her hands caressed my entire body and we wound our legs around each other and against our crotches.

Gradually she undressed me, kissing all my body as she did so. I was giddy with rapture. She undressed, too, and I gasped to see the long, graceful lines of her nude body. Ever so gently—and yet with a persistence and insistence that excited me even further—Birgit parted my legs and placed her mouth (that same mouth) directly over the front of my cunt.

I was already so hot and wet I thought I would come immediately. Her mouth closed over me and I felt her tongue run like an excited animal all over my clitoris. I *ached* with pleasure and moaned as she sucked gently. Then, here tongue thin and dartlike licked me back and forth and tongued my vagina. I thought I would explode and then faint.

Suddenly, on the very edge of coming, I knew I wanted *more* and, magically, Birgit knew it too. Her mouth, those encircling lips and that darting tongue, rested again at that special place and three of her fingers—knitted tightly together, hard and impassioned—slid deep into my hot, soaking wet vagina. My entire body shook in a spasm of sublime ecstasy and I screamed with pleasure as I sank back, spent.

I was in a swoon of delight and amazed myself that I was able to coherently plead: "Don't go away. Don't come out yet."

"Darling," Birgit muttered in a way no one had ever called me "darling." She kept her hand there for a long time as I lovingly caressed her head resting on my stomach.

Then I wanted her to come out. I wanted her to lie full against me. We clung to one another that way for quite a long time. I revelled in the sensuality of her nude body on me. Suddenly I seemed to awaken with a little shudder. I was embarrassed, apparently, I had fallen asleep. I started to apologize. Birgit only laughed gently and—again staring at me with those blue-green eyes—with a funny shake of her head she said, "Lillian. Oh, God!—the way you responded. I could make love to you the rest of my life."

I started to answer. She placed a finger in front on my lips and said, "Not now." She lit us both cigarettes and I lay close to her, grateful that I did not have to talk, for I did not know what to say.

*

I had spent the night with Birgit, and when morning came I found that I could not bear to leave her. I spent the entire day there. We did not get out of her convertible-couch bed except to shower and to eat a little.

It is strange that, just when you feel you've experienced the ultimate, there is yet another ultimate. Birgit seemed to be indefatigable, and continuously brought me to new heights of soaring. Sometimes I tentatively caressed her, and often initiated our kissing, I did nothing more. I did not feel uncomfortable about this because I sensed Birgit's tacit approval. I mean, it did not seem that she felt any urgency to be on the receiving end. I was grateful—partly because that idea panicked me, and also because I was feeling positively gluttonous about my new-found means to ecstasy.

When I finally returned to our apartment—after a parting kiss that lasted half-an-hour before either of us could open her door—I went immediately into the bathroom and took off my clothes. I studied myself closely in the mirror. Were my lips swollen from so much kissing? Were there any marks on my body? I kept running my fingers over my lips and each time I did so I recalled Birgit's mouth—the way it had been there, the way her lips played against mine. Each time I thought of it, an orgasmic sensation surged up, in, and over my entire body.

I studied my face and thought how unusually pretty it looked. I noticed one stray hair between my eyebrows and plucked it out with tweezers. I kept turning in different directions, looking at my body from every possible angle. I took a hand mirror and looked between my legs. My crotch was red and slightly swollen, and I parted the lips to look at that tiny organ that had responded like a center of my universe when Birgit's mouth or fingers had been there. I touched it hesitantly and felt pleased when—tired as it might have been—it seemed to yearn for more.

Feeling more and more excited, I crawled into a warm tub and, as idly as I had plucked my eyebrow, I began slowly to masturbate while the water lapped around between my legs. I thought how long it had been since I had done this. Then, because I had some aesthetic objection to touching myself with myself, I used the penis-shaped handle of an umbrella that had come apart.

It was that image that recalled what Sallie Cruikshank had been telling over bridge the winter before. A large drugstore on Lexington Avenue was selling something called a Vibraplexie. She even drew a picture of it. Roughly seven inches long, maybe an inch thick, tapered. They were advertising it as something that women should carry around for massaging tired feet! Runs on batteries,

$7.98. Her drawing had looked absolutely obscene, and we had all laughed uproariously. But obviously I had tucked the information somewhere in the back of my mind, like Heidegger or the E-flat Quartet, I thought with amusement, but not embarrassment.

That was the answer. I jumped from the tub and ran to look at a clock. Yes, there was time. I quickly pulled on a dress and dashed outside. I was beside myself with worry: Would they still have them? How could I *ask* for it? Would it still be $7.98?

It was with great relief that I rounded the corner of Lexington Avenue and saw the store's window display carried a full line of Vibraplexies—pink, white, and blue. I shuddered at the blue.

I approached a clerk. "I see you're still selling the Vibraplexie for $7.98?"

"Yes, madam," he replied with no more interest than if I had asked for a pack of cigarettes or a tube of contraceptive jelly. "Would you care to see one?"

"Yes, the pink."

He got out a packaged pink one, but commented, "You understand these are sold without batteries. They take a regular Type C flashlight battery. Would you like to see a demonstration model?"

I nodded and muttered a "Yes, please" and he produced a rather dirty white model which he flipped on. It vibrated wildly, and I asked if I might try it. Casually as I could, I stroked my neck and an arm just as the ads had shown. "Hmm," I said, "It seems to work quite well."

The clerk obligingly showed me how to undo it and insert the batteries, and how easy it was to turn on by flipping the bottom section counterclockwise. I thanked him, paid for my precious package, and hurried from the store.

I remembered the batteries and fairly *jogged* to Third Avenue, where I had once noticed a hardware store selling purple toilet seats that George wouldn't let me buy.

"Two Type C flashlight batteries, please—on second thought, make it four." I wasn't going to take any chances.

I felt calm and pleased with myself as I took the elevator back upstairs. I undressed quickly and inserted the batteries into the Vibraplexie. It turned on easily. I was about to go lie down and then decided I'd better *wash* the thing. "One can never be too sure," Aunt Grace always said about everything that existed, but in this instance I thought she would probably be right. I dried it off on a towel and while standing there placed the tip of it just barely into my crotch, hard against the clitoris, and turned it on.

The vibration was maddening in its insistence. In two or three seconds I gasped and shivered—I had come. Not a big one, not a "real" one, but I couldn't deny that it had happened. I felt cheated.

I went into the bedroom and lay across the bed—I even tried letting my legs dangle over the side of the bed so I could approach myself from different angles. I enjoyed it thoroughly. I was determined not to pull it off so fast, so I played teasingly—inserting and withdrawing the Vibraplexie, sometimes turning if off midway, and then on again. I found that I loved drawing the tip quickly across the clitoris—ever so lightly, let's not ruin it again—and then plunging it slowly, slowly, deep inside me. It was a delight to experiment. I wondered how it would feel against my nipples. Not bad, I thought, but nothing like a mouth! I laughed out loud as I thought, "What do you expect for $7.98?" I returned it downward.

By this time I had played too long. I was a little sore, for one thing (and not just from the Vibraplexie), and I had been holding back too much since the disappointing-too-fast happening in the bathroom. Now I wanted like fury to come, and I couldn't.

The "playing" was a nuisance now, more annoying than pleasurable. The vibration that had initially been so titillating was bothersome. I flipped it off and began using it as a phallus—in, out, in, out, *hard*. Then in and around: around and around and around. I started to bound about in bed, moving my pelvis like I really were being fucked. Suddenly, quite without knowing why, after plunging it hard in and out, I put it so the tip was just barely inside me and the rest of it covered my whole cunt. I then flipped in on and writhed with pleasure: the vibration seemed to penetrate all the way up through my body. I tightened my thigh muscles to cling to the ever-mounting orgasm. Then, just at the very height, loosened them as I plunged the vibrating thing up as far as it would go. I moaned a long howl and sank back against the bed. I flipped off my precious Vibraplexie, but kept it there awhile, re-enjoying the sensation.

I lay there only briefly and then went to the bathroom where I carefully washed the instrument, put it back into its pretty pink box and placed it deep in my lingerie drawer—next to the old umbrella handle that had not been used since George and I had married.

I showered quickly, ate some Mrs. Paul's fish sticks with a small salad and a glass of domestic white wine, and went to bed. George would not be home until late, and I considered it a good idea to be asleep. Besides, I thought, surely I'd have some interesting dreams—maybe enough to send me back to an analyst, if I could just find one who wasn't all fucked-up.

*

I found my new life not at all confusing. When George was there, we made love and I enjoyed it. When George was out of town on business, Birgit and I slept together (always in her apartment) and I enjoyed it. By tacit agreement, she and I never made love when George was in town—although we did continue occasionally to get together for iced tea on her terrace, and we did go to one Wednesday matinee together. She was pleasant to be with. I enjoyed her attention, her flirtatious glances, the touch of her arm against mine as we sat in the theatre.

I found that I had no sense of conflict about juggling two situations. I still liked being fucked by George, at the same time I sensed an overwhelming feeling of *being in love* with Birgit. I never made any kind of "commitment" (other than saying "I love you" to her, which I felt was true). Nor did I seem time to regard her or myself as a lesbian, nor our affair as homosexual, though I realized that, by definition, it was. One afternoon I did muse that it was rather a pity we're all slightly too old to fit in with the "younger generation;" they seemed to be so marvelously free, slipping easily from one mode to another.

My days were filled with the usual trivia I had for years found to be so fulfilling—chuckling at *The Village Voice*, seriously studying *Esquire*, puking over *House Beautiful*, feeling comforted by *Time*, whiling away extra time with *War and Peace* and *The Brothers Karamazov* (I like to alternate them). I continued to shop at Bloomingdale's, but I found myself devoting more of the important hours of the day to contemplative pursuits. One day I invented a recipe:

Break one Grade A Extra Large egg into martini glass. Whip briskly until well mixed and slightly foamy. Take two 2 × 2 inch sterile gauze pads and combine. Dip into egg mixture. Apply with steady, circular motions to entire lips-parted vulva.

I tried it and found it to be a successful replica of oral sex. That, with the Vibraplexie, and one's equipment for self-satisfaction is quite complete.

Early August brought the promise of an extended out-of-town trip for George. He would be gone nearly the entire week. I mentioned this to Birgit one afternoon as we sipped iced tea on her terrace. She asked, "Say, I wonder if you would enjoy going over to Paul's with me on Tuesday? You know, I rarely go to parties and"—she looked at me closely—"I don't know how you'd feel about this kind of party. Well, I mean, it will be gay. But *nice* people, and Paul's *so* lovely, and"—she again looked at me closely—"Well, I'd be so . . . *happy* to be able to go there with you."

I couldn't imagine how this had been so hard for her to say. I sensed that she realized this was my feeling when I quickly replied, "I'd *love* to go with you, Birgit."

Birgit was obviously relieved. She lit a cigarette and sighed as she exhaled the smoke. She smiled faintly and turned to me, "Well, I didn't know. I was a little afraid you might not want to, well, associate with such a crowd."

"My God, Birgit, I wasn't born yesterday. After all, I *know* about such things. Besides, I've been damned bored with that—that other crowd." I paused. "You know, all those *straight* people." I said it with some emphasis.

Actually, it was true. I had been bored with all of George's and my friends. I felt *ready* for something new. I even idly wondered whether Carl might be there. Probably not, that was so many years ago. Still, I was curious. If he *was* there, I'd be sure to reach over and kiss Birgit at some appropriate moment—maybe while picking up a martini with my left hand, which is my better hand so I do prefer to show it to the fore whenever I can. (I'm sure that's why I hold a cigarette in my left hand.)

That Tuesday evening I made-up with extra care. (George had been gone since early Monday, and Birgit and I had already enjoyed a night and morning of exquisite lovemaking.) Birgit commented that she liked my gray eye shadow, so I used it. This time I used irridescent *orange* lipstick. It looks good with black hair and was especially effective with the suntan I'd acquired, spending so much time fussing with plants on our terrace and drinking iced tea on Birgit's.

The orange dress was perfect. It was a low-cut slip dress copied from the black one that two fags on Third Avenue had designed for me two years before. The original had created a sensation. All I had to do was walk into a living room and every cocktail glass was lowered while people stared at my nearly exposed and unbrassiered bosom. I had ordered five more in different colors. I put on bone-colored high heels and brushed my hair back so it looked like I just stepped out of a speeding yacht. It was a good effect.

I buzzed Birgit and she emerged in a sleeveless green linen sheath with a V-neck that plunged almost to her navel. I thought as we left the building and got into a cab, "My God, what a beautiful couple we make." I had never thought of it that way before.

When we arrived at Paul's huge, high-ceilinged and many-roomed Upper West Side apartment the host answered the door.

"Lillian, Paul," Birgit said simply.

Paul took my hand and placed his other lightly on my arm. He smiled broadly. "I'm *so* glad you came!" he said.

I was somewhat taken back by his youthful appearance. I knew from things Birgit had said that the man *must* be the same age as everybody else in the world—that is, 29 to 41, give or take a year—but, except for the slightly receding hairline, he could have been a college boy. His waistline seemed to me to be about the size of George's wrist. He was beautifully tapered from his broad shoulders down, and his shirt had been tapered to fit such anatomy. His face was ruggedly handsome—not at all "faggish," although neither had Carl's been—and his entire bearing was wholly masculine.

The assembled group was much the same as any I'd seen at cocktail parties, except they were all better looking, better dressed, and possessed of a kind of youthful verve that did not conflict with the dignity and seriousness that were also evident.

Paul saw to it that I met everyone there with an easy, nonfussing kind of attention. I chatted with a number of the guests—*none* of whom asked what I did or where I was from. I especially enjoyed the tall, somewhat older man whose political views sounded like what might come out of Gerald Ford if the latter had suddenly been given the gift of articulate speech.

It was much later in the evening, when everyone, myself included, was floating high but curiously still able to talk—that I happened to overhear Paul telling about some of his experiences with "daddies." I knew that he was not discussing older men, but rather the *married* men he always seemed to be picking up. Business meetings, walking down Lexington Avenue, on out-of-town trips, everywhere. It seemed that *they* usually "cruised" *him*, and the acknowledged glance and chit-chat over a drink always culminated in sex. But, Paul was contending, they usually wanted to be fucked. Not a mutual thing, they'd never do you—they wanted to be *fucked*.

He was saying, "Christ, just last week I got a phone call from that guy I picked up that afternoon in June. You know, the one who wanted to be fucked so badly. I didn't even know he'd made a note of my number, or knew my name. He called and I said, 'Sure, come on over.' Well, we had a couple Scotches and he started *begging* me to go to bed. Well, we did, and I did him a couple of times, but then he started saying, "No, no, I want to be *fucked*.' So I did. Then he took a shower, and asked if he could have another Scotch. He was getting a little high by then, and I said, 'Sure,' but I started to tell him—just like I did last June—that I really don't go for this one-way bit. Well, he damned near dragged me into bed again and carried on about how much he wanted to be fucked. So I did. Then I started to cuddle and he drew away. Don't want any of that stuff,' he said. So I hopped right out of bed and pulled my trousers on, and said, 'Okay, if that's the way you want it. But I don't like to play that way.'

"Well, he finally got out of bed and took another shower and then he asked for another Scotch. I gave it to him. We sat and talked awhile—but I made it damned clear I really didn't want to see him again, and that he'd better never call."

The small group around Paul muttered, and one of the men asked, "Well, who is this guy? And how do you always manage to find them?"

"I don't know," Paul said as he shook his head. "He's just another one of the daddies who has this big thing about being fucked. Name's George—lives over in the East 50s. Believe it or not, he works for the *phone company*. Some V.P. in charge of public relations."

Birgit's eyes shot questioningly over to mine, but I merely smiled and blew her a kiss. I wasn't annoyed; I was *intrigued*.

ANDREW HOLLERAN

Proof if any more is needed of the growing strength and vitality of gay literature is the meteoric appearance in our midst of Andrew Holleran. So much has been said and written about his dazzling premiere novel, Dancer From The Dance *(Morrow, 1978), that I will only add the following: the summer it was published, I saw muscle numbers I didn't think capable of reading ferry schedules to the Pines, with copies of the book under their arms.*

His pieces for Christopher Street, especially "Dark Disco" and "Nipples" also caused comment, by their unusual form (the personal essay at its most reflective) and by their trenchant criticism of aspects of gay life. The apparently superficial made intensely important—and a silver-tipped prose style are Holleran's most evident gifts, and he displays them to the hilt in the hilarious story published here, "Someone is Crying in the Chateau De Berne," one of the funniest country houses in literature since Noel Coward's Hay Fever.

Holleran's concern with the fixed institutions that gays construct for themselves and how those institutions can trap even the most wary, is the profound understatement of the story. Hadley, like Sutherland in Dancer, *gives a hint on how to get out of the trap: survival lies in being absolutely realistic—and slightly larger than life.*

SOMEONE IS CRYING IN THE CHATEAU DE BERNE

Hadley van Ness had the most beautiful hair—he went to a barber on Astor Place who charged only two dollars (Hadley loved a bargain, and could afford little more) but his hair was so thick and luxuriant, he always looked better than the people who paid fifteen dollars at Sebu. There were those who, out of envy or cynicism or both, claimed he was the only person they knew who once stayed in bed for three days with a bad haircut. It is hard to imagine this being true; but what they meant by this tale, of course, is that Hadley was shallow; too sensitive to his appearance. But who among us has not, on some days, considered his barber only a shade less important than, say, his doctor? Hadley was always a pleasure to look at, and when I caught sight of him at Grand Central Station one morning last March (we were going up the Hudson to visit friends of his) I noticed as I approached that the color of his sweater—a cinnamon crew neck with touches of gray—matched the color of his hair. The effect, as he looked up from his newspaper with a warm and reassuring smile—was stunning. "*Darling!*" he said to me, and held out his arms.

"No longer late for trains," I murmured as we embraced.

"No longer late for trains," he said with that dazzling grin, "and smart enough to travel with very few things." He hoisted his canvas overnight bag. "And considerate enough to bring gourmet cheese and appropriate books for our hosts. God!" he said, holding up an illustrated survey, *The English Garden*, "in the old days I was awfully rude, but now I'm so thoughtful I could puke!"

He took my arm and led me toward the gate to our train to Brewster. Only Hadley van Ness could have produced me on the spot with but twenty-four hours' notice; only Hadley, despite my deep affection for the country, could have persuaded one to visit the house of people one did not even know; for whenever Hadley van Ness pulled up on his motorbike, or telephoned, out of the blue, to ask for a loan, or a coat, or my company at a party, I always said yes. There was something about him I could not resist. "Now I must explain," he said, as we sat down in our seats and he took my hand in his and patted it, and looked straight at me smiling, "I must give you a little history. I don't want you to be alarmed, but these are *not* my favorite people we are going to see. They're all perfectly nice, and ten years ago I wanted to belong to their little group more than anything on earth. In the last decade, however, I've grown up, we're all grown up, and they strike me as just a teensy bit dull. This used to be their summer house, but now they live there permanently and they're even duller. They've always thought me mad, anyhoo. Wilcox is fun, and Roger I adore, but the rest are beasts. However," he said, "once a year—the way other people go to San Francisco, or Provincetown, or whatever, I go up to see Roger's new lover. He always has one, and he's always worth the trip. We'll just stay one night, play charades or something and leave, and anyway, you *do* enjoy the country, don't you?" I assured him that I did. He patted my hand again and said: "Well, it's all right then. Brewster is awfully pretty," he said, and with that he settled back to read a back issue of *L'Uomo*, and the train lurched forward and began to slide out of the station.

The journey we now commenced was up the Hudson—into the countryside north of those crumbling, mellow towns along the river whose mansions are now open to tourists on Sunday, up into that peaceful farmland dotted with reservoirs—lakes on which no sailboats sail, no swimmer intrudes, since they contain Manhattan's water—like the covers of packages of butter: the somber forests of

Brewster, where horses, farmers, and homosexuals retire when they have been too long in city pent.

The journey takes an hour and we read the entire trip, exchanging magazines, newspapers, letters from mutual friends, with the comfortable silence that is one of the legacies of a long friendship. So pointless did talk seem, Hadley merely handed me his calendar for the month, and I read the news that way. Not only was each event—dinner, opera, cocktail party, tryst—noted, but rated in the bottom corner with an "Ugh!" or "Golden!" I asked why he did things which were an "Ugh". He said: "Well, one doesn't know in advance. If one did, one wouldn't. But sometimes you find yourself in a loft in Soho with two video artists, waiting for a hustler with a ten inch dick to show up. You know." I handed him the calendar and said: "Of all my friends, Hadley, you're the only one who hasn't changed. You still go out to all these parties, you still have your heart-throbs, you still go to Soho and wait for hustlers with ten-inch dicks."

"*And* he had a pimple. Here," he said, and with that the train came to a stop in Brewster. It was lightly snowing, and there was no one to meet us. We called a taxi company and sat down on a bench. "How like them to meet us at the station!" he said. "How courteous, how chic!" He sighed, and said in a quiet voice: "You know, in all my years in New York, I've never fitted in to any group. I never felt I belonged." At that instant the taxi appeared. We were silent as we drove through forests of fir, over hills which gave us views of little lakes, and finally to a white clapboard house which sat at the end of a long driveway in a gloomy stand of pine trees. "Hello, Hadley," said a man with reading glasses and a magazine in one hand when the door opened. "welcome to la Casa de las Reinas Muertas. A name too silly to translate. There's just the two of us here now. Roger and Nick are out, and Wilcox is sleeping. Let me show you your rooms." We went upstairs after introducing me, to a room whose two windows looked out on an enormous oak. "Oh Clayton!" said Hadley dramatically. "It's so pretty I could die!" And, when the door had closed behind our host, to me in a low and serious tone: "I won't get a minute's sleep. I have to have a *very* firm mattress for my back. *I'm* sleeping on the floor," he said grimly.

"The floor?" I said.

"Absolutely," said Hadley. "Otherwise I'll have lower back pain for days."

It was not my first contact with Hadley's whims—but it brought to mind a remark made by a man who did not even know him, but who said, on learning I planned to attend Hadley's birthday: "You mean you still know Geminis? I got rid of my Geminis years ago!" I asked why. He said: "They're all very charming, but so inconsiderate!"

To briefly describe life in the house its occupants had christened Casa de las Reinas Muertas (a name I will not translate either) let me simply say that that afternoon—after introductions and gossip had dwindled to silence and we all sat reading in the living room, I looked up to see Harry sitting in an old red armchair as he stared into the fire with an index finger to his lips. "What are you thinking about?" I smiled.

He looked up at me. "I was trying to remember if I've masturbated today," he said. "I don't *think* so—but perhaps I did. Oh well," he said, and went back to his book.

Hadley looked up from the scrapbook on his lap—he loved scrapbooks more intensely than anyone else I knew—and said: "Here's Joe Clark! I haven't seen him in years! I wonder how he's aged."

"He's dead," said Clayton.

"I see!" said Hadley briskly. Then, after a moment: "Who got his apartment?" Clayton looked at him. "That divine apartment on Twelfth Street," said Hadley. "Who got it?"

"I haven't a clue," said Clayton.

"What a steal that place was," said Hadley. "Five rooms for eighty-seven dollars, and trees on both sides of the block."

"Why at the age of thirty-seven," said Clayton in his foghorn of a voice, a voice from the tomb, hoarse from cigarettes, slowed by life in the country, "is one suddenly a horse that has run free till that moment, but which is now saddled, bridled with guilt, discontent, self-reproach, and the nervous consciousness that one's time is limited? Why does that all become evident at once?" he said, his head back as he addressed the grandfather clock against the opposite wall. "Why isn't it gradual? Why is it overnight? To suddenly realize one's time is up, and one is about to be whisked offstage by one of those hooks they used for bad vaudeville acts?"

Hadley put down the scrapbook and said: "I've always said there are two things one should never talk about—hemmorhoids and age. Both may be troubling you, but do not mention the fact to others."

"I'm sorry," said Clayton. "But sometimes I get frightened."

"So do we all," said Hadley. "But it's a dreary fact which calling attention to only makes worse—so let's remember, these *are* our golden years."

"Hadley," said Clayton, "you said our twenties were our golden years."

"Clayton," said Hadley, "they're *all* golden. Life just gets better and better."

"Hadley," Clayton said, removing the cigarette from his lips with the slow, measured dignity of a man who deplores haste, "is it true you collected money for a Christmas tree from all the people in your building, and then gave a dinner party with it?"

"Well," said Hadley, "it doesn't take news long to travel from city to farm, does it! It *is* true," he said, as he looked up from the scrapbook. "I'm a van Ness, I *must* entertain! Besides, I got them a tree, a perfectly beautiful tree. I took it from the lobby of the Emigrant Savings Bank on Fourteenth Street."

"Was it a pretty tree?" said Harry.

"Very," said Hadley. He put down the scrapbook. "A girl's got to live, don't you see! I was destitute and it was Christmas and the apartment was deserted. I used white poinsettias. Simple. Classic. I had twelve for sit-down, twenty-four for charades, and got nothing but raves. I've saved all the thank-you notes! I've put them in my scrapbook. Wish I could remember the cutest," he said, as he stared off into space. "But I have no memory. That's why I left the theatre. I couldn't remember my lines."

"You have no memory?" said Harry.

"For most things," said Hadley. "I can remember the veins on the wrists of the boy I spent last evening with. Every one! To recall the veins on the wrist of Pablo Marcovici, the neurons rush to collide with one another. Not for *Hamlet*." Hadley stood up and ruffled the back of his thick, beautiful hair with the fingers of one hand. "Mmm," he said, "it's three o'clock."

This fact elicited no response.

"Would you like to take a walk?" I said.

"Oh, why not" said Hadley, and started up the stairs. "Let me just get my shoes."

Hadley disappeared upstairs. Clayton sighed, and said, putting down his copy of Mary Renault: "Where would Hadley be without his hair?"

"I beg pardon?" I said.

"Where would Hadley be without his hair? That magnificent head of hair?"

I had never thought about it, but when Hadley descended the stairs, I could not stop thinking about it: indeed, as we went out into the snow I stared at his magnificent hair and wondered if it did *not* explain his life. It was impossible to imagine Hadley bald, and it was evident he never would be. As we walked down the snowy road, the wind parted his hair briefly, like the fur of an animal blown into tufts by a breeze, and then it fell back into place. "To think," said Hadley, "I once wept that I was not included in that group! I used to see them in their blazers walking down Ninth Street on spring evenings with daffodils and champagne in hand, on their way to dinner! *I* was on my way to the Upper West Side to give some old man a massage! Well, weep no more! Don't get me wrong," he said, turning to me, "I know there are far worse things to be, they are not mean, or selfish, or thoughtless, but darling, they are *dull*. Do you know they watch a soap opera?" he said.

"Clayton told me," I said.

"I asked him what they did during the day," said Hadley, "and Clayton said, 'Well, we all watch "Another World" from two-thirty to four.' Can you imagine? That's why I live in New York. In New York one doesn't watch a soap opera. One sleeps with the actors!"

He threw out his arms to embrace life. I took a tree branch in hand, shook it, and watched the snow shower to earth. A sparrow flew up from an evergreen and perched on an oak limb to watch our progress. The air was sharp and clean. Hadley pulled a train schedule out of his pocket and read it. "I don't know about you, dear," he said, "but I'm going to take the one o'clock tomorrow."

"Oh Hadley, no!" I said. "You have to relax, they're all very nice, you have to undergo a sea change and give the place a chance."

"A sea change?" he said.

"Yes," I said. "New York is so fast that it takes a while for you to slow down, to get into this other rhythm. You see, we're—or at least, you're—still going sixty miles an hour, and they're all going ten. But it's so beautiful here," I said. "Look at those distant hills!

Just breathe the air! How clean it is! Feel the cold on your face, look at the pheasants grazing there!"

"*Aren't* you good," said Hadley in a flat voice. "Aren't you the perfect houseguest! I suppose I will give it another go," he sighed.

But when we returned to the house after our invigorating walk, filled with energy and good spirits, our hosts were in the same chairs, and seemed to have hardly changed position since we left; nor did they even look up from their reading at our entrance, or at the appearance of Wilcox Trent at the top of the stairs as we stood there unwrapping the scarves from our necks. Wilcox stopped on the stairs, held out his arms, and said: "Darling."

"Sleeping Beauty," said Hadley, holding out his arms. "Were you awakened by a kiss?"

"Gas," said Wilcox as he descended the stairs. "We eat nothing but bean sprouts and I fart day and night. When did you get here? What time is it? What day is it? What is my name? And where are we?"

"We're in Sleepy Hollow," said Hadley, "in a town called Coma." He crossed and embraced Wilcox. "Don't you look marvelous!" said Wilcox. "Having lots of sex?"

"Enough," said Hadley.

Harry looked up from his volume of Plato's *Dialogues*, and said: "Do you think happiness is virtue or sensation?"

Wilcox and Hadley looked at each other—years of madness between them—and then Wilcox said: "*I* think happiness is a pair of silken balls, resting on my chin. If you want *my* opinion."

"Well," said Hadley, with a smile, "I wouldn't go that far. I would say it's the right sweater on my way to Tea Dance."

And the two of them sailed off to the kitchen to gossip about people Wilcox had not seen in months. Silence descended over the house. Hadley came back to the living room to retrieve his cigarettes, and, after lighting one, sighed, and said, "Will we ever get to Moscow?" He rolled his eyes and went back to the kitchen. A log shattered in the fire. The deep domestic peace deepened. Around the windowseats stood pots of flowering azaleas, bright pink against the snowy panes, and African violets. A white cat dozed in the corner. A bird cage filled with a stuffed parakeet, two walls of books, and little alcoves in which a comfortable old chair and a floor lamp promised hours of happy reading, completed the decor. It was an old farmhouse, and even the fact the floors slanted was charming—like the imperfection in handmade lace. Wilcox went up to bathe, and Hadley fell in with the regimen by leafing through old copies of *L'Uomo*. "Hadley, can you cook yet?" said Clayton.

"No, I've never really got beyond Jello," he said.

"Who's cooking tonight?" said Harry.

"Roger," said Clayton. "He and his boyfriend should be back soon. He's doing an Argentinian pancake called *pantoche*. They're just delicious. And some fowl. He hunts, you know."

"I'll say," said Hadley. He put down his magazine and said: "Tell me. What is the new lover like?"

"Like all the others," said Clayton.

He elucidated this remark no further, but Hadley made a face at me behind the newspaper he held. We both knew that, at least in his opinion, all the others had been glorious.

"He knows a lot about plants," said Clayton. "He knows, for example, that a waxy begonia requires partial shade. I just learned that today."

But this was all he offered, and as silence resumed, Hadley picked up the newspaper and read parts of it he never glanced at in town—the business section, for instance, sports, science, obituaries—and the log in the fireplace hissed and popped. The white cat rose, arched its back, and, receiving no inspiration from the humans around her, lay down again in exactly the same spot—as if, its day's exercise complete, it could now go to sleep. The light grew dim in the room, and when I looked outside, the sunlight lay in long, low, slanted bars across the snow. The trunks of two oaks glowed a ruddy brown in its light, and then they faded to pale gray, and the early winter darkness arrived.

Just then there was a piercing shriek, and we ran upstairs to the room from which it came. Wilcox stood in the center of his bedroom, arms outstreched to a Delft vase of flowers on the mantle. "These azaleas!" he said, putting a hand to his head. "Are gorgeous! Did Nature have to go *quite* this far to attract a bee?" He swept out of the room and left us standing there. "Aren't these people mad?" said Hadley.

"I feel like an appraiser for Sotheby's," Hadley said in a whisper as we went into our bedroom to nap. "In the mansion of a mad old woman whose silver we want to auction. I've just come to see the pieces, and then I've got to leave. Where *is* Roger? And his new beau? What is taking them so long?"

We lay down on the comforter and he began to recall the lovers he had admired in the past: the Japanese swimmer on a scholarship to Columbia, the Argentinian cab driver who had left the seminary in Buenos Aires, the carpenter from Colorado, the naturalist from Oregon, these creatures so rare on eastern shores, these silent blondes with whom he had always fallen in love. "They were so special, you see, because they had a quality, a quiet masculinity, a lack of pretense," said Hadley. "They were not always *brilliant*. I remember the boy he met in Montauk in—1966." He sighed. "The last time I was in Montauk was fifteen years ago. I find it most upsetting that fifteen years separate me from *any* event other than my birth." He drew the comforter up to his chin, and said: "Well, he had absolutely nothing to say. I once had to spend the day with him, and found it a chore. But the others—the others were all, let's face it, mere gods."

There was noise downstairs and we raised our heads: voices in the kitchen, stamping of boots. We sat up and listened. "It's Roger!" Hadley said as I heard a hearty voice asking if we'd come. We got off the bed and bounded down the stairs, like children about to meet their father. "Hello!" said Roger. "Hello, Roger, hello!" we warbled. A young man with curly blond hair on which snow was still dusted came through the door and stopped. A single drop of water zig-zagged down his temple, golden in the firelight. "Nick, this is my old friend Hadley, and Steve," said Roger, and in the silence that occurred after we shook hands, and Nick said, "Hi, Hadley," and "Hi, Steve," one heard with utmost clarity the single pop of a log in the fireplace, in the great, breathless silence that sometimes follows the apprehension of beauty, or the peculiar knowledge—like the moment you know you have caught the flu again—that you have fallen in love. We turned to Roger and went on with life, as one must, as if the earth had not opened and swallowed us up. Hadley behaved as it Nick were not there; he interviewed Roger about his teaching post, his car, his plans for the summer, and mutual friends now living in Carmel, Key West, London. It was not until Hadley and I were setting the table, and we were alone, that he put a knife between his teeth and bit it. "Darling, he's *direct* from heaven," he whispered to me as he passed on his way to get more plates. Hadley began to pale, and I sensed this was more than the usual delight in a comely young man; in fact, he held his temple a few moments later and said, "I've got a splitting headache." Half an hour later he grimaced and touched his spine. "My lower back," he said.

"Next you'll have a fever blister," I murmured, by now familiar with my old friend's symptoms. By dinnertime Hadley had retired upstairs and told everyone not to worry. Nick went up with a tray. Downstairs we talked about New York until Clayton, coming in with a bowl of hot biscuits, said, "Who wants to take these to our sick friend?" and I volunteered. The dialogue within the room stopped me just outside the door. "You *must* go to Flamingo once," Hadley said, "if only once. I hardly go more than twice a year myself, I used to go every week, but now there's Studio too. And the White Party next week, and the Sleaze Ball after that, and the opening of Pravda. These are things someone your age *must* see, just as you must see Paris, Rio, the Sistine Chapel. You understand. They are wonders of the world! Imagine a gigantic space filled with perfect men at six in the morning, at nine they are still dancing, glistening with sweat! Everyone should experience it once, and who knows how long it will last?"

"I would like go to the city," said Nick in a quiet voice. One could hear his smile. One could feel the joy flooding Hadley van Ness (the wrong van Nesses, a cousin from Cincinnati once said coldly) at that moment.

"You know, you're quite welcome to stay at my flat," said Hadley. "I've almost always got a houseguest from somewhere, but it's no problem to find room for another. We'll have *such* fun! But you mustn't delay! In two months, it will all be over, and they move to Fire Island, which is a spectacle of a different sort. Have you thought of living in the city?" he said.

"Well, Roger-"

But this was too much: I entered at that moment and yelled, "Look at these biscuits!" Hadley shot me a look. "My food must be cold," said Nick, getting to his feet. "Has Hadley been enchanting you with fairy tales?" I said, Nick smiled. Hadley narrowed his eyes. "I hope you feel better," said Nick. He then excused himself and went downstairs. "You *couldn't* have entered at a worse moment," said Hadley in a gloomy tone, putting his hands to his temples.

"Hadley," I said, "there are ethics. Roger is your dear friend, and—"

"I *merely* invited him for the week-end," said Hadley in that same dead serious tone. "I think he should be seen. One rarely finds things like this in the provinces. That boy is magic."

"Earlier this evening, Hadley, you spoke of 'The Three Sisters.' May I remind you of another play by Chekhov? 'The Seagull'?"

"Is that the one," mumbled Hadley through bites of his chicken Marengo, "where the boy commits suicide—"

"And the girl falls in love with the sophisticated writer from the city, follows him to Moscow, and then returns, a broken bird, when he has tired of her."

"Darling, *I'm not going to do that!* I'm not sophisticated! I'd just love to have him for three days, and put his thank-you note—next to a photograph, of course—in my scrapbook. Some people collect butterflies."

"I collect thank you notes," he went on. "You know very well I'm not interested in the kind of long, and deep, relationship which is Roger's forte. I live for my scrapbooks! And I always will! The reason Roger has all these exceptional lovers, these gods, these angels—you must have wondered how he does it," he said, dropping his breast of chicken and picking up a buttered biscuit.

"I have," I said.

"It's simply that *he* is as single-purposed about having an intimate relationship with a serious young blond as *I* am about having twenty-four for Charades, and twelve for sit-down. Now you must realize that because Roger *has* this genius, for that is what it amounts to, because Roger *can* give himself to these fellows, he is never without one! Simple as that! What most of us fail to realize is that each and every one of us has a talent—"

"Which is death to hide," I said.

"Death to hide," he mumbled through his second biscuit, "and that we aren't competing with each other! And remember dear, a young man wants to be attached to an older guy, he feels secure, he learns, he meets people he never would otherwise—people like us! Remember how attractive *we* found older men when we were two and twenty? Thirty-five was the *acme* of attractive, in our eyes. A graying temple, a slight puffiness beneath the eyes, was *heaven*. Now *we* have the graying temple, the bags under the eyes, and we're looking for a recent graduate of Long Island University! Altar boys! No matter! *I* can't give Nick what Roger can. *I* haven't the time! A week-end with me in the city is *hardly* the plot of 'The Seagull,' dear. Try again." He finished his biscuit, licked his fingers, and sighed. "That was absolute heaven," he said, looking up as happy as a child. "I feel quite restored. Do you think if I went downstairs after coffee, we could persuade these girls to play a few charades?"

But this remained only a thought—even he decided they were too heavy a mass to raise to the heights Hadley demanded in charades—and he was still beside me leafing through an issue of *L'Uomo* when I dozed off. I was awakened by his hand on my arm. "Shhh!" he said. "What is it?" I said.

"Someone is crying," said Hadley.

I listened harder, and discerned the sound; it grew louder, then subsided.

"Someone is crying in the chateau de Berne," said Hadley.

"What?" I said.

"Someone is crying in the chateau de Berne. That was the name of our house at the beach, summer of '71," he said. "I remember lying in bed one night after a marvelous party, in this house filled with young, stylish, drugged beauties—and hearing that sound. Someone had just broken up with his lover. He wept. Who could it be now?" He turned to me with a frown. "Do you think Wilcox is weeping over the crow's foot he found this afternoon?" he said.

"Of course not," I said.

"Then who?" he said. "These people are full of gloom to begin with. They've retired to this house in complete despair, having concluded they are no longer young—as if a messenger from the gods knocked on your door one day with a telegram to that effect—and they must therefore retire from the scene. *Tant pis! Quelle dommage*! They're so loaded with regret, nostalgia, and remorse over their wasted youths, I suppose weeping in bed is not uncommon around here!"

"It *is* sad," I said.

"What?"

"That even among friends, even among families, there is often a secret sadness, a grief we can share with no one."

"But one does *not* sob over a receding hairline," he said.

"Over what then?" I said. "It *is* sad that so many of the men we considered wonderful, handsome, are now recluses. Replaced by eight hundred boys with black moustaches, who are all twenty-two and all named Luis."

"How thrilling," said Hadley, returning to *L'Uomo*.

The house was still, but for the tapping of an oak branch against our window. Hadley, untouched and unperturbed by the passing of the years, sat upright, ears alert, like a detective in an English murder mystery; only it was not murder he wished to detect, it was grief. There was a knock on the door. "Come in!" said Hadley. Roger entered. His face was calm. He said, "Hadley, I have a favor to ask. Can Nick go into the city with you tomorrow, and stay a few days? He's been wanting to for a while now, and I think the two of us should have some time apart."

"But darling, of course!" said Hadley. "I'll show him all the sights, we'll have a marvelous time!" Hadley put down his magazine, and went pale. He said: "Roger, I must be quite candid. May I be perfectly frank?" He took Roger's hand and laid his over it.

"Of course," said Roger.

"I invited Nick to stay with me, and urged him to come to the city, and told him he'd have a wonderful time."

"I know," said Roger.

"You do?" said Hadley.

"Yes. He just told me."

"Oh. Well, let me just say I in no way wanted to cause a rift between the two of you. I would never forgive myself. I do find him dead attractive, as who does not—the angels weep—but relationships, rare as they are, are sacred to me, and—"

"Our relationship is over," said Roger calmly.

We gaped. "No!" said Hadley.

"Yes," said Roger. "You'll be doing me a favor to take him to the city. We've simply been alone out here so many months, we've devoured each other. I'm grateful to you for your invitation." Roger squeezed his hand. "Thanks for your concern."

Hadley sat forward and embraced Roger and said, "*What's* a friend for?"

Roger said good night and closed the door. Hadley turned and said, "Now I know why I was asked this week-end. Roger knew this would happen!"

"What?" I said.

"This! I wonder what's wrong with him."

"With whom?" I said.

"Nick! I wonder why Roger is finished with him. Kind of like buying a house, don't you see. You always want to know *why* the owner is selling."

"Roger isn't *selling* Nick to you," I said.

"Of course he isn't, dear," said Hadley, as he put a finger to his lips and frowned.

"Hadley," I frowned.

"Yes?" he said.

"You shouldn't think of Nick as a used car."

"Well, one *does*, don't you see," said Hadley, with a frown and a sigh.

"What exactly *are* your plans for the boy?" I said.

"Nothing unusual," he said. "Just take him around. The weekend was all I had in mind, although it would be so easy to fall in love with that one. His eyes—I simply swam in them. Did everything but wear flippers and a face mask."

I broached then the wisdom of painting the city in such bright colors; in describing positively a life whose limitations we all saw very well by now; in leading him to believe that there was happiness to be found in such places as Flamingo, or at the White Party, or the Sleaze Ball. "Oh," said Hadley, "I won't send *him* to the Sleaze Ball. *I'll* go to the Sleaze Ball. These things must be done in stages. I'm not sure he even shaves every day! He'll go to the White Party. And anyway, you say all of these things are empty and meaningless and emotionally void, but dear, you didn't think so when *you* were twenty-three! They were fabulous! They were ecstasy! You had a ball! I find it very amusing that all you boys suddently decide in your middle and late thirties that the life you lately led was silly, sordid, and a waste. Easy to dish the host, dear, after you've left the party! Anyway, that's your opinion of it all, not mine! I think it's still divine! I want to die on my knees in a back room with dead babies oozing from my lips!"

There was a crash in the corridor—I leapt up, opened the door, and found Clayton kneeling among the tea things, which lay around him and an overturned tray on the carpet. "I . . . was just . . . putting these away," he mumbled, and, after helping him put everything back on the tray, I returned to bed. "Well," I said to Hadley, "Even eavesdropping has it's risks. . . ." "What do you think happened to all of Roger's previous lovers?"

"They're probably buried in the basement," said Hadley with a wave of his hand. He turned out the light. "At rate, it's clear to me who was crying."

"Roger?" I said.

"Nick," he said. "He's scared, probably, of leaving what is, no matter what else it may be, a very stable home. But the break up was not our doing. It never is. My conscience is clear, my calendar for next week *black* with entries. I shall take Nick everywhere!" And with that he sighed and—as only he could—fell asleep at once. Hadley could fall asleep in discotheques. He snored beside me in noisy slumber, oblivious to melancholy, regret, nostalgia, or concern over the price of veal.

In the morning we ate blueberry pancakes, and shortly afterward caught our train back to the city. Nick told Hadley the story of his life. Hadley composed drafts of his thank-you note as he listened. "I was *born* to write thank-you notes," Hadley explained to me.

I did not see Hadley for several months after our return. He owed me two hundred dollars, but I could not find the words to tell him so. That summer I saw Hadley in Central Park. "What happened to Nick?" I inquired. "Nick?" said Hadley. "Roger's boyfriend. From Brewster!" I said. "The week-end in January!" "Oh Nick!" he said. "He's living with a man and his mother in Brooklyn," he said. "He was so handsome!" I exclaimed. "But very dull," said Hadley. "The magic wore off pretty quickly, dear, and thank God I placed him with someone who loves him." "Hadley, you're not talking about a pet," I said. "I know, dear," he said. "But the man is very rich, and has already bought Nick ten thousand dollars worth of stereo equipment. And a BMW. Nick stays at home with the mother. They're all Greek, and she's a great cook, and Nick is as big as a house. But he wrote the most charming thank-you note after he left! I have it in my scrapbook next to a nude photograph of him—when he was skinny!" And with that we parted, and went our separate ways.

Eventually I came to see very little of Hadley, except from a distance, on the street, and on those occasions I did not stop him to ask for my money, my lamp, or my parka. Of Hadley a friend once said: "He tries so hard to be superficial, he has *depth*." But the friend who said this has long since disappeared up the Hudson, to one of those sleepy little towns with an abandoned factory beside the train station, on which the light becomes a ruddy gold on those quiet autumn afternoons when you step down off the train, and stand astonished by the silence and the beauty. He lives now in one of those little towns that recall the stories of Washington Irving, where the bricks of the buildings are faded and the aqueduct that runs down to Manhattan forms a bridle path between slender sycamores shedding their leaves on a warm October day, and the river is flat and blue and somnolent.

He lives there now—as do I—and only Hadley remains in the city. Even Nick, who has also been swallowed up by it, is sequestered in Brooklyn, fat and no longer beautiful.

JANE DE LYNN

Jane De Lynn's first novel, Some Do, *Macmillan, 1978, was that rara avis, a political, lesbian novel that punched first and asked questions later—and never, never preached at all. Her tense style and deadly accurate aim on the perversities by which the human mind amuses and sometimes destroys itself signalled a strong new voice in literature. The story is about a group of women who find themselves in Berkley at the end of the Sixties, in crises of different sorts, and who willy-nilly become feminists out of sheer frustration with their lives and begin to act out— outrageously at times—their conclusions about the oppression of women. De Lynn portrayed the relations between men and women as one of communication lines totally shot down—misunderstandings between them caused abortions, rapes and murders. Yet, even among the women, dialogues were often outrageously misunderstood too.*

In the story printed here, "The Designer and The Typesetter," De Lynn is still concerned with the impossibility of men and women reaching any kind of understanding—and its bizarre consequences for one of them. The designer's story is so sad, so possible, so beautifully distanced it reads like a fable out of some jaded Fin de Siecle La Fontaine: *one with De Lynn's unique, blacker than black sense of humor.*

THE DESIGNER AND THE TYPESETTER

The typesetters were so incompetent his anger had no recourse but to quickly change to resignation, then humor, and finally indifference. He was doing design and lettering for a small leftist organization that insisted on using what in the late 60's would have been considered Movement printers. The Movement printers (walls splattered with Viva Cuba posters) took a week to move the copy to the typesetters, three blocks away. The typesetters took two weeks before returning the first set of proofs, and the margins were so off (three-quarters of an inch wide) the designer could not have adjusted them to his lay-out. At this time he started dealing directly with the typesetters. It took another week to get the columns reset, but most of the initial typesetting errors had not been corrected; also there were new ones. This was the point where his resignation had changed to humor. When he brought the copy back he patiently explained each of his proofreading symbols to a tall fat girl with freckles who said they were quitting early since this was Friday, but they would fix up the copy Monday as soon as the work day began, somewhere past noon. As she talked he stared at a short girl with wire-rimmed glasses who was holding a razor blade in her right

81

hand. On Monday he showed up at five but was told to come back Tuesday. This time the girl with the wire-rimmed glasses was biting her fingernails in front of one of the typesetting machines. As he walked down the stairs of the building they shared with other anti-Establishment binders and plate-makers he realized he was in love with her. So far he had only spoken to her once, over the telephone.

Deliberately he came late on Tuesday. He hoped the copy would not be ready so he could yell at her. Then he could make up for his rudeness by taking her out for a drink, and maybe dinner.

When he arrived at five-thirty the only person in the room was a curly-haired girl he had never seen before. She totally ignored him as he aimlessly re-read his copy hoping the girl with the wire-rimmed glasses would appear. She did, carrying two cups of coffee, as he was blue-ing in an unimportant comma. He remembered with intense vividness the one conversation they had had, about margin widths. Then he began to talk to her in the over-precise tones with which one spoke to children, lunatics, and telephone operators. His head had the same kind of buzz he got when he held his breath too long underwater. It had been six days since he had stopped worrying about his deadline.

The girl was very understanding about his being upset with the errors in this—the third set—of proofs. She admitted three weeks was an excessive amount of time to set seven thousand words. She held the copy almost to her nose as he explained the corrections to her, paraphrasing each sentence twice as he had been taught to do on college papers. Then he sat down on the floor in the middle of a square of sunlight. He shut his eyes and pretended he was on the beach. People stepping over and into him as they walked in and out of the office only contributed to his impression.

The girl worked quickly. He stood next to her as she cut out bad lines with her razor and fitted in new ones with clear tape. The top of her nondescript brown hair, when she stood, was under her chin. Not only wasn't she his type, she wasn't even particularly attractive. His friends would think he was crazy.

He was nearly out the downstairs door before he realized he had forgotten to ask her for a drink. He stood on the stairs, trying to make up his mind whether to go back to the office. He moved up a few steps, then down, like a rat in a double bind situation. The longer he stood there, the stupider it would look when he went back to ask her for a drink, as he knew he would. She said no, as he had expected, which made him feel even stupider.

As he walked down the stairs a second time he thought about love's uncanny ability to limit the imagination. But even his thought lent the dark, graffiti-speckled walls a romantic, melancholy splendor, which he thought about with sophomoric poignancy as he sat on a bar stool with a mug of beer in his hand. The sun came horizontally through the plants hanging in front of the windows. His feet dangled above the floor. If he shut his eyes he was on a beach with the girl in the wire-rimmed glasses, on a hammock under trees he had once sat in, in a tiny town outside Acapulco whose name he had forgotten.

The next morning he decided it would not matter if he delayed production one more day, so he invented some plausible copy changes and for good measure added a paragraph he would never use. If she wouldn't go out with him, at least he could find out her name. Then he could call her up on the phone and hang up when she answered.

The girl was taping copy when he arrived. He promised to pay extra for the new paragraph if she would have it ready by that evening. When he came back at six-fifteen it was as if she had never moved. He looked her full in the face for the first time. They were alone in the room. Her hair was stringy and her face was smudged.

He knew he was thinking slowly and ponderously. He invited her for a beer, which sounded less official than "having a drink." It had been a hot afternoon for the 22nd of May, 83 degrees at one-thirty, and she accepted.

He took her to the same bar in which he had had poignant thoughts the afternoon before. The waitress was blonde and talked like she came from Mobile, though, according to the typesetter, she was born in the Bronx and had a yen to race stock cars. They each had a draught beer, light.

The designer had nothing to talk about, so he made jokes about the inefficiency of women typesetters and the job he was doing for the small leftist organization. He realized she wasn't paying attention to what he was saying, not that he blamed her, for he wasn't either. When he stopped talking as a kind of experiment to see what would happen she didn't say anything. Women could do this. He envied them this ability. He couldn't. He was too nervous. He started talking again about his job, his dog, India, Christina Rossetti.

He was sure he had never been in such close proximity to someone who had such little interest in loving, or perhaps even liking, him. Even if she loved him, he decided, it could never be in the way he wanted to be loved, for the certain quirky qualities for which he wanted to be loved. Unfortunately, this knowledge did nothing to alter the situation. She smiled at his jokes in a distant way at the appropriate times to show she knew he was joking. In the past at a time like this he would have bought a pack of cigarettes. The typesetter did not join him in a third beer but she smoked like crazy. Thank God she liked Indian food.

Over dinner he found out she knew nothing about art. She was interested in feminist self-help clinics. He listened patiently as she earnestly described various hassles with the legal profession, city council, and journalists. As was often the case when he was in love, he was bored and irritated. He wanted to brush the hair out of her eyes and tell her how out-of-sight she looked when she got caught up in something. It had pleased the girls in college but you couldn't get away with stuff like that now. A week ago he would not have believed he would by buying dinner for someone who had never heard of Robert Rauschenberg.

"I thought you were gay," he said for no particular reason after swallowing some mango chutney.

"I am," she said.

He drank some water and dipped the paratha in some green stuff that looked like watery pea soup.

"Me too," he heard himself saying.

"Really?"

"Really."

The girl had no current lover and he told her he did not either, as in fact he did not, nor was he into cruising.

They went to movies and an occasional concert on the pier together. The longer he delayed telling her he had said he was gay only to fill a nervous gap in the conversation, the more difficult it became to say it, and so he never did.

Soon after he found himself marching in the annual Christopher Street Liberation Day parade to celebrate Gay Pride Week. It was the kind of sunny Sunday afternoon in June he usually found himself on some part of Long Island. He chose to walk with the girl and her typesetting collective rather than with the men, he told her, as a sign of solidarity.

A broadcaster from ABC's Eyewitness News stopped them on 34th Street as they were the first male-female couple the broadcaster had seen in the parade whom he was absolutely positive were neither transsexuals or transvestites. The designer said he had recently come out, thanks to Gay Liberation. His parents lived in Sacramento and didn't mind. The girl said her parents had kicked her out of the house when she was seventeen, in Grand Rapids, when her father had seen her kissing a girlfriend on the kitchen floor, nude. She had not seen them since then, though last year they had sent her a check for Christmas. The designer was forced to admit that he had gone to Pratt.

When the parade was over the designer, the typesetter, and the collective headed for the collective's favorite Village bar, which was packed for the occasion. The designer was surprised how deep his voice sounded on the six o'clock news, and how short the girl was next to him. When she saw their faces on the television, the bartender gave them a free round. It was the first time the designer had ever been in a gay bar.

One lie the designer had told on television was that his parents were living in Sacramento. He had used this name because a picture of a sixteen ounce can of peeled red tomatoes flashed in his mind for no reason at approximately the same time as the newsman's question. In fact, his father owned a drugstore on the upper West Side of Manhattan. There was no way that neither the designer's mother or father nor one of their friends or customers would have not have been watching the last quarter of the six o'clock news.

That night the designer cried for the first time since his dog had gotten run over. He wet the pillows with his tears and let the damp dry around him like sweat after making love. His parents would never believe it was all a mistake. Nor would he ever have the girl, who bored him, whom he loved, who would never love him because she had stopped sleeping with men two years ago. Not that she hadn't had sex with a number of them; she just didn't like it very much.

Since he had had these thoughts before and knew where they were coming from and going to, and he didn't want to have them any more, not even one hour, he took out the automatic he had acquired in his leftist days, shoved in a clip, and stuck it to the side of his head.

In his final fantasy the designer saw himself standing in the early morning sunlight next to the girl as she cracked eggs in a creamy-blue bowl that itself had a crack along the side. He would have bought her some nice Norwegian glass bowls if he hadn't been about to kill himself, but as it was he just stood and watched her crack the eggs. "I'm straight," he told her. "Really?" she said. "Really." Then she laughed. She laughed so hard she knocked the cracked bowl with the eggs on the floor where it cracked even more. She laughed so hard she had to lean her head on his shoulders as tears poured out of her eyes and onto his shirt. He had never seen anyone laugh so hard in his life. But even then, she did not fall in love with him.

If that was the kind of fantasy he had, thought the designer, he didn't want to go on living. And he left two notes to that effect, one to his parents, one to the girl. In the split second between the pulling of the trigger, and the convergence of the bullet with his brain, he had an unpleasant intuition that what he was doing was a mistake, in the very same way (but more dramatically) other things he had done had been mistakes, and the anguish of this realization jerked his soul and his head enough so that the angle of the bullet spared the medulla oblongata, while forever terminating the higher-brain activities—the ones involved in thinking, speaking, seeing, moving.

The designer's mother was furious. She stood at the foot of the bed and raged at the useless conglomeration of protons and electrons and neutrons that had been her son. She raged: at the designer's desire to kill himself, at his failure to do so, at the fact that she could not scream at him about it, now or ever. The designer's father said nothing. There had been doctor, hospital, and there would be nursing home bills for the next forty years—the biological life expectancy of his son—long after he and his wife were dead. Although he supposed it didn't matter whether the room a vegetable got its food and oxygen in was clean or dirty, empty or crowded.

The girl was furious too: at the designer's shameless body that refused to die (despite the myriad of tubes running in and out of his arms, his side, his mouth, his nose: how could it take him so long to die?), at the profound irony that the greatest love anyone would ever be likely to feel for her should come from such a jerk. For the rest of her life she could not stand people telling her they loved her, or even acting like they did: not because she didn't feel worthy of being loved (though she didn't), or because she didn't love them in return (sometimes she did), but because of the awful places love might drive them to. Far better to be lonely than follow them there! (The designer, she knew, would rather have been lonely.)

ROBERT HERRON

Gays have always been known for their sense of humor. Susan Sontag apotheosized one aspect of it, but other kinds are as important. Perhaps it is the part of the oppressor-oppressed relationship that we often do amuse — if only each other. This anthology is filled with different kinds of lesbian and gay humor, from the campy to the gentle to the delicious to the mordant. Robert Herron's excerpt "Moritz Goes To A Garden Party," is yet another kind: earthy, sly, a little like Boccaccio or is it Evelyn Waugh? But after all rather up to date, too.

Noel Haig's penthouse garden to-do for the titled Mag Ritchie-Hoare is all maiden aunt dates and fortyish fag antiquities collectors. Moritz's rooftop shindig next door is an afternoon drug orgy, starring porn flick deities and featuring S/M equipment. The two gay worlds represented collide in a mock Homeric battle that is set up as cunningly as any backwoods tall talesman, and released as tastelessly and amusingly as anyone could desire — with the added fillip of a surprise connecting link among the participants.

Herron is best known as a playwright. Among those works of his of special interest to readers of this book are his comedies Arrangement For Children, *premiered at the Eugene O'Neill Summer Festival, and* The Softness of Damion's Underwear, *1974. Herron has been researching the physiological and evolutionary determination of human sexuality in recent years. His conclusions, presented in public lectures are sensible, provocative and worth hearing.*

MORITZ GOES TO A GARDEN PARTY

Spot and Rover shared the same diet, shelter and cultural stimuli. So, you might expect them to have similar personalities. Nothing could be further from the truth. Take toilet behavior, for instance.

Rover would leap into the litter box without so much as "Here I come." She would perform her functions then shamelessly shirk the cover-up. Hardly catlike at all, she would flip a few inconsequential grains of sand over her fewmets, flatten her ears, glare about her with wild eyes, and cry, "Away dull care!" Whereupon she would tear around the apartment until Spot thwacked her and told her to remember herself.

Much different was studious Spot. Spot approached the litter pile with an almost reverential seriousness of purpose. She sniffed the box to make sure it was indeed the toilet box. If Master had changed the litter, she would defer the solemn joy of making doodie until she had reshuffled the sand to meet her strict esthetic demands.

Then she would do her duty. She did it with a severe lowering of eyelids which told the densest onlooker that it was a duty indeed.

Two divergent personalities, Dionysian the one, Apollonian the other. Which animal, then, would be most likely to cause ill-will between Master and Mr. Haig, who lived next door? Anyone would automatically guess Rover, the giddy pussy. Rover seemed like a troublemaking, self-centered cat. However, the delinquent kitty in fact, the pussy cat who could not let well enough alone, was none other than stolid, high-principled Spot.

Spot's sole moral flaw was an irresistible impulse to wander. When a cat lives in a 26th floor penthouse whose terrace is separated from a well-planted neighboring one by only a ten-foot wooden fence, it is not hard to guess where her wanderlust will lead.

A curious fact about Spot's delinquency was this: Every time guilty Spot slipped into Mr. Haig's veranda garden, the wicked kitty had to take a crap in one of his planters. Even then she was consistent. She always dug a deep hole to doody in. Hence, whenever Mr. Haig found a pile of compost-rich soil on the terrace deck, he knew that Spot had left her calling card in a planter above.

Spot's behavior would be deplorable even if Mr. Haig were an ailourophile. But Mr. Haig cherished a vivid dislike for cats. Spot's forays did nothing to convert the man to a more tolerant disposition.

These details would be of little interest to the friends of Moritz Jellico did it not happen that Spot and Rover were known to him. Their master was 28-year-old Napier Beddoe. In the May following Moritz's emigration to New York, Napier Beddoe was by way of being Moritz's regular sex mate. They were not lovers. But they had been enjoying sex together at least once a week for two months prior to Mr. Haig's elegant afternoon party for Mag Ritchie-Hoare.

* * *

Mr. Noel Haig trafficked in medals and decorations. He was what the Germans call a schmuckmeister.

Mr. Haig flogged schmucken more for love than money. He relied on a sizable competence left him by a grandfather to pay for his comforts.

Mr. Haig's source of merchandise lay across the Atlantic. There he spent three summer months every year sniffing among families of high name and low fortune, making himself agreeable to the wrinkled nieces of once-famous statesmen and generals, and allowing himself to be shown the shabby honors of much-daughtered and hyphenated aristocracy. Mr. Haig loved the enameled and encrusted bits of metal which passed into his cases. He paid good honest prices for them. So, he was able to effect their purchase tactfully, with as little embarrassment to the sellers as possible.

Brittanic trinketry was an especial passion of Mr. Haig's. He devoted half his scouting time to the British Isles.

On a routine foraging trip through the border country Mr. Haig solicited Mag Ritchie-Hoare for her family geegaws. Mag lived in a hugely dilapidated old stone castle and owned a broad collection of pre-Jacobean items. Most had been fabricated to reward piratical rustlers against Scottish cattle in the 15th and 16th Centuries. Mag knew exactly which medals to keep back from Mr. Haig for the family inheritors, and which represented historical garbage. Even the garbage she cannily relinquished only a few at a time. After several years of these amiable transactions, Mr. Haig established himself on a genuinely friendly footing with Mag.

When Mag wrote to say that her nephew with the British Mission to the U.N. had finally persuaded her to visit him in the States, Mr. Haig had reason to show her more than ordinary courtesy. Toward that end, he determined to throw an afternoon cocktail party in her honor.

But Mr. Haig was somewhat hard/pressed to decide whom to invite. Mag was a type not uncommon among rustic English aristocracy, a horsey lady with straw woven into her working tweeds. In many respects she was naive. She knew her animals, she knew her family, and she knew her garbage medals. But in many areas she remained innocent as any sucking babe, with the fresh forthrightness of a child. Being aristocratic, English and horsey, she could form her mouth around intelligible human sounds only with great pain. Mr. Haig could decipher Mag's throaty emanation and snortings. He wondered how many others could. Other Debretted equestrians would make suitable company for Mag Ritchie-Hoare, to be sure. But on his own side of the Atlantic, Mr. Haig did not hobnob with nabobs. Which was a shame. Because Mag Ritchie-Hoare, being reclusive and rare, was a great catch for the man to show off.

Mr. Haig settled on only the politest and most genteel of his own American circle — professional men mainly, with a few medal enthusiasts thrown in. The chosen ones followed a single pattern: unmarried men of his own generation who squired their elderly mothers to functions where female presences were required — certainly an unexceptional group who could give no offense to his bluff guest of honor.

So, Mr. Haig had invitations drawn. Runners were dispatched across the face of the mighty city, and a caterer engaged. At 4 p.m. on the last Saturday of May, the recipients were invited to drink tea with the Lady Margaret, Countess of Dump. R.S.V.P.

"Let there be champagne punch, tea, and other liquors," he instructed Mr. Perfection, the caterer. "Let there be Spring strawberries supported by dollops of crème fraîche. Let there be canapes and gateaux aplenty. Let there be colorful festoons attached and a great awning hung. Let there be a centerpeice of salmon mousse. And let me make it myself."

Salmon mousse was Mr. Haig's culinary specialty. He had served small molds of it many times on the terrace before, with his fresh fennel sauce. Mag lived in great salmon country, of course. As a tease, Mr. Haig would deny that the Scotch was as tasty as the North American variety. His party would provide Mr. Haig opportunity to uphold the reputation of Cisatlantic salmon. It would make a nice surprise for Mag, Mr. Haig thought. Mr. Perfection could only agree.

Acceptances came in, plans went ahead, and Saturday arrived. On the appointed day, all was expectant Rossinian bustle at one end of the 26th floor penthouse terrace.

* * *

A far different mood prevailed on the Beddoe side. There, only Wagner, dark, Fafnerian Wagner.

Four men were sleeping off a night of depravity. Mouldy clumps of vermin-infested dust clotted their arteries. In their heads, leprous cooks stirred cauldrons of steaming pus and phlegm. Ah, God, what a night it had been!

Moritz and Napier Beddoe had dressed in their hardest clothes on Friday night. They intended to do the bars of West Chelsea.

Between West 23rd Street and West 18th Street, in New York City exists a community of rugged bars. These establishments attract actual and presumptive sadists, masochists, bike freaks, leather lovers, cowboy cutups, and other hard-core role players. All these bars support lively fuck rooms in the rear. A few bars highlight extremely narrow-interest activities, although the oft-heard rumor that one is devoted to the ravishment of young male ungulates was always malicious and is now untrue. Even so, this Chelsea strip is just the place to take a date provided he is as insatiable a sex maniac as you. To Napier Beddoe, the strip had the further attraction of being only two blocks from his apartment near the Ninth Avenue seminary.

Moritz and Napier wanted to hit three of the bars before the night ended, The Bucket of Blood, Tanna Leaves Forever, and Thong & Thew.

As it happened, they entered Thong & Thew first. There they encountered Knut DeLacey. Knut was a former trick of Moritz's, and had just made a name for himself in a gay porn version of an old movie classic. Knut had got the Fay Wray role in *King Dong* because he was the only actor in New York City who could sit all the way down on the Empire State Building. Knut stood about six feet four in his bare feet; Moritz thought of him as a giant. Lo and behold, Knut had already taken up with an even taller fellow, one Magnus Richards. Magnus was six feet seven — surely a titan among faggots.

Knut remembered Moritz's enormous schwantz. Straightaway it was agreed among the four men that they should leave Thong & Thew and repair to Napier's place, there to charm away ensemble the hours of darkness. Knut explained to Moritz, "Magnus wants to get fucked a whole lot tonight, as who doesn't."

Napier laid out the dope. Then he and Moritz sat back to watch the giant disrobe the titan.

Magnus was wearing basic black, of course — leather. Knut had undressed many a man and, with his actor's background, knew how to sustain a visual scene.

Knut embraced his partner, to start undoing the titan's leather vest lacing. At last, the lacing fell free. Knut slid his hand across Magnus's chest. And discovered chains.

The dark-haired titan had nipples which stood out sturdily half an inch; they were pierced with silver pins. Hanging from the pins and connecting them was a catenary of heavy silver links. Magnus was superbly constructed. Black curly hair swirled in cyclones across his chest. Everybody was awestruck by the muscularity, proportion and expanse of the man's mineral-laden chest.

Knut played with Magnus's nipples a moment or so. But not for long. In measured determined pace, Knut divested the titan of all his clothing but a cap and a jockstrap. Knut bent to the jockstrap as though it were going to present an enormous problem in logistics. But black leather jockstraps never do, actually. He ran his finger around the top of it. He cupped the hard cock inside it. And Knut slid his own cock underneath it.

Now came the moment to Reveal All.

Knut crouched in front of Magnus. He held his head low so Moritz and Napier could follow the revelation. The blond actor grabbed the titan's cache-sex by the waistband on both hips. He yanked!

Gasp!

Part of the gasp was in honor of Magnus's ten-inch cable of a cock which sprang out and almost knocked Knut over. But most of the gasp went to the credit of Magnus's scrotum.

It lit up.

Not really, but almost.

Some fellows who are into chains and studs decorate their scrotums with metal jewelry. Clearly, Magnus counted himself among that number. Like the floor of heaven, his scrotum was inlaid with gold patenes, and metallic memorabilia.

After appropriate whistling and a series of muted goshes and gollies, Moritz wanted to know, "You wear this stuff all the time?"

"Most pierce guys do. Every piece down there means something personal. This St. Christopher's I got from a Minnesota lifeguard when I was only 15. This provincial emblem is from a Mountie in Ontario. Just a week ago a cute little junky gave me this one; said he couldn't fence it because it wasn't real gold at all. I like my hardware."

From his foreskin, Magnum removed a crucificial fibula and tacked it into his earlobe, so he wouldn't lose it. "Hardware's great for identity reinforcement," he explained.

To help Magnus reinforce his identity even more, the three men began to kiss and polish his *objets de vertu* with their tongues.

The night had begun.

It did not end until six hours later. The last orgasm of the night was achieved by Magnus and Napier on the terrace. Moritz and Knut, lying on the living room floor, caught the scene in silhouette against the rising sun.

Magnus's orgasm, with Napier and the sun between his legs, brought festivities to a close. Everybody was gloriously exhausted — from sex, from drugs, from booze, from dawn, from mortality.

They slept. All together and all naked, in Napier's huge water bed. They slept as soundly as they had dissipated.

* * *

Consequently, none of them remarked the noise at noon when Mr. Perfection's staff arrived to set up for the tea.

Nor were the sleeping men disturbed by the sounds of awnings and banners being emplaced on Mr. Haig's terrace. The ten-foot wooden fence damped what little noise drifted in Napier's direction.

Mr. Perfection's forte was handling hosts. He made Mr. Haig feel perfectly comfortable in his own home. Meanwhile Mr. Perfection kept him from getting in way of the three handsome Greek boys who comprised his Very Efficient Staff. Mr. P. told Mr. Haig he must not squander his energies; he must preserve them for the great task of creating the salmon mousse. Think only of the salmon mousse. Mr. Haig allowed himself to be confined to the kitchen. Mr. Perfection's boys did their work.

They raised the awning, a lovely thing with springlike patterns of white and grassy green against a background of jonquil yellow. Beneath the awning they arranged makeshift but sturdy serving areas, planks lying across sawhorses. Then they spread out a long tablecloth perfectly coordinated with the awning. Coordination was Mr. Perfection's middle name.

Onto one end of the serving bank went the tea area. At the other end, the bar. In between would lie food.

After laying the table and flying the buntings, the Perfection team did last-minute cleaning up. The boy who swept beneath the middle serving table did not give a second thought to the small pile of planter soil he found on the terrace floor. He assumed one of his coworkers had somehow disturbed the flowers and made a little mess. He cleaned up the dirt and kept his mouth shut.

Well, of course, the Phantom had struck again. How could Spot resist the siren's call from OVER THERE?

Spot had been interrupted before she was able to complete the cover-up. Her castings lay hidden well enough for the time being.

Soon their tell-tale odor would work its way through the thin layer of soil which buried them.

Spot returned home, her trespass unrecorded save for the dirt pile which the waiter swept up. Cats being gifted with foresight in these matters, Spot had chosen to make her deposit in the planter against which the centerpiece table was pushed.

* * *

On that selfsame table an hour later, Mr. Perfection, with dignified flourish positioned the hugh silver tray which held the large salmon mousse of Mr. Haig's personal fabrication.

"It's lovely, Mr. Haig, simply lovely."

Mr. Haig agreed. The new large mold from Hammacher's for this single occasion had been money well spent.

Mr. Haig had done what he could for the guests' comfort. He could do no more. Now he must go and change, and make himself ready to receive them. Yes, to change his clothes and to ponder once more the rather embarrassing problem which might arise this afternoon.

Mr. Haig rarely found himself in a compromised posture. Forethought and safety. Those were concepts dear to Mr. Haig. But even a Haig steps off the curb now and again. Mr. Haig had stepped off a curb, and now he was faced with embarrassment.

It was all Virgil Price's fault, actually. Virgil Price lived only a few blocks from Mr. Haig in Chelsea. Virgil was an accomplished hustler who catered to the mature man. It was not unexpected, then, that his calling card might find its way into Mr. Haig's permanent reference file.

During Mr. Haig's New York months, Virgil came to his apartment once a week. Mr. Haig depended on him once a week. Mr. Haig's whirlwind days of sex were well behind him, Lord knows. Yet, a fellow likes the lash of a dulcet tongue once a week.

But Virgil had absented himself for a while. He'd accepted a two-week invitation to cruise the Greek Isles with another regular customer, leaving Mr. Haig bereft of his service.

On his regular Virgil night, Mr. Haig had gotten lonesome. So he stepped off the curb. There was a neighborhood youth whom Mr. Haig had seen many times but whose references he had not had occasion to inspect. The youth put himself in way of Mr. Haig's reach and came home.

It was all a horrible mistake. As soon as the kid took off his shirt, Mr. Haig saw the scars on his arm. In bed the kid hardly touched Mr. Haig, forcing Mr. Haig to assume Virgil's role. Then, when the sordid scene concluded, the brazen youth demanded a fee that was far out of line.

Worse came the next day. Mr. Haig had tried to keep his eye on the little bastard every minute. But he discovered that the dreadful creature had ripped off the Cheviot Commemorative. The Cheviot Commemorative did not belong to Mr. Haig. It belonged to Mag Ritchie-Hoare.

Last summer the Cheviot Commemorative caught his eye at Mag's. The Cheviot had been highly prized but stingily awarded during its period of issue in the days of Henry VIII. One border lord felt slighted at not having been recognized for his contribution to the Cheviot campaigns. For revenge, he got hold of the medal and had his smithy forge half a dozen imitations. These he distributed to his swineherds. Thus he was able, in one fine gesture, to display his contempt for those who had received authentic medals and to debase their rarity. Naturally, as time wore on, the forgeries became more valuable than the originals.

Mag would not part with her Cheviot, authentic or not. But Mr. Haig's professional curiosity burned bright. He begged Mag to let him bring the bauble to New York and research its provenance. He wanted to satisfy his own curiosity. With misgivings, Mag agreed. It was the Cheviot which the junky hustler had purloined. Mr. Haig had already spread word among his fellow medailleurs that he was in the market for a Cheviot Commemorative of any extraction. None had yet turned up. All too likely, Mag would interrogate Mr. Haig on the Cheviot's whereabouts today.

Mr. Haig was sure, though, that he could cover himself from the Countess's reproaches until he found a replacement. Mag could hardly dress him down if the subject arose—not during a lovely party he was giving in her honor.

Yet, Mag was British. She was titled. She was a Hoare. And she was Mag.

Halfway through his dressing, Mr. Haig got a telephone call from Tony MacSinnett, Mag's nephew at the U.N. He would not be able to come to the party—U.N. business. However, on Mag's flight to the States, she had met a young American fellow and had been taken by him. Would it be all right for this young man to act in place of Tony?

But of course.

Tony gave Mr. Haig the charming American's name and rang off.

Oh, good, thought Mr. Haig. This means I *am* in Mag's good graces. She would never invite her own guest unless she felt perfectly comfortable with me.

A knock on the bedroom door: "Mr. Haig. The first of your guests are now entering the building."

* * *

Six feet away, on the other side of the double wall from Mr. Haig's bedroom, four bleary men were weighing whether to get out of bed or to slit the plastic and drown themselves. Their druggy euphoria had turned into ashes of lead. Very heavy Wagner. Low rumblings of saurian arousals, sluggish stumblings of semiconscious reisenwurms, hot mephitic breath from foul monstrous mouths, stinking tails and feet, dragon flakes. Napier had not dispensed amphetamine last night. Everybody was crashing anyway.

However, never underestimate the motive force of full bladders. One by one the men had to get out of bed.

Napier brewed punishingly thick injections of Kenyan coffee. Nobody paid any attention to the sound of elevator doors constantly opening and closing. Napier had no idea his ill-tempered neighbor was throwing a do.

With great caution, the four men slowly got their circulation up to andante. Everyone took Alka-Seltzers. Each man stayed in the hot shower twenty minutes. Through the miraculous synergy of coffee, scrambled eggs, two loaves of whole-wheat toast, and all the milk in the refrigerator, the dragons slowly turned back into human males.

They felt human again, but lazy ones. They were men with no purpose that golden, slow Saturday afternoon but to lie on Napier's small, floating terrace high above the church where Clement Moore wrote "A Visit from St. Nicholas" and take their first nude sunbaths of the year.

Napier turned on WNCN low. It was playing "Gotterdamerung." The reviving orgiasts dozed while Valhalla tottered.

Not a creature stirred. Not even a mouse. One cat though was feeling restless.

* * *

Mr. Haig stayed by the door greeting his guests. Dozens of pallid middle-aged professional men escorted genteel elderly ladies wearing white gloves, filmy flowing afternoon dresses, and great summer leghorn hats—old lady finery for meeting a countess.

What a lovely terrace! Mr. Perfection's minions had outdone themselves. It could not have been prettier.

Mrs. Devou, Toddy Devou's mother, poured tea as though to the manor born. All the newcomers took tea first, finished it fast, then got down to important drinking at the far end of the serving bank. Stabs of hunger could be stilled from the array of catered delicacies on the board.

All of Mr. Perfection's canapes and hors d'ouevres moved briskly. But, alas, Mr. Haig's beautifully molded salmon mousse betrayed not a single bite of the serving spoon.

People were too polite actually to say as much to each other, but an impression had gotten abroad that the unseasonal warmth of the sunlight had over-powered the delicate fish dish. It had gone bad sitting on the terrace. "Oh, I must have a bit of that lovely whatever it is, there!" The epicure approached the centerpiece, took the serving spoon, and leaned over the handsome comestible. At that point her hand froze and her nose broadened. "But first, I'll try those marvelous stuffed mushrooms!"

Mr. Haig was not aware of how badly his mousse fared. He could not leave the door. Certainly not until Mag herself arrived. The elevator door opened without fanfare. There she was. The Countess of Dump. "Noel, how good of you to have me."

"Mag, my dear! Where's your friend?"

"He'll be on, he'll be on."

"You look enchanting." Mag had soaked off all her horsey smell. She was wearing a dress not at all tweedy. She had even put on lipstick, although thank heavens she had not tried to improve on that pink English complexion. Hat and white gloves? Yes. Mr. Haig knew Mag wouldn't disappoint him.

Mr. Haig sent a waiter to fetch a cup of tea for her, and introduced her around.

The delighted little old ladies kept Mag pinned in her corner of the terrace for over an hour. At home Mag did not entertain much. But she knew the obligations of her caste, and she could show the flag of British etiquette with as much grace as any woman in the realm.

Mag snortled from the back of her throat and made incomprehensible noise at the guests. They smiled in turn and commented favorably among themselves on the dear Countess's democratic affability.

Nobody had any doubts that afternoon who the man of the hour was. Mr. Noel Haig had done it. Even Mr. Perfection was impressed. He could almost forgive Mr. Haig for having done such a pathetic job with the mousse, spoiling Mr. Perfection's otherwise superb presentation of food and drink.

Finally, each guest had been met and provided with a titled snort or gurgle to treasure. Now, Mag wished to draw Mr. Haig apart for a short private talk. They went into the bedroom, keeping the door a discreet few inches open.

"I was wondering, Noel, whether I might have the Cheviot to take back with me. I've been bothered, letting it out. Should never have let it go. It is a prize."

"Ah, well, Mag, there you've caught me. I don't have it."

"Not have it!"

"Not here. It's turned out more of a mystery than I counted on. So I've shipped it off to an analysis laboratory, for positive identification."

"Shipped off? Without consulting me?"

"It's standard procedure, dear lady. The lab will scrape off the merest flake of the metal . . . ."

"Really, Noel!"

"I promise you, the medal will not be damaged in the least. The lab analyzes the sample and determines the exact composition of the item. We already know the originals were copper-lead. If this one shows a percentage of tin, then it will be a forgery beyond question. Keep your trust in me, Mag, I beg you."

"Oh, very well, Noel. But you must return it to me at the soonest possible moment. I shall be sorry until I have it back in the vault."

"Of course. Come. I have a little surprise for you out on the terrace."

It was an off-hand remark. Mr. Haig was referring to the salmon mousse. He knew Mag adored good salmon. They left the bedroom.

Salmon mousse had been much in the air that afternoon. Although Mr. Haig had served his concoction on the terrace in the past, he had never made such a large mold of it before. The massive mousse naturally gave off a more powerful fishy cream odor than had those of the past. With the result that more of the delicious salmon aroma drifted through the wooden fence, where it caught the attention of Rover, the finicky cat.

Ordinarily, Rover would not give salmon a second sniff. But such was the craft of Mr. Haig's cooking that this particular salmon had a precious, inviting herbal curl to its odor which overcame Rover's usual indifference to snacks. When Rover detected the salmon mousse, she knew she must have it.

Rover detected another odor along with the mousse. But, unlike humans, she could discount Spot's noisome fraction and focus exclusively on the food. The guests smelled a deadly stink about the fish. Rover smelled only irresistible temptation.

And she knew how to get to the mousse. She had watched Spot travel the Haig route many times. She tensed down on the floor, looking upward and shaking her head a little to make sure of the distance from ground to fence top.

While Mr. Haig is leading Mag Ritchie-Hoare from the bedroom for her surprise, let us ride a traveling shot onto Napier's terrace.

* * *

There, too, things were looking up.

Minutes before, all four men awakened from their slumbers. Their afternoon nap had refilled their seminal cups to the lip of excess. All four awoke horny.

Their debauch of ten hours before might never have occurred. They smoked a little pot, which made them hornier still. And a little buzzy. The only question which needed answering was, who would give and who would take?

While the radio plowed quietly into the latter depths of "Gotterdamerung," Moritz, Napier, Knut and Magnus enflamed themselves into a mood for intensive group sex.

Moritz's dick took pride of size. He must fuck somebody. Knut and Napier had already gotten themselves occupied in a side-by-side sixty-nine. So Moritz must bugger titanic Magnus — hardly a hardship.

While Magnus greased and arranged himself for this recreation, a number of things happened throughout the 26th floor terrace area which would affect the outcome of Magnus's diddling by Moritz.

Mr. Haig intended to surprise Mag Ritchie-Hoare with his flavorful salmon mousse. But he told her only that he had prepared a surprise.

When he stepped onto the terrace, free for the first time to lift his head from greeting guests, Mr. Haig saw, on the food bank, that his mousse centerpiece remained virginal and untouched. Why? he wanted to know. Was Mr. Perfection shilling people to his own dishes, leaving Mr. Haig's to rot? Where was Mr. Perfection? As it happened, an awning flap had come untied. Mr. Perfection was now on the penthouse roof tying it down. To tell the truth, though, Mr. Perfection's attention centered less on the awning than on the scene taking place on the other side of the wooden separator fence. Mr. Perfection's sole imperfection was a debilitating weakness for big men.

Mr. Haig dragged Mag with him to inspect the fish.

"Why has no one eaten of the mousse?" Mr. Haig demanded from a Greek waiter. But Mr. Haig did not need an answer. It assailed his nostrils.

Like Rover, Mr. Haig could tell the difference between spoiled fish and cat shit.

That damned cat had been over here again! Mr. Haig grew greatly wroth. If he ever got his hands on that damn cat he'd wring its neck and throw the pieces to New Jersey!

"Oh, Mag, I'm terribly sorry. Something seems to be wrong."

Mag had a nose, too, one inured to the olfactory facts of animal life. Evidently a cat had lately been about the terrace. But Noel said something was wrong. What can be wrong? This congealed concoction has an appetizing odor. Why is no one eating it? And where is the surprise?

Mr. Haig looked again for Mr. Perfection. It was Perfection's job to keep cats off the terrace.

That worthy man was watching Magnus Richards, huge, solid and naked, get down on his knees. Magnus lay his torso and head forward on the terrace, leaving his ass to fly high, winking for Moritz's big dick to enter. Moritz had moved back a few steps, voluptuously smearing grease on his cock preparatory to ramming it

101

as a benefaction into the depths of the dark titan's bowels. He did not rush. When these moments of anticipation discover us, what clod does not wish to prolong them?

The party crowd had all eyes on the dear countess and Mr. Haig. Mr. Haig seemed agitated. His guests felt vaguely guilty. Guests generally do when their host starts unaccountably to clench his jaw and pop his eyes.

A hush fell over the group, quiet and deadly. Not because of anything Mr. Haig was doing. It was the hush of a crowd watching, helpless to intervene, the approach of certain doom.

Oh, Rover. Poor Rover. Turn back from that salmon mousse.

Mr. Haig saw where everybody was looking. He turned.

Even a woman who moved as little in society as Mag Ritchie-Hoare knew that cats were not ordinarily treated to the buffet table. It was bound to be planned. This was part of Noel's surprise, surely. Mag reached out her hand to pat Mr. Haig's arm in acknowledgment. Her restraining hand saved Rover from a much worse fate than actually did befall her.

Mr. Haig's strongest impulse was to grab the cat's tail and fling the nasty beast over the side of the building. Mag's hand, and the shocked gasps of all the little old ladies, moderated his intentions. He seized the purring cat by its tail and, with a whiplike snap of his forearm, flung the indiscreet intruder in a high screeching parabola back over the wooden fence to where she belonged.

This movement coincided with Moritz's tensing for attack. His cock was greasy and glistening now.

Magnus was spreading his cheeks with his hands, to facilitate Moritz's anticipated penetration. The handsome, expectant titan pulled his cheeks wide, wide apart. He exposed a center circle of sensitive, pulsating pink membrane as big as a silver dollar.

A violent sound splintered the air. Rover protested with decibels of injured innocence, "This is not just!" she screamed, "I am abused!"

Before the four lewd men could ascertain the screams' source, Rover landed. With all twenty nails out, sharp and flailing. Like an electric fan with blades made out of chili-dipped cactus spikes.

The alert reader will no doubt be asking himself at this point, *Where* did the cat land?

Ah, the pen drops.

* * *

Viewed in a slow motion shot from Mr. Perfection's rooftop vantage point, here is what happened next.

Magnus leapt up with demonic energy and the sound of twenty terrible trumpets.

Rover sprang from Magnus's bleeding cheeks to the valley made by the bodies of Napier and Knut as they lay in 69. Hence, she was able to inflict maximum injury on both men around their midsections and produce broad flesh wounds which bled copiously and smeared luridly. The excited cat hurled menacing yowls at Moritz as it fled inside.

Napier and Knut rose as one. Doing so, they knocked the radio table, turning the sound up to full volume. It was the end of "Gotterdamerung." Valhalla tumbled with noisy crackling and crashing thunder. Napier and Knut advanced to help Magnus.

Moritz was so startled that he stumbled backward a few steps against the wooden fence. Flimsy to start with, it could not withstand the heavy impact of his lurching body. As Valhalla disintegrated with a mighty rumble, so did the 26th floor terrace partition.

A waiter reflexively darted away from it. Sad to say, he jostled against the serving bank so violently that the dishes and glassware went all ajangle, adding to Valhalla's din. Worse, the young waiter's inertia impelled Mr. Haig's magnificent centerpiece across the planter toward the terrace edge. With quick agility, the waiter grasped the tray and prevented ten pounds of lethal silver from falling 26 floors to the street beneath. He caught the tray.

But not the mousse. It slid off the tray, into the air, and vanished from sight.

Few people on the terrace noticed the evasive mousse. They were all watching the tableau unveiled by the fallen fence.

They heard loud turbulent music. They saw four naked young men, two of them gigantic, three of them displaying wounds of blood, and all of them still with enormous erections.

Mr. Haig could not speak. Mr. Perfection back on the terrace, could not speak. Nobody on the Beddoe side could speak. Only one person could speak. The Lady Margaret, Countess of Dump, spoke.

Mag had been expecting a surprise but nothing like this. The timing was so marvellous (the cat on the table precisely on cue), it must have been rehearsed many times. True, Mag could not quite interpret the deep symbolism of what she saw before her. But of the scene's symbolic nature she had no doubt. The blood, the chains, the dear reference to fertility. The giants: Perhaps, in honor of her British blood, Noel had done something with the myth of Gog and Magog. The cat might represent Brute, as a visual pun. Mag Ritchie-Hoare did not pretend to be a learned or artful woman who could expound all the elements of a symbolic tableau without her clever nephew's help. But Mag could certainly express her appreciation for work well planned and executed.

"Splendid, Noel! First rate!"

Being Americans, the other guests knew in their deepest hearts that British nobility understood things that they did not. Something was revealed to the dear countess that was not revealed to them. However, the little old ladies were not going to admit that a countess's intelligence was a bit more penetrating than their own. A warm round of polite applause circled the terrace. Grey-blue heads nodded approval of the entertainment. Clucks, of goodwill clattered toward Mr. Haig.

Four persons could not add their kudos. Moritz, Napier, Knut and Magnus were immobilized by surprise, shock, pot and pain. One minute they were happily engaged in swinish behavior. The next minute they were performers in front of all these strange people wearing Scarlett O'Hara hats.

And now what's happening? One of those old women was advancing on them.

Mag Ritchie-Hoar spied something in the tableau which confirmed her notion that Noel had taken more than a little trouble putting together this complex and taunting puzzle.

She moved closer to make sure before she mentioned it to Noel. She bent her head down and directed her curious face toward Magnus Richards' effulgent, metal-bedecked scrotum. The Countess of Dump showed intelligent interest in the titan's balls.

Magnus knew only that a woman with clear pink skin was sniffing his crotch and babbling something about her Chevy. "Is that my Chevy?" she asked, sticking her nose closer.

With a seraphic smile of discovery, the Countess turned to call her appreciation to Mr. Haig. The crowd could not make out her remarks fully. They too understood her to say something about finding a Chevy. The strain of jet lag was taking its toll of the dear Countess.

Mag wanted everybody to see the Cheviot Commemorative which Noel had incorporated into this living memorial to the House of Hoare—for surely that is what it all came to.

Before their very eyes, 85 refined and well-bred Americans saw a belted Countess turn into a psychotic sex fiend. The Countess of Dump grabbed for the Cheviot Commemorative. Its displayer fended off her attack. He inadvertently knocked her off balance. Instinctively the Countess reached for something, anything to hold on to.

Alas, alas, alas, she found the catenary chain.

That was when the little old ladies and Magnus all started to feel faint at the same time.

* * *

Mr. Haig signalled his friends and the serving staff to help him bring Mag back to his terrace and her senses.

Fifteen men and three waiters advanced cautiously upon four naked bleeding men and one terribly confused lady. Mag was trying simultaneously to stanch Magnus's new wounds and to get back the Cheviot so she could return to the Pierre. The Cheviot seemed to be stuck. She pulled hard. In agony Magnus knocked her backward, into the advancing forces. They pinned her arms.

All hands now seemed turned against Mag. Are Americans mad, after all? She would not have them treat her in this impossible manner. The Hoare blood grew hot in her veins. Mag struck out.

The Beddoe men were returning to their senses. They saw only that this one funny woman was being mistreated by all those bald-headed fruits in seersucker jackets. In an instant Moritz, Napier and Knut set about to free her.

Across the fallen fence and into the fray. Mr. Perfection saw the beautiful titan standing vulnerable and unprotected. Mr. P. just wanted to touch him, only to touch him once. He led the waiters against the invading nude host, with Magnus's capture his intent. For his effort Mr. P. was rewarded with the champagne punch dregs poured over his head by a furious Mr. Haig.

Cross-purpose fighting can be lots of fun to watch for a few minutes. But it is the nature of misunderstandings eventually to get themselves sorted out. Combatants get winded, they run out of missiles to throw, explanations start getting through to the other side.

Within a few minutes the 26th floor would have reached that conciliatory state except for one thing.

The salmon mousse.

* * *

Few who have flung salmon mousse will vouch for its cohesion. If it is at all light and fluffy like Mr. Haig's masterpiece, it flies apart at the first touch of wind resistance.

When the gelatinous mold fell from the 26th floor, it broke apart into hundreds of small harmless gobbets.

The Countess had met an American during her flight to the States. He was scheduled to join her at Mr. Haig's and escort her back to the Pierre. This same man had just alighted from his taxicab. He was getting his bearings by looking up at the colorful awning 26 floors above when, without warning, he was attacked by a school of flying mousse.

Knowing the ways of teenage gangs in Chelsea, the taxi driver sped away. The young American stood on the sidewalk dumbfounded and growing very angry. He wished a policeman were at hand.

Two soon were, in a cruiser. They saw that somebody was throwing shit on people. The 10th Precinct had lately come under severe criticism for dawdling when teenage gangs threw stuff on people over by the Chelsea bar strip. Here was the 10th Precinct's chance to show that it did so care when people threw shit on other people in Chelsea. They called into the station house.

Within two minutes sixteen NYPD officers with billysticks held high burst upon Mr. Haig's terrace. "Complaint about somebody up here throwing shit, sir," and then the cops saw the fight in progress. Clearly, they had to break up the fight. This introduction of new blood renewed the fray, but with a different orientation.

Now everybody fought simply to get away. The more percipient little old ladies knew that the party was composed mostly of sons and mothers; they saw naked flesh on every hand; and they could envision the headline of tomorrow's *News:* FUZZ BUST CHELSEA INCEST ORGY.

Thus, the little old ladies attacked the cops. The cops wanted to arrest the Beddoe troupe for indecent exposure. Napier and his gang tried to raise the fence and cut themselves off from the melee on Haig's side. The awning got torn down almost at once, and the remaining goodies on the serving bank went for instant ammunition against the fuzz. A lot of it went astray.

The mousse-covered American arrived with the cops. He tried to embrace the wild-eyed countess to tell her who he was. Not on your life, laddie. Mag flattened him with a good right clip, then went on, while the ancient Dump fit was on her, to deck Noel Haig, too. Old Mrs. Devou got her face pushed in the crème fraîche by Mr. Perfection in his hunt for Magnus; a couple cops loaded up on valuable-looking medals from broken display cases; and the young junky just happened to show up hoping to squeeze another ten dollars from Mr. Haig.

If ever it was time for a young faggot to save his own ass, it was now. The fence barricade was a loss. Every man for himself.

Frequently two sides of a battle become so engrossed in the details of war that the object of their fight is left unprotected. For about a minute the elevator stood empty, unguarded. All the faggots' clothes lay in the living room. Moritz grabbed them and dashed toward the lift.

He collided with the mousse-drenched American, who struggled with him. With help from the blond giant and the dark titan, Moritz threw the man aside and reached the elevator. Two frightened cats tried to sneak in with them. Bleeding Magnus returned them to the terrace with a couple superb place kicks, his love for cats no more.

* * *

The three men dressed enough in the elevator to run toward the bar strip when the lift reached ground. There, Magnus's ripped nipples and his bleeding asshole blended unnoticed into the regular early Saturday evening pedestrian traffic of Eleventh Avenue.

They convened in the Bucket of Blood. Their bloody wounds and the dazed panic in their eyes were much admired. Knut was recognized and was asked when he intended to take on both towers of the World Trade Center. The customers kept them supplied with restorative drink until they regained a fitting composure. Within an hour the episode on Napier's terrace seemed like a rather imaginative episode in a gay farce. Magnus was already speculating on the advantages that might accrue from being the only kid in his parish with hinged nipples.

Eventually Moritz said he had to get home for a cleansing shower, as did Knut. Magnus looked at a clock. "My lord, I'll just have time for the midnight mass."

"Do you go every Saturday night?" Moritz politely inquired.

"No, darling, I celebrate it, at St. Stephen in Chains. And if you think I didn't have to kiss a lot of parish ass to get the midnight show. . . . well, my dear!"

In front of all, Magnus took the crucifix out of his earlobe and replaced it in his foreskin. He fingered the medallion which the old trout on the terrace had groped him for. He lifted his face, now transfigured as though undergoing enlightenment.

"Say, maybe this has all been a sign. Maybe this year we ought to raffle off a Chevy."

SHIRLEY POWELL

The second poetry reading I did in 1975 was under the auspices of Lambda at Hunter College, a gay and lesbian club. Present with me as reader was Shirley Powell. She read a dozen or so poems of great beauty and strangeness, and a remarkable short story. I forgot — during her reading — where I was, who I was, and slipped back into the universal unconscious role of story listener. Her work was filled with the omnipresent magic and bizarre logic of fairy tales; even though her material was contemporary.

In 1977, Mouth of the Dragon published her book Parachutes, a collection of poems and prose containing the works she had earlier read. When it came time for me to begin to solicit work for this anthology, I wrote to her asking if she would be a contributor. She sent me "Solitaries," wondering if I would want it: as it didn't deal directly at all with the lesbian/gay experience.

And it doesn't: except by association. In Shirley Powell's world, we are all solitaries; temporarily distraught middle-class women, dead junkies, street bums and poets. The boundaries between the respectable and the not, shatter under Powell's cool, often dryly humorous vision. For those gays and lesbians who feel they require no sympathy or relationship to transvestites or costume queens, et al. "Solitaries" is a gentle reminder that being a freak is merely the angle of perception.

Avon Books will publish Powell's new novel in 1981.

SOLITARIES

When I lived on Ninth Street near Cooper Union, one not infrequently saw women standing often wearing boots, mini skirts, and a lot of makeup. There was at that time a building on Twelfth Street where they took their clients. Now it's closed; I don't know where they go when they find a customer. But they still work the corners. I often see them as I ride by on the Fourteenth Street bus.

I said the women were almost always young, but one wasn't. She was at least 40, and she wore black; all of her flesh except her face was covered. She wore a large floppy black hat, black raincoat, long black skirt, and black boots. Her face was pale. She sometimes smoked a cigarette, but never spoke, and she never sat down. Beside her was a battered black briefcase. For a week, she stood on the corner (northwest) of Ninth and Cooper Square. Then she was gone.

Two prostitutes had an early morning business going near the Port Authority one Sunday while I was a cabbie. One stood at the curb watching for cops while the other used a deep doorway to provide a stand up quickie for a john in a neat gray suit. I wanted to see him come out of there, face forward, but had to move up to stay in the cab line before he'd finished.

Sure enough two police officers were on their way. The girls split, and the one in a shortie fake fur over long chocolate legs which ended in immaculate white boots came our way. "I've got a warm cab here," one driver offered, as others laughed.

"I don't know how to do it lying down," she said, hurrying on to the next way station.

For awhile, several years ago, I drove a taxi four days a week for a fleet that was then established on West 47th Street. It's not there any more; the owner died. But one winter day while I was driving day shift, a bum moved into the street just beyond our garage. He was filthy and in tatters that didn't completely cover what needed to be covered. He couldn't speak, or chose not to, but he had sufficient cunning to get himself boxes of cardboard which he fashioned into a rude shelter. We took him some blankets one morning which he accepted. Someone probably reported his plight, for after about two weeks, I came to work one brisk morning when one's breath became clouds, and he was gone. Only one piece of soggy cardboard thumped across 47th Street, as the wind swung out toward the Hudson.

When I worked in Brooklyn, I got back to Manhattan about 4 p.m. each work day. As I left the Brooklyn Bridge, I'd take the ramp to Chatham Square. There, on a traffic island, a young black man usually stood. I got so I looked for him; days when he wasn't there, I felt cheated. Each time he wore a different costume. Once I remember he had on a frilly dress and an apron. Once he urinated proudly into the path of passing cars. He talked to himself a lot, and seemed oblivious to the city life around him.

Where did he come from? Did he spend all day on the island? Why? How had he become solitary?

One summer day on the Bowery at Houston Street, near a number of bums waiting to wipe off windshields whenever cars were caught by the light, stood a young blond, a handsome fellow with a magnificent body. He was completely naked. When we passed again several hours later, the young god was still there among the derelicts. This time, though, he wore a bright red bathrobe.

Before school one morning when I arrived early, the secretary met me in the lower hall. "I'm glad a teacher is here. I'm having a terrible problem. There's a man downstairs in the bathroom across from the cafeteria. I've threatened to call the police, but he won't come out."

Inside the boys' bathroom, the man, having shed four coats, was washing his hair.

"This isn't a public bathroom," I began.

"I'm going, I'm going!" He scrubbed at his face with a paper towel. I saw that his feet were bare; he'd put his shoes on the overturned wastebasket while he was washing his feet which still glistened with moisture.

"The police will be over shortly. The precinct is less than a block-"

He struggled into his coats and his shoes, combing his long graying hair with a leftover hand. "Jesus!" he spat as he passed me. "I'm leaving. I'm leaving!"

After a performance at a theatre on St. Mark's Place, some of us went to a nearby coffee house that our friend Margot knew. A grotesque man stood just outside the door, trying to get money from people entering. One of our group gave him a coin. While we were drinking coffee, he knocked on the outer door, begging to come in. It was quite cold outside, and whenever a waiter would try to get him to leave, our sympathies were rather with the panhandler. "We don't dare let him inside," a waitress told us. "He's ruining our business. If we call the police, they chase him away, but within a half hour, he's back."

While she was talking, a patron went outside and gave the old man a handful of change. He came charging inside, his whole manner changed. "You can't keep me out now, for I've money!" He ordered tea with lemon and sugar and milk, complaining loudly because the place was full, and there was no place for him to sit. He soon got a stool from a departing customer, and commenced cursing and flinging cups about the small cafe. At last a waiter twisted his arm and took him out, arms flailing, mouth wide in a high pitched scream. He was back at his first station now, piteously asking to be let in out of the cold. We left, glancing aside as we edged by him. His harsh laugh ran along behind us for most of a block.

There was once, and perhaps still is, a man who attended poetry readings in the Village in order to read his own incomprehensible poetry, full of allusions to Descartes. He usually spelled the one syllable words for his listeners, but otherwise read as rapidly as possible in order to get in as many poems as possible before he was chased off stage.

He was a bald man who wore a variety of ill-fitting wigs. His face was as smooth as a baby's ass, and it was not possible to guess his age. He once said that he had a job, and he seemed to live in a church on Seventh Avenue. He would talk of ideas, but was offended at the slightest personal remark, and pretended not to hear such pleasantries as "How are you feeling?" Once he told me his theory of Kennedy's importance in history. I didn't understand anything he said.

There was a woman called Jean who often came to the church basement on 22nd Street when our group held poetry readings there. She had a shock of white hair, and was twisted small with arthritis. She carried all her belongings about with her, and slept wherever she could. By the time we knew her, she had lost all of her teeth and most of her sense. She'd mutter all through the readings, sometimes in a distractingly loud voice. There were other equally witchlike noises she made, mostly through her nose, unlike any I've heard from anyone else. People ignored her as much as possible.

One night, though, after a particularly loud outburst, she suddenly said, "You'll have to excuse me; I get confused sometimes. But I love to hear your words."

It was the first time she'd ever said anything coherent in the time she'd been attending the readings. At intermission, everyone there managed to say something to her. She sat on her folding chair receiving us, serene and smiling like a queen returned from exile.

Going to a deli on Second Avenue, I nearly walked into two men fighting each other in front of the little store. They were burly fellows, breathing hard as they wrestled across the sidewalk, one trying to get some sort of strangling hold on the other while his opponent struggled to find room to land a punishing blow to the other's gut. A crowd happily gathered, calling out suggestions and encouragement.

An old bag lady on the periphery of the on-lookers pushed her way closer to the action. "Get up outa that!" she screeched, whacking each of the men with her stout cane. To our surprise, the men got up. She continued to lay about her till they went off, in separate directions. Someone gave the hag a dollar, and then others handed her money. A prowl car came by, an officer leaning out of his window to see what was happening. "Will you be taking me in for arranging assignations?" she bellowed, and shuffled off, swinging her bags and cackling.

On Fifth Avenue and University Place one day last summer, some friends and I were headed for the beach in my car. When I stopped for a red light, a well-dressed woman about 65 caught my eye. As soon as she realized I was looking at her, she ran to the car. "Will you please help me? You look like lovely people. I need you so much."

We asked how we could help.

"Would you take me wherever you're going? Let me come with you, please."

We said we were sorry; we were leaving town and couldn't take her along. As the light changed, she sadly returned to her corner. We made a call to police before the Holland Tunnel. Remembering her jewelry and stylish clothes, I said to the quiet voice on the line, "Someone might rob her. She's alone."

It was my custom a few years ago to take an early morning walk along Jane Street. When my knee was giving me trouble, I walked with crutches. For convenience, I carried a change purse tied to a crutch and wore an orange backpack. During this time, I somehow got a bit of poison on my face in the form of an unattractive rash which my doctor treated with a still less attractive purple medication. One morning in winter, I was bundled up in scarf, coat, knit hat, poison medication, crutches, purse, and backpack. Though I didn't know it until later, I was also trailing a long streamer of purple crepe paper, caught in a crutch, which must have followed me like an unshakable idea.

"Look at that today, worse than ever," a man on the corner opposite the Waverly Inn said to his female companion.

They each stepped back so that I could pass between them.

"Poor thing," the woman murmured. "Looks almost respectable."

I very much wished I'd been wearing my roller skates.

There was a solitary sitting dead on the subway one rush hour a year or so ago. He was about twelve years old. Everyone pretended he wasn't there. I suspected glue sniffing, because he clutched a brown bag of something in one hand. When we got off at 96th Street, my friend called someone to take the kid's body away.

As I left a hotel on Gramercy Park one morning, a black man strode by, his hair tied up in many tight pigtails, each fastened with a bit of rag. He wore a dark coat festooned with gay patches of cloth, he was shod in Western boots, and his pants were jeans painted with wide white stripes. As he marched emphatically along, he shook a gourd, rolled his dark eyes, and chanted. When he saw that I intended to cross his path, he shook the gourd wildly in my direction and hurled me a killing voodoo curse. All the way down the block, he cursed the trees. As far as he knew, everything behind him had instantly withered.

Today as I am leaving my apartment building, a man approaches. He is wearing the long fireproof gloves of a fireman, carrying a yellow slicker stenciled with the letters NYC FD on it, also wearing black rubber boots, and carrying a long metal hook. He walks along Avenue D in the late afternoon. He is bareheaded and very dirty. Glancing around him every few steps, he frowns fiercely. A stranger meets him at the corner; the fireman suddenly raises his hook. The other awkwardly hoists his umbrella to fend off a blow that after all doesn't come. They cross the street at right angles to each other. Only one looks back.

The man with the hook thumps it on the pavement as he walks. He enters a parking lot. There he glances about him once more, then pries up the grating over a sewer. He stands for a long moment, looking down. Then again he gazes keenly around; is anybody watching? I am, but I look away, and slide under the steering wheel of my car. The booted solitary lets fall the grating. He stares without fear at the gaping holes everywhere under his feet.

PHILIP KRAVITZ

"Steven Fisch Jr — thirty, plump and balding (incognito Nymphet D'Amor)" is how Philip Kravitz describes the subject of this bitter but also rather loving story, "Fisch." Now that the image of the macho gay male has all but eliminated any other possibilities, a character such as Fisch is sneered at by critics. Yet he continues to exist all around us, if we bother to look: fossil, anachronism or not. The muscleman who suddenly prances like a twelve year old in a pinafore, the sudden icy hardness in the prettiest and most femine lesbian — occurs in reality — and reveals to ourselves (if not to others) that we do seem in some ways to contain more of both genders within ourselves. Platonists would say it is natural: some of them would go so far as to declare it the best humans can be.

This story, along with another equally as good, was sent to me by Phillip Kravitz, I forget exactly through what channels, and I liked it immediately for the absolute clarity of its vision and the detailing of the grim reality that is its world. Fisch sees himself as a "vision of virgin and slut", and his eventual, inexorable encounter with the badly dressed, unattractive man he meets on the subway is both religious and sordid without being arty or fey.

Kravitz is a technical writer. This is his first story in print.

FISCH

The man on the subway . . .

isn't his type . . .

short . . . greasy . . . fat . . .

Puerto Rican . . .
teeth: black and chipped . . .
thin moustache . . .

How many lamplights in a city
Barrooms per square mile
How many strangers to an evening
Cigarettes, the same dull story
Drinks to a rendezvous
How many cups of coffee
When You're feeling blue
I know the score
I've been here before
The story's always the same
Lovers come and go
This you come to know

While Steven Fisch Jr. — thirty, plump and balding — (incognito nymphet D'Amor) sits across the aisle, humming to distract himself eyes bloodshot . . . pockmarked face
. . .
                      How many teardrops

He surmises he's coming from work
. . .
The man sits groping his crotch . . .
The downtown local from Pelham to Manhattan, on a stifling summer's night, almost empty.

Make a parting
When it all must end

How many lamplights in a city

Wearing a purple shirt, tails out; and black skintight pants with white tennis sneakers (all of which suggest to Fisch if not propriety then stardom: a vision of virgin and slut) he scans the ads while eyeing the man who casually pinches his bulge. BRAS — "For a fuller figure" . . . A Smoking Man's Smoke . . . Home Appliances . . . Shirts . . . A request: Visit Your House of Faith Today — none of which impress him. But a Red Cross appeal

FOR HEAVEN'S SAKE — GIVE!

offends his cruising eye.
 And haven't I always, he huffs. Imagine, asking ME that! Why, my dear, I AM the Red Cross!
 Indignant, he shifts his position and readjusts the books on his lap, the traveling bag hanging across his shoulder, aware that, although obvious, both are indispensable props. The bag because it's scarlet and gay, positively wanton. Because it announces a propensity to wander and enables him to carry medicinals, decongestants, a brush, some pills, a tiny vial of Aphrodesia Cologne — and to collect books of matches. Not that he smokes . . . He's allergic to smoke and to dust . . . to roses and a host of fruits and spices. Allergic, moreover, in the swelter of a heat-wave, when the five day outlook is up in the 90s, the air-count "unhealthy", the pollen-count "horrendous". His eyes and throat inflame, his face breaks out — but collects matchbooks to recall where he's been, what he's done, to keep — in his fashion — a diary.
 And the books? This time: *Swann's Way* and *The Eternal City?* They sum up the other half: the habitual student. Not that he reads on trains. The poor lighting makes reading a strain, which only brings on his migraines. He carries them instead, should he grow nervous, to relieve tensions, like now, when the heat and filth, the litter and stench engulf his sensibilities, when like now, as usual, it took hours before to rewire nerves disconnected the previous night;

to work off sleeping pills and sedatives his psychiatrist prescribes (for a full night's rest) with alka-seltzers and cups of milked tea. Hours to reassemble his mind into a functioning facsimile of himself. And then, to start things off, the phone rang at midnight (three in the afternoon) — and he nearly went nuts. For today, the first time in weeks, Fisch saw daylight, and the sun — so vital — had made him nauseous. He took two Seconals. But Thank God, Hail Mary, say a thousand Amens, his parents and brother were out and he blessed his lucky star. Not because they ask where he goes, what he does, criticize or nag — at least, they don't — not any more. Nor do they press "Find a job!" — "Finish college!" — "Marry!" The hysterical scenes, the shouts and screams, the excessive demands are over. And yet, that shrug of defeat . . . his mother's pitiful gaze . . . that glare of disgust his father can scarcely suppress. That even his weekly allowance (which his father hands him filled with self-reproach and meant as a bribe to avoid confrontation) must be accompanied by his father's complaint "Things cost an arm and a leg!" Yes, there's suppressed annoyance. That same expression of his father and brother whenever they enter his bedroom: with his socks, shirts, underwear, handkerchiefs neatly folded on fine white cloth in designated draws. To shelves of arranged colognes and lotions . . . Jasmine, Aphrodisia, Intoxication, Wild Herbs. To his desk where papers and dateless memorandums are meticulously bound; to his bookcases in which the books are dusted daily and always alphabetically arrayed. Yes, his compulsive order irks them both, and so he avoids them, as they, in turn, avoid him. Except when he used to use the family phone, tying it up for hours. "Must you always gab?" his brother would chide, and Fisch defied "It's MY phone as much as yours!" His brother would mimic and rage "It's MY phone as much as yours!" and THAT TOO had been an issue until his father saw fit to give him his own private number. Since then, he might as well be a ghost — and he knows it. And often he's said that if not for his mother, he'd leave . . . find an apartment . . . live a life of his own. But he feels that she needs his moral support, is dependent upon his inner strength — yes, especially when his father and brother argue — (which Fisch finds ludicrous "since they're so much alike"). Worse still, although he vows not to get involved, he invariably does, stepping in as his mother's stead and attempting, like her, to restore order. It always works. For no matter how upset his father and brother are, once he intervenes, they both grow silent and sullen. Such scenes are draining enough, he feels, at night when he's fully sedated and prepared. But he doubts he could survive one in mid-afternoon. So whenever he sees one approaching, he dresses and flees.

Yet he knows, as time goes on, dressing takes longer. Like today. Hours of coldcreams, ointments, massages. Hours of soaking in warm baths of lipodermic oils. In between a bit of reading, browsing through his cherished books — most of which he steals from public libraries and hides in the back of his bedroom closet. Or listening to opera or jazz . . . especially Corcovado . . . or squat on his bed picking through pubic hairs for crabs, checking the front and back for clap ("Although," he bemoans "it's so difficult to tell.") And then, to shave, to tweeze nostrils and eyebrows, plucking a few grey hairs from his chest and drenching himself in a fragrant mood — usually Aphrodesia. Then, to inspect his face: his puffed cheeks, swollen lips (naturally too full anyway) and a victorious attempt to hush a few wrinkles about the eyes and mouth with Woman's Care (a new and sensational cosmetic). And when finally finished, naked and posed before the bathroom mirror, has to conclude — all in all, it's still an attractive face, still a tempting body. Still good enough to make out with. Yes, he can still pass for twenty-nine, and a good day after a good night's sleep, or a good night after a good day's sleep, for twenty-eight, maybe seven. Of course, for some months, he's been touching up his hair, and that certainly helps. Yet still — that hideous spot, that minor balding at the crown of his head. "Yes!" he accuses. "What about that!" Even holding a mirror behind his head while combing (thereby securing a double reflection of both the front and rear) he hasn't been able to conceal it completely. Not that it warrants over-concern or has become a preoccupation. No, he can still brush his hair in such a way that nobody can detect the spot — and so feels confident of his youth. But he views the balding with resigned distrust, as if it's a cruel warning of what is to come.

As for "This Creature!" — the man who sits opposite him now — NO! — Fisch sincerely has no designs on him. For the man, despite his gross attempts to arrest his attention, isn't Fisch's type at all. Yet what makes an ugly man attractive! That although Fisch keeps flipping through *Swann's Way*, he keeps inadvertently glancing at the Puerto Rican's thighs and oily forearms. Often enough (it's happened before) for some reason a man whom he otherwise considers a loser unexpectedly arouses his interest to the very extent—just a moment before—he found him repulsive. Whether it's due to the way the stranger walks, with saunter, like a hustler, or takes a cowboy stance, leaning his weight to a side, his hand hooked to his belt, a cigarette poised between stalwart lips as if he were an advertisement, or whether the way a strand of delinquent hair obscures an eye or how he sits, confident and defiant, with legs spread—there's always that singular and irridescent gesture which illumines the stranger's presence and sets him apart. Well Fisch apprehends that even ugliness, when tinged with the illicit, possesses the prospect of allure and attains to an aesthetic ideal. That the chiseled, refined features of a handsome man might leave him flat precisely because the features are too self-contained, too arrogant, that in their perfection, the features are unnatural and estranged. "Ex perfecto nihil fit," he concludes and passes perfection by. But the Puerto Rican's thighs—brutal, massive, reminiscent of a bull, thighs which can pound unremittingly against perfumed flesh—THIS Fisch imagines "exciting."

Yet right now, considering the heat, the unbreathable stench, Fisch is enjoying merely the intrigue (for that's all it is)—the role of White Goddess, naked and alluring, teasing the man on. Already he's slinking through venomous leaves, pricking nettles, herbs of hemp. In the distance the throb of beating drums as the Puerto Rican pursues—dying, thirsting, killing for him.

—Just too too divine, muses Fisch. Though, of course, if I want, I could get him to a tearoom, one two three. But . . . no . . . Not tonight! No quickies. You've had enough.

For throughout the past few weeks he's been in and out of orgies, and just last night, compelled by what? the heat? the relentless need to exert a charm? —he carried on in Central Park with two seventeen year old negroes: tall, lean, smelling of beer and pomade. He picked them up on West 86th as they sauntered along with wide rhythmic strides, their white tight pants with back pockets bulging worn just above their waists; their red shirts falling loose about bony hips. With lewd, obvious gestures—like those of the Puerto Rican's—he lured them into the park and there among the bushes had them force upon him the fate of a woman. How sharp were their nails. How hot their teeth. He can still see them: slanted eyes, hairless frames. Still hear their snorts and giggles. Cannibals through and through. Harlem trade. Immoral and beautiful niggers. How he had loved it!

But tonight? Tonight he seeks something else, something more. Yet what he can't quite say. It stirs the persevering saint in him: coy, demure and chaste. Yet, not that either. For hasn't he when feeling most pure been usually misled to the greater degradation? Yes, doesn't it happen in flights of resurrection that the sense of seduction and being seduced converge, becoming in the convergence and its gathering out-leap, interchangeable and one? Then alleys and subways trap him. Then pills deplete the strength he seeks to preserve. Then all his needs invert — as if by closing his eyes he can't be seen. And so, through the years he's come to discern that to save means to seduce; to be the saint, the whore; to defy, to inevitably succumb.

Warning's enough! He knows the scene by heart. Vowing to remain on the train until he reaches the Village, he decides to change cars. He's promised to meet his friends, especially Larry and Lows, at the Bali, and tonight, the first time in ages, has a fair chance of arriving as planned. But fearing he'll run into Warren — a recent extrick — he isn't that enthused about going and wouldn't be if Lows hadn't phoned and insisted. No, he would have stayed home, cloistered in his room like an Epicurean monk — or, at least, would have tried, perhaps winding up on the Grand Concourse about two in the morning and making out with a taxi-driver, or as lately is the case, the guard in the back of the Court Building where the police rarely patrol. But the thought of amazing his friends with his unexpected punctuality augments his image of being the star: the commotion and screams, the spotlight of novelty. Besides, he's showered and shaved, and moreover douched, and isn't about to waste it all on a fifteen minute trick.

— For what! he snaps. — For what! To mess your hair? Get stinking like a latrine? You'd be a fool, you slut — don't even consider it! Thought it would serve you right, it certainly would . . . but since you're here, you're staying put . . . right where you are, understand? And besides, he needs a bath. Just look at those hands . . . those teeth . . . those nails. He most likely smells . . . has bugs . . . Oh, THINK. And yet, he keeps playing with that thing of his, throbbing it up and down and this heat . . . Oh, don't look! Think of something else . . . think WHITE, TENNIS, HANDBALL,

FAIR SKIN . . . BLUE EYES . . . DIGNITY . . . BLOND. Read Proust! But THINK, damn you, THINK! Must you always be a slut?

Stating to himself "Definitely Not!"—he defiantly uncrosses his legs, straightens his shirt and gets up to leave. Only for a second does he eye the man and then with such contempt, he's abashed by his own temerity and quickly looks away.

—Serves him right, the spick! Like all the others with their cocks . . . all those you've desired and despised . . . construction workers . . . mechanics . . . pizza boys . . . high school bums . . . (oh, but you're drifting . . . drifting . . .) . . . on and on down the line . . . symbolic of them all . . . yes, those you've robbed . . . who have raped me of my will . . . my self-respect . . . my . . . but now . . . I want no part of him. I can't stand to be here . . . in the same car . . . the same train. I want out!

And indeed, Fisch is passing him by. Triumph quivers his lips. Despite himself he smiles. The Puerto Rican is smiling back.

Exhausted, Fisch leans against the door, his underarms soaked, his concentration fading. And although he'd concede that should someone offer "Look—you can have him . . . Take him right now. His name is etc . . . He lives at such and such"—then as sure as he has cock between his legs, Fisch would refuse. Instead, he just feels trapped.

—But this is absurd, he reflects. Do something or simply shut up . . . Leave the car! . . . Sit down . . . Or . . .

Comes the next stop, Fisch gets off. He doesn't turn to see if the man is following—he takes it for granted. The station's deserted, the men's room (luckily) unlocked. "Ah Heaven"—he sighs as currents of urine make him reel. "And now to wait."

He places his bag and books on the floor beside the last latrine. He's carried on in how many tearooms—with men: semi-, straight and gay . . . and always he's desperate for AIR. He filters the stench through his fingers. In a few minutes he breathes more relaxed amid the dirty walls, dim yellow lights, urinals, sickening smells—Yes, he's looking about: and THIS he's noticed before: No two tearooms look alike. Each is unique. Each with its own charm, its own *fleur de lys*. Especially those near 125 Street. They have a character, a special aroma of urine plus. He can spot one sight unseen.

—It's almost an art, he observes. But this one—ordinary, confining, not fit to piss in . . . Black messy floors . . . unflushed shit . . . the walls covered with obscenities . . . numbers, sizes . . . an almanac of subcutaneous lives . . . in other words, history . . . hieroglyphics . . .

Suddenly, he pauses. The image of himself: beaten, bleeding, lying on the floor—

—Think slut!

Quickly he wedges his garnet ring, money into his sneaker. The door is opening, he inches back, cursing himself, the nightmare terror, the joy—he's rooted.

To run, scream, be violently pushed—trampled even. He yearns for hell, divine degradation. Yearns for sweated thighs clutched around his neck like a necklace with a long dangling pendant.

The Puerto Rican enters—sheepish, half-smirking—he's twisting his wedding band.

Immediately Fisch perks up, his confidence is returning, and yes, is now transformed—a courtesan—a priestess—here in his luxurious brothel. For he is as he knows himself to be: Nymphet D'Amor.

—But no preludes, please. No 'Mira, mira'—and all that jazz. No 'Te quiero mucho'—just that sumptuous flank of flesh and Nymphet will manage the rest. Nymphet: seductress and saint, seduced and sedated. Nymphet, lovely and alluring—who is now approaching and about to unzipper your fly—

The man, his body tense, backs up against the door, arms folded, legs astride—

—Nymphet D'Amor. Known to more elegant circles as Steven Fisch Jr.—eternal student—

He touches the Puerto Rican's thigh, feels him quiver, and is perfectly enraptured with the foul stench, the sea of urine blending with—garlic, he winces. Oh, he stinks. Utterly stinks. Thank God for Aphrodisia. Not that it'll stop me now. It just means no kissing . . . no intimate stuff—

He kneels.

—Besides, it's just as well. One two three and bye-bye. I give it fifteen minutes—not a second more.

MICHAEL GRUMLEY

"Public Monuments," brings out another aspect of gay life—being abroad: what the displacement means, what consequences it can lead to for worse, and eventually for better. Grumley evokes the city of Rome with its glamorously setting suns and colorful temptations, its incipient violence and lush bafflements as though it were a tone poem by some forgotten contemporary of Debussy. At the same time, he writes about the fine line that exists in our lives between the ordinary and the utterly unpredictable. Gays and lesbians are no strangers to crime, violence, police or prisons. Our activities are often crimes in themselves. Our existence certainly brings about crimes against us. Natural aliens wherever we are, we are more so in foreign lands where we often cannot even comprehend how we are perceived. That Grumley can see love emerging out of this anxiety and despair is some kind of testament to the spirit underlying our lives and hopes today. "Public Monuments" is an excerpt from Grumley's novel-in-progress A World of Men.

Michael Grumley's earlier books are the highly praised and soon to be filmed After Midnight *(Scribners, 1978), his study of sado-masochism, and the leather life,* Hard-Corps, *(Dutton, 1976),* There Are Giants on the Earth, *(Doubleday, 1974) and with his lover, Robert Ferro (also in this anthology)* Atlantis, Autobiography of A Search *(Doubleday, 1970).*

PUBLIC MONUMENTS

You are six feet tall, with dark hair that will one day be white like your grandfather's—if there is truth in heredity—and weigh one hundred seventy-eight pounds. Your only distinguishing scar, and one which the Roman jailers found especially interesting, occurs half an inch above your navel and to the left: the three letters S E C are barely discernible against your skin, the S being the most pronounced, the other two fading out so that the C is incomplete, a moon with horns retracted; letters half an inch high, type-face from the printing factory in which you worked as a teen-ager.

There were a dozen men running the printing machines, young men mostly, and you all stood along one side of the long low room on the third floor of Regal Manufacturing. Women sat at presses behind you, rolling the acetate ribbon onto spools, stapling rosettes to banners for livestock shows and county fairs across the country. The air was thick with the smell of sizing, and bits of gold leaf clung to every surface; an old man named Cecil walked among the workers frowning and complaining and blowing his nose in his grey handkerchief when he was especially upset. The years of surveillance had dropped his chin low on his chest, and his back rose behind his neck in an odd hump. He was a short man, without a shred of authority in his bearing, and no one really paid him much mind. The man at the type desk was called Frankie; he worked year round in the factory and was the same age as you. How he got out of attending high school you never knew; he was there when you came to work in the Spring and still there when you left in the Fall. It was Frankie's job to fill each case with the line or lines of type specified on each order, and he was very good at pulling the letters out of the type tray, grinning and joking all the while. He had one story which he liked to tell about deflowering a girl named Alice in the back of his Buick. He would hold his nose between his type-stained fingers when he got to the point of it, that she had been reduced to incontinence by his onslaught, and so stained the back seat with her exhuberant evacuations that he'd had to sell the car.

The day you got your scar, you had been riding around during lunch, with your bag of french-fries and a root-beer float, in a car that belonged to one of the workers from your side of the river. Carl was tall and good-looking, and had let his flat-top grow long on the sides so it could be swept back into a D.A. Girls from the other factories and from the offices would be out walking on their lunch hour too, and it was Carl's delight to approach such a group from behind and, if they ignored his whistle, to lob his half-finished malted at them over his left shoulder, and then speed away. You threw one or two shakes and malteds yourself, all the boys did; no one ever got caught and you didn't do it every day. Carl was in high spirits that afternoon, and pulled his line out of the press with a flourish, bumping the arm of the printer next to him, who was called Skeeter.

Skeeter was a few years older than the rest of the boys, and was done with high school. He had been off from work for a period of weeks, had been back only a few days and was more than a little morose. He had blue-black hair and milky biceps; he kept his sleeves rolled up almost to the shoulder, and his shirt unbuttoned in the heat, as did most of the other workers. He turned when Carl bumped his arm and swore at him with such a vengeance that no one laughed, but paused at their own presses to see if anything would happen. It was a run of 4-H ribbons that day; thick red and purple and white rosettes above streamers that proclaimed BEST OF BREED or HONORABLE MENTION-HEIFERS, as well as the usual grade of prizes — first through fifth. You were next to Carl and stood back to watch, pulling out your own stick of type by its smooth wooden handle. Skeeter stood for a moment with his face growing dark. You fuckin creep, he said quietly, and yanked out his white-hot stick and thrust it up close against Carl's face. How'd you like to lose that pretty hair, creep? he asked, his voice low and menacing amid the sound of the other machines. Carl had dropped his stick on the type table, and Frankie had begun to break it down with his hammer, the steaming metal letters falling against each other as they cooled. And you put your own stick in Carl's hand as he stood facing Skeeter, and started to back away. But Skeeter's fury caught you; as Carl moved backwards and away from him, Skeeter swung around with his stick and hit you across the stomach, and you cried out. The heat singed your open shirt at the buttonhole, and you looked down to see a wisp of smoke curling against your skin. Then Cecil was yelling in the background and the other boys had grabbed Skeeter from behind, and Carl was trying to get at him with your stick, but couldn't. Then Frankie got up from behind the table, holding in his glove the cooling type from Carl's stick and in one motion emptied it down the front of Skeeter's jeans. He howled and screamed and that took some of your pain away. When they let him undo his pants, the women began to clap and whistle, and Cecil came running over, and told everybody to get the hell back to work.

In Regina Cieli prison fifteen years later, after the first three days when you saw no one but through the hole in the cell door through which they handed in your food, you were asked what the letters meant by the guard they called Porcile. You had not enough Italian to reply, and so he called you Secco, the dry one, and grinned and put his finger to his cheek and then slammed shut the door. The other guards would not speak to you; neither the ones who took you out into the yard for exercise, nor those who came through at intervals to run a club along the bars of your high window. You could climb up and look out of the window into the yard if you made no noise, and moved your head slowly upward. The wing in which you were put faced the yard over a series of small pie-shaped open-air cubicles in which the solitary prisoners were made to exercise; you could only see the shadows of this movement against the concrete. The hands stretched upward, or flailed back and forth, as shadows; there would be the beginnings of a line of cigarette smoke, and then the guard would appear and take the cigarette.

The thin line would disappear, the hands reached upward once again, into the empty air.

When you were arrested, you were wearing jeans and boots and a shirt, but no underwear. You didn't want to sleep in your jeans and boots; the single cot in your first cell was high up off the floor, and you had to jump down from it each morning when they first banged on the door. The morning guard seemed to you intelligent; when you jumped down the first day, he looked at you naked from the waist down and said nothing, except with his club he lifted your shirt in front, and thrust out his chin slightly and raised his eyebrows, in the way that Italian men do when they expect some explanation or clarification. You smiled; his club was the first physical contact you had in the time you'd been there. He lowered his club, and motioned with it for you to turn around, and then lifted the shirt-tail out away from your body with it. He let the club press against your skin below the small of your back, and he said nothing, and you said nothing and then he was gone.

The next morning, when the banging came on your door, you jumped down as before. The first nights you had been so terrified that you'd gotten little sleep, but this night's wakefulness was tinged now with a specific sexual apprehension, not unpleasant in the way the general terror was. You had decided that whatever he expected you to do, you would do; the incredulity at being in prison at all was now being replaced by the fear that you would never be let out, and you were desperate to act in some way, to be able to put things in some perspective. The door swung open, and he stood a few paces inside the cell. *Scifozo!* he barked, and his lips were drawn together tightly. With an angry gesture he pointed to where your jeans lay against the wall. *Sei scifozo. Vestiti!* He called you a pig and told you to dress yourself. His look was now a sneer. Trembling, you zipped up your jeans, and from then on slept in them, until you developed a rash, and were finally able to secure a pair of shorts from the English-speaking priest, when he passed through with books and cigarettes some weeks later.

The morning guard never touched you with his club or with his hand again. It was Porcile who held your arms tight behind you in the shower, and forced you to bend over, and he who put one of the cigarettes he collected between your lips, afterward.

You had been in Rome a year.

The full still moon above the city, transfixing its movement. You imagined the Via Appia and the Via Condotti, the scruffy young men lounging on the Spanish Steps, the flow of young men and women crossing over the Tiber on the Ponte Garibaldi. On nights such as this you had often stood watching cats gather in the sunken temple of Diana in Largo Argentina, their thin bodies gliding like serpents over the ruined columns and plinths. You thought of the cats and of all the city's painters and artists and expatriates, of the jumble of bodies along the Tiber's bank, bodies locked in brief anonymous embrace: of the hands of men upon each other in public places, hearty and thrusting in the Mediterranean way, hands moving, illustrating emotion, bold gestures over red and white tablecloths and saucers of salt.

But all images dissolved to those of the zoo, fragmented by terror of the place, the place in your mind where fat policemen stood next to the cages of animals, grinning stupidly at one another, spitting at the ground. No images, then, but only the sweet clarity of the moon. You moved toward madness as toward the distant light, tracing with your finger on the damp wall the letters of your name, and then abandoning all sense.

Lying in your cell, you were mad for many nights — all men must be mad all nights in prison, and all days. To accommodate the taste of sweat and urine in your dish of nameless soup, to feel the odor of Nazionales clinging to your body like a shroud of smoke, and each day and night to feel the guard's club as it rattles across the window's bars as if it ran across your ribs instead — to do every small and every large task as if it were the same: surely this is the madness of prison. And closer and closer each night coming something like death.

The first time you saw Luke, he was sitting in the yard. His face was turned in profile, and his hair was light enough amid the group of dark heads, that you thought he might be French or even American. But as you saw him talking to the other prisoners and laughing and gesturing with them, you decided that he was Mediterranean after all.

The men in the yard spent the time walking up and down in pairs or singly, turning within half a step of the wall that separated the main yard from the building you were in. Their faces were discernible in the sunlight. Luke's hair was the color of chestnut and the color of copper at once. His smile was broad and even, and that made him seem finer than the men about him. He wore a white undershirt and what looked like khaki pants, and boots.

He had been on his way from his home in Athens to New York when he was arrested. He was staying with friends in Trastevere, drawing in the Roman light, tracing with conte and charcoal the folds of marble fabric that are everywhere in the city, fattening his portfolio with sheets of intricately bedaubed vellum. When these friends were arrested on suspicion of drug possession, he was arrested too. Though no drugs were found on him, he had been detained for three months by what was called the American Law, making proximity a crime, and any citizen's denunciation, or *denuncia*, a sentence of guilt.

He later said he had watched you while Porcile held you against the wall of the shower stall, watched as half a dozen wretched felons threw themselves into you, cursing and joking. He would not come close to you those first few days, because you talked to no one he said you were thereby more beautiful. He had been in the prison, the *cancelleria*, for two months when you arrived, and had fucked and been fucked, and then grown fierce in sexual disavowal, turning with fists clenched and lips drawn back if anyone tried to provoke him. You saw this later, in the yard, from the window of your cell where all action was framed by the bars and stucco.

You took your exercise at different times, and it was only on shower days that you passed in the yard. You were aware of him and not aware of him at the same time; the ordeal of showering and what went with it kept you blinded and you moved slowly from your cell, across the yard and through the long tunnel, prodded by the guards, in that dazed state that had become your habit. When no one came near that day, you were suspicious; Porcile laughed in his corner, beyond the stalls, and shook his head, and even handed you a thin wedge of brown soap. You dressed quickly, grateful to fate or circumstance, or whatever had spared you the attentions of those other prisoners Porcile had traded you to in previous weeks, and hurried back along the tunnel where rats and waterbugs ran in the half light.

Outside, in the morning light, Luke stood with his arms behind his back. He looked solemn. The sun was behind him and shone through his hair, into your eyes when you looked at him directly, so that his features lacked detail, except for the soft nimbus of his hair. The solemnity was inscrutable. He reached out his hand and gave you a folded piece of paper.

The note said:

> You are like a statue.

Back in your cell, you flattened it out and placed it on the bed. He had said nothing to you, and you nothing to him — you'd walked on past him a few steps before opening it, and then turned, but he was walking away.

When he gave you the drawing the following week, you didn't walk on, but stopped. He smiled. It was of you, your body bent as it had been the first time in the shower, but drawn out like a figure from El Greco, simplified and rustic. The sound of your own voice jarred you, you were so unused to using it.

So you came back to yourself, and were like the other foreign prisoners, and came to talk and joke with them for the rest of the time you were inside.

In prison, all men are innocent, or so they say. One may be guilty of other crimes, true enough, but not the one for which one's been put away. The anarchist Valpredo came up to you in the yard one morning. He had the look of a fox, his dark hair sticking out in thatches. He wanted to know about the American consulate lawyer; he spoke only enough English to ask if the man were good or bad, and when you didn't recognize the name, and couldn't help him, he swore and turned away. The Turk with whom you'd been speaking said that this Valpredo whom the press called the mad bomber was not happy with the party lawyer he'd got, but could not change. This was during the first month. He was moved from Rome to Milan not long thereafter; later, when his case was tried in open court, he was one of the men who sat inside a great iron cage and howled at his persecutors in front of the Italian and German television cameras and the men from RAI.

When your case finally came to trial, after forty-seven days and nights, the three judges sat on a raised platform behind the wooden bench. It was a high room, painted with indifference. The manacles were like some beast that had got itself clamped to you, its jaws imbedded in your flesh, pulling your fists down in front of you with its weight.

You came to justice with your beard shaved and your hair cut that morning by the prison barber. He was a young man and he held a cigarette clenched between his teeth as he moved the clippers over the crested manes of the men who sat before him. On the floor, men's hair lay in mats. The judges rose like a cake of reason as you were finally thrust into the room. They knew what you would never know, that you were innocent.

There is a screeching in the air, and Italian words crawl up the walls like insects.

This is the sequence that keeps recurring:
You sit with a *caffelatte* at a table in Piazza Navona. Beneath the figure representing the River Plate at the center of the piazza, a boy crouches over a match and inhales sharply, cupping the flame in the wind, then throwing it away from him. It lands beside the rose woman where she stands surveying the tables of tourists, painters and actors. She jerks her head in the boy's direction to see if there is malice behind the gesture. Finding none, she ambles over the stones towards Domiziano, intent on a table of white-haired tourists.

"*Qui e la piú bella?*" she asks, turning up the corners of her rubbery lips in a smile. She bends over the small table, holding up one red rose. It is dusk; the petals have been peeled since mid-day. Who is the prettiest, she wants to know.

"Clara! Clara!" shrieks one of the women at the table, and the others join her as she laughs and points to the woman opposite, who in turn smiles vacantly and cups her ear.

"How nice," Clara exclaims as the rose is handed to her. Those of her companions who have understood the question nudge each other. Her hair has a yellowish rinse and she wears her glasses on a chain; she holds the flower to her nose, trying to draw some scent from its dark petals. She is the least beautiful of the party, deaf to irony and insult, a homely woman in the midst of grandeur. The rose woman is given a coin. The flower is passed back and forth, then pinned to the lapel of Clara's cloth coat.

The boy at the fountain watches the women, tossing back his dark hair and letting the blue smoke escape from between his clenched white teeth.

When he comes to your table, he continues to watch the women, standing in front of you, turned in profile. He waits for you to offer him a seat, and then feigns surprise. He has an espresso, and then a glass of Anisette. You are somewhat taken aback when he asks you to come with him to the zoo, after a half hour's rambling conversation about automobiles and American films and the problem he is having with his fiancée. You ask if he would like another Anisette before you go, and you have one with him. By now the sky is dark, and the stars above the church of St. Agnes are beginning to show in the deep vault of sky above its spires; within the church, the glass eye of her holy replica glistens with the light of the candles lit before it. Small flames dart up in the misty darkness, ignited by Roman wives and mothers, by tourists fascinated with the twisting martyrdom of the Saint's rack; the flames depicted and the stars are of the same greenish gold.

It seems a wonderful idea, to go to the zoo at night; you have been there before, during the day, and have watched the flamingos, and the women sitting on orange crates beside the gate, basking in the sun. There is a llama one may ride, you remember. You leave Domiziano and the rose seller. In the zoological park within the Villa Borghese Gardens, the lair of the wolves is situated at the bottom of a long grassy incline, not far from where the Viale Rossini and Via Bellini converge. (Outside the park, across the city toward the Forum, another more well-known wolf resides inside a wire enclosure at the base of the Capitoline Hill; she is languid and honorary, a living symbol of the she-wolf who is said to have suckled Romulus and Remus, and she is called Luperca Dea. The zoo wolves are too thin, but not particularly mean-spirited, whereas Luperca Dea is running too fat and will snap without warning at any human limb). The zoo at night is closed to visitors, but there is access to where the wolves are kept, through the parking lot behind the Belle Arte gallery. Roman cypresses rise up on all sides, and the early evening breeze catches the scent of zoo and park and something else: the odor of the city as it changes from night to day. Exhaust fumes blend with pignole nuts and chocolate and cheese. Close by the acrid odor of decay and damp rutting.

The boy has his favorite among the animals, a female, and he calls her to his side once you have gotten to the lair, a low moat and fence between you. When she doesn't come, but stands instead beside her pen regarding you with blood-red eyes, he says she won't come because he's not alone, that if he were, she'd doubtless come over and lick his hand as she has in the past. Intrigued, you offer to walk away, up the path, but something in the way you make your suggestion seems to offend him, and he rubs his palms on his trousers and says, no, let's go.

    The sky never darkens over Rome. There is always some reflected light, and the ocean at Ostia must contribute as well to the radiance that never completely fades from the air. The cypresses in the parks and along the sea take all blackness to themselves and stand against the softer sky like incisions in the night. They are what you remember, and the smell, and the chirping of cicadas that ceases and then begins again on its own miraculously aligned metre: the night is circular, a great dome in a city of domes, and within its polished orb is repeated all eternity.

    You walk up the path with the young man—whose name you will never know—he calls himself Draco, but that is no doubt an affectation—and where the Pére David deer are housed you stop and have a cigarette, and as you light it, you see that he is trembling. There is a feeling of panic; the walkway stretches upward to the pachyderm house near the entrance, and you visualize the children there at the moat on a sunny day. Children and animals and oranges being peeled: comforting thoughts to dispel the warning coldness at the base of your neck. He inhales, and throws the cigarette from him with the same gesture you have seen in the piazza, and then he is kneeling in front of you without a word, the bravura discarded as a mantle is thrown off. The cicadas cease and begin, cease and begin, and you try to feel that it is all right, to move at one with his motion, but it is too jagged—too rigid. He continues and you brace yourself against his shoulders, but through his light jacket you can feel his skin recoil at the pressure—why is he doing this; you repeat the question to yourself; and feel yourself building to a climax that somehow horrifies you because it has nothing to do with love and little to do with sex. This boy is *working*, you think, and you try to pull away, though of course it is too late, and with his hand he jerks the wet skin back and forth, claiming the outcome, spilling you with a harsh intensity onto the thistles and moss beside the pathway and whirls away from you, regaining his feet as you still in the spasm of orgasm are unsteady on yours, he whirls away and then turns back, with an ugly sneer drawing his features down, and pushes against you with one hand while with the other he pulls at your wrist, at your watch, pushes you backward, silently, all malevolence gathered in his fists.

Pulling away, trying to free yourself from him, feeling foolish in your naked vulnerability, you start to bellow into his face, and you choke on whatever words rush out. He steps back a pace, and you see the glint of metal in his hand.

The words continue to pour from your mouth, as rage and fear confound you—your voice is remote and thin, not your normal voice at all, you think, remarking on the phenomenon to some objective arbiter within. Your body is only a machine now, and moves as it will. When the knife comes, you twist away, and slide on the gravel, and are on your feet again turning as he turns. The high wail that is your speech seems to come from some other source: noting this you throw yourself against another blow. The knife is deflected, turned, buried in his throat. A sound like the soft pop of old threads in a fabric, a seam loosened, a hem let down. There, before you, his body jerks like the headless chickens of your uncle's farm long ago, the blood black in the darkness.

Stumbling along the path, you are overjoyed to see the man in uniform at the gate. When you remember to check the sound, your scream that rises to the cypresses, it is too late. Then there are other uniforms, and they too are aiming their fists at you, but there are no other knives. He is not dead, but mute. The tendons, severed, cannot be re-connected. The motor activity of the left side of his body is impaired as well. His eyes remain when the other images have ended, burning out from the chair in which he sits slumped, making sounds which—you cannot be sure now whether this is true, but it seems as if the cry he makes is little more than an exhalation of breath, really—making sounds like the sound of a wolf. You see him only once, in the court-room, and it is unlikely that you have heard what you think you have.

When your case is dismissed, it is because the weapon was not your own. Another charge, resisting arrest, is pressed; the time you have served is considered sufficient by the court. The embassy appointed lawyer is pleased. Before he leaves, he mentions that you will, alas, be required to leave the country within twenty-one days of your release. It is standard procedure, he explains: the innocent are expelled with the guilty, as a matter of course.

As it turns out, there is no question of self-defense when obscene acts are involved. Because the boy is Italian, and because you are a *straniero*, the court must assume for its own reasons of honor and machismo—*figura*—that it is you who have taken advantage of him, have indeed attempted acts which, if not exactly justifying his knife attack, have at least induced it. Such is the way of the world.

Your lawyer's confidential opinion is that you are lucky to be at large.

When, on the forty-ninth day, you are set free, you pass through iron gate after iron gate to the last building, where whatever of value you have had when you came in has been kept. The man who stands behind the counter and hands back your watch, ticking and correct as if it has never once faltered, smiles, and the glint of metal in his mouth picks up the four o'clock sun slanting in through the high window.

He stands regarding you as you sign your name on the form in front of you, drumming his thick fingers on the table between you. He coughs, and though his skin is robust in hue, you see that he puts his fist to his chest in the way of those men who have been inside longest, those to whom the stone walls have imparted their parasitic damp.

He picks up the form, and satisfied that everything is in order, that you have served your time and are to be released, makes a quick nod of his head. He says, *Adesso sei un Romano.*

Now you are a Roman.

When Luke comes out two weeks later, he repeats the same words that the clerk has spoken to him as well; you are standing in the train station, getting ready to board the Palatino for Paris together, on your way west. The steam hisses on the track, and an old man with orange juice and mineral waters is calling out his wares.

Now you are a Roman. And it's quite true. Now—for the rest of your life—you are.

RICHARD UMANS

I'm pleased to be introducing Richard Uman's writing to readers of this anthology, as I've been acquainted with him personally for several years. His work comes into the book in the following manner. One evening at the Sandpiper at Fire Island Pines, we both left the humid dance floor to sit out on the backdeck and cool off. There, we caught up with each other's lives over the past year. Very shyly — and surprisingly so to me, since Richard is a large, handsome muscular man usually confident in even the most daunting static attitude fields of the Pines — he admitted he too was a writer.

Months later not this, but another story appeared in my mail from Richard. It dealt with a complex subject even the most accomplished writers would have difficulty pulling off. But it was ambitious, sensitively developed and finely written. In the midst of our exchange of letters about revisions on it, "On the Door" suddenly appeared in my mail, and I instantly chose it instead, for its precision and perfection.

Gay life has many institutions. Bars and bonding and the art of acquaintanceship are three of them. Uman's story of Warren and Jess, the bar they work in, and how we are affected by other relationships are disturbingly tied together here. Emotion flickers dangerously under the surface of the objective style and narrative distance. I've seldom found the fire/ice of the gay male personality and relationship as well portrayed as in "On the Door."

ON THE DOOR

The dark street behind the Boston Public Library throbbed dully to the Bunkhouse's disco music. Barrow Street was hardly more than an alleyway, but it was lined with cars every night, despite its darkened buildings. On one side of the street bums huddled by the library steam grates, and on the other side leather — and bomber — jacketed men walked quickly to or from the Bunkhouse's black metal door.

I opened the door, and a wave of disco music washed into the street. Stepping into the pornographic glow of the vestibule, I shed my gloves to dig for the dollar cover charge. But Warren Higgins was on the door tonight, arranging a pile of ones in the drawer of the old brown cash register, and he motioned me past. I smiled, thanked him, asked how he was doing.

"I've been better," he murmured, jaws locked and lips parting to reveal a grim cage of rubber and metal strips restraining his teeth.

"What happened to you?" I asked.

"Broke my jaw," Warren pronounced carefully. He looked like he'd tried to chew up a Cadillac grille.

"Jesus. When?"

"Last Tuesday. This is my first night back."

I had a pang of guilt for not noticing his absence over the weekend. "Are you okay?"

He dismissed my question with a nod and took money from two men who'd entered behind me. I shuffled out of the way and started to take off my coat, then changed my mind. If I was going to be talking to Warren for awhile out here, I'd need it. The little space heater on the office stairs behind Warren did something against the January cold, but not much.

"Look," I said, "I'm going to go in and get a beer. Do you want something?"

"I guess I could use another Coke. Just ask Jess, he'll give it to you."

"Sure, but how about a real drink?"

"Nah, I'm still on pain killers. I'll pass out."

The Bunkhouse had recently expanded, breaking through to the restaurant next door, and was now more than twice its size on opening two years earlier. It was a Western-style cruise bar: levis and light leather, dressing down from the chic image of nearby Copley Square but not far enough down to bring out the hardcore leather dinosaurs. Jeans and T-shirts in the summer, jeans and flannel shirts in the winter, most of the leather ending up checked in the coat room. A quick glance showed that the expansion had changed the dress code not at all. The music, though, was a good deal louder, and there was a white tile dance floor in what must have been the kitchen of the defunct restaurant. A second bar now ran along the long wall of the new section, balancing the old oval bar still in place in the original area. There were more pinball machines, two electronic games, and a new pool table. The interior had been repainted from the brown and white of the old Bunkhouse to a high gloss black and royal blue. Probably meant to evoke leather and levis, but it was so oppressive that they'd begun lightening it with touches of white. Too late; the opening night crowd had appraised the gloomy color scheme, and in stores and offices all over town men were telling each other, "I'll see you tonight at the Black and Blue Room."

I took a leisurely lap around the place to see who was in tonight. Wednesdays didn't bring out a really distinguished crowd. Tonight's featured a sparse and familiar group of earnest post-teens — waiters and busboys and students and hairdresser's apprentices — dancing and chatting with each other, lording it over the few lonesome beer-clutchers and enjoying having the bar more or less to themselves. I spoke for a moment to Mike D'Anastasio, whose interior design business let him sleep late during the slow season. I waved hello to Teddy Gray, a nightly fixture at the Bunkhouse since he'd left his public school administrator's job. He was throwing his bulk around one edge of the dance floor in hopeless emulation of a boyish partner. A pair of slim young blacks had appropriated most of the floor to practice an elaborate dance routine. Teddy's and Joe's were the only faces I recognized. I'd have to wait for the weekend to see many more of my aging, post-thirty peers.

Jess was tending bar alone and bored. The weekend would see him and another bartender charging around their oval course like model racing cars. Tonight, for once, it was easy to get his attention.

"Hi, Jess, how you doing. Listen, Warren asked me to bring him a Coke, okay? And I'll have a draft."

"Sure thing," Jess replied, swinging automatically into the motions of filling beer mugs. He was wearing a tight black French-cut T-shirt with the Bunkhouse logo stenciled on it in white. The shirt went well with his black hair and moustache and his milk-white, blue-veined skin. Still, one of the small pleasures of the Bunkhouse was watching Jess at work with his shirt off. He looked very good for a guy in his late thirties, with a stomach like mortared bricks and flat, hairless, sharp-cut pectorals. Beady eyes and a low-bridged, pointed nose gave his face a snakelike quality, but the rich black moustache framed it with a hanging judge's dour authority. With the black T-shirt on he was a forbidding figure, but come the weekend's hard work he'd be flashing that bare, creamy torso again, and his whole look would lighten.

"Thanks," I said when he placed the two mugs in front of me. My dollar lay on the bar.

"On me."

"Oh, hey, thanks," I said, but Jess had disappeared to the other side of the bar.

Warren thanked me for the Coke. He transferred the plastic straw from the Coke he'd been drinking to the one I'd brought. He'd be using a lot of straws, I realized.

"How do you eat?"

Warren gave his monster's grin. "I've learned a lot of things you can do with a blender."

"How long will it be wired up?"

"About another month, I think. I go back to the doctor Friday. He'll tighten it and tell me how it's doing."

"Is it painful?"

"Not too much anymore. It hurt like a bastard at first. When I got out of the hospital they took me off Demerol, but Dick Wilson got me some codeine, so I'm okay to work."

He didn't look it. He was sitting slumped over, supporting himself against the cash register, his eyes unfocused. He was speaking a little drunkenly, but that might have been the awkwardness of forming words over the portcullis in his mouth. Or it might have been the codeine.

"Are you back at work?"

"Yeah, I went back half a day Monday and Tuesday. Today was my first full day."

"Jesus, what the hell are you doing here, then? Why aren't you home in bed?"

"I need the money."

"Weren't you insured?"

"Yeah, but there's still expenses."

I knew that Warren and Jess were workaholics—that's how they'd gotten involved in bar work in the first place—so I figured Warren just couldn't see sitting home alone. He and Jess had been lovers for eight years, thirty-year-old Jess having scooped up little Warren fresh from the Navy. They'd been a couple long enough to be virtually an institution among the people I knew. They both had day jobs of long standing, Warren in the women's shoe department at Filene's and Jess as a chef in a restaurant in the financial district. Jess had taken the bartending job at the Bunkhouse two summers ago when he was out of work. He'd stayed on part-time when he went back to his old job, and Warren had followed him, taking the door job when it opened up. Neither of them got to sleep much on their Bunkhouse nights, but working there was probably the only way they could have enjoyed the bar scene. They weren't active socially, and they had few pleasures outside their work. They did have a sailboat they'd bought together—the Bunkhouse money had helped with that, though their work schedules prevented them from sailing it much, and they both drove new cars.

Warren had driven me to New York in his new red Rabbit just a few weeks before. He'd been so proud of it, I hoped it hadn't been wrecked in a crash.

"How'd it happen, Warren?"

His eyes regarded me sluggishly. He was preparing to repeat the story he'd been telling all week when the door opened to admit a little rush of customers, overdressed for the Bunkhouse, tourists or bar-hoppers.

"A dollar cover!" protested the first one, reading the sign. He was a short blond in a tweed sportcoat over a pink sweatshirt and a tight pair of Calvin Kleins. "When did that start?"

"Three months ago, same as all the other bars," Warren said tiredly.

"They do the place over, and we have to pay for the decorator!"

"Yeah, right," Warren said and slouched in his chair while the new arrivals huddled over their finances.

I waited alongside Warren, feeling official. It pleased me sometimes to man the door with Warren, postponing the booming disco and the familiar conversations waiting inside the Bunkhouse. It also pleased me to go inside when I felt like it, but it was at the door of the Bunkhouse that I'd actually gotten to know Warren, after years of acquaintanceship. Slim and close to pretty, with neat sandy hair, large blue eyes, and a heart-shaped face, Warren had earlier existed for me only in Jess's shadow. The people who knew them both said that Warren was in fact the more personable of the two, but Jess was the one people remembered. The job at the Bunkhouse had been good for Warren in that respect, since he worked apart from Jess, and he'd met a lot of people on his own. Once I'd gotten to talking to Warren, I'd been surprised to find him a witty and quite likable person. I'd always expected him to be the supporting player he appeared next to Jess.

It was during one of those conversations on the door just a few weeks earlier that Warren and I had found we were planning to visit New York the same weekend, and he offered me a ride in the new car. On the way down we talked about life in the depressingly similar towns we'd grown up in at opposite ends of New England.

We talked of our escapes, mine to college and his to the Navy. And we talked of the comforts of life in Boston, a cultured and stylish city without the frenzy of New York or the claustrophobic gayness of San Francisco. I asked Warren what he was planning to do that weekend in New York.

"I don't know. Go to the baths, walk around the Village, I guess. I haven't been there in so long, I don't even know where to go anymore."

"What made you pick this weekend?"

"I just needed to get out of Boston. It was as good a time as any."

"Jess couldn't get away this weekend?"

"No, had to work. I needed to get off by myself anyway. But he'd sure be a lot better at this than I am."

"What do you mean?"

"He'd know where to go in New York. Or he'd know how to find out."

"It's not that hard to find out."

"Yeah, but he's so much more sexual than I am. He'd enjoy it more. I can hardly even get it up for sex lately, but Jess could probably spend all weekend at the baths."

I remembered a wild party several years before when, knowing neither of them, I'd made a pass at Jess and gotten no response. Warren hadn't been there, yet Jess was one of the few at the party who hadn't paired off with someone. Apparently things had changed, perhaps since the Bunkhouse job.

"Well, Warren, you may get to like the New York thing. A lot of people go down there once in awhile to let off steam."

"Yeah, maybe. Anyway, I have an old Navy buddy who lives in Brooklyn. I can always visit him."

"Sure. He'll probably be able to show you around."

"He's straight."

Warren knew I was going to New York to visit a guy I was seeing, so he didn't suggest we do the Village together. When we reached Manhattan, Warren dropped me off at my friend's place on the Upper West Side and came up to use the john. Charlie offered Warren his couch for the night, but the apartment was small, and Warren said thanks anyway, looking like a starving man politely declining a dinner invitation. Charlie and I watched with arms over each other's shoulders as Warren left manfully for his big weekend in New York. We felt like we were sending an orphan into the storm.

"How'd it happen?" I prompted Warren when the Bunkhouse's vestibule was clear again.

"Oh, yeah," he said and took a slow draw of Coke through the mangled straw. "Well, I was working the door here, and around 1:00 this guy comes in and walks right past me. So I get the coat-check guy to watch the door, and I get a bartender, and we go up and tell the guy there's a doller cover charge he hasn't paid. The guy says okay, okay, and starts reaching around in his pants, but he doesn't come up with anything. So we tell him he'll have to leave, and he says okay. Oh, yeah, he was carrying, like, a walking stick when he came in, and it's lying there on the bar. I pick it up and we walk him out. He asks me for the stick, and I say I'll give it to him at the door, and wham! he lets me have it."

"With the stick?"

"No, I had the stick. He just slugged me. We were so surprised we just threw him out. Then it started to hurt, so I went home early to lie down, and the next day my face was so swollen you couldn't even recognize me."

"What about the guy?"

"I don't know. Nobody knows him."

"What if he shows up again?"

"I don't know. I guess I'll go up to him with a few more bartenders this time. I hate this fucking job."

"Was Jess working?"

"Yeah, but he didn't even hear about it till it was all over. He was pretty pissed at me for not breaking the stick over the guy's head."

"Why didn't you?"

"I don't know. It never occurred to me. But believe me, it's occurred to me since. I go over it in my mind sometimes, and I think how great it would feel to smash his skull into a million pieces. But I had no idea then that my jaw was broken."

"It doesn't look swollen or anything now. It'll probably heal fine."

"Yeah, the oral surgeon said it'll be okay. And they only had to take out one tooth. But I didn't need this right now."

The black metal door opened again, a rush of cold air and a new customer came in. He was a big, heavy-set guy wearing a blue windbreaker that was far too light for a Boston January. He smiled at Warren and me and walked past us.

"It's a dollar cover charge," Warren called out as sharply as he could with a clenched jaw.

The guy stopped and turned. "A dollar, huh?"

Warren just nodded and pointed to the sign on the wall.

"Well, I'll tell ya," the big guy began, "I'm from out of town, and I've spent all my bar money for tonight. How about letting an out-of-towner in for a look around?"

"Sorry," Warren said. The guy stared hard at him. Warren's eyes were half-closed with boredom, fatigue, or something else. The guy's hands formed slowly into fists, then slowly released.

"Okay," the guy finally said and turned to leave. He sneered over his shoulder, "Thanks a lot."

"Fucking asshole," Warren said quietly, taking a sip of Coke.

"Jesus," I whispered. I caught myself straightening up and trying to look tough, completely after the fact. "Warren," I said, "what the fuck are you doing here tonight?"

He just looked at me, eyelids still at half mast, his whole face frozen, immobile as his jaws.

Then Jess appeared. He strode across the narrow vestibule as he must have just traversed the bar, shoulders squared and head high and slightly forward. He halted at the cash register and stood looking down at Warren.

"How ya doin?" he said. The question was for Warren, since Jess hadn't acknowledged my presence. He wasn't so much rude as gruff, concealing a basic shyness. The gruffness went better with the image.

"Okay," Warren said. "Slow."

"Yeah, it's dead in there," Jess said morosely.

A customer came in. He reached around Jess and handed Warren a dollar. "Thanks," Warren hissed through the metal frame. Jess hadn't moved.

"Is Kevin coming by tonight?" Warren asked him.

"Yeah. Thanks for letting him in for nothing, by the way."

"No problem. Did you talk to the guy about the boat?"

"Yeah, it's all set. No problem."

"You sure?"

"Yeah."

There was a moment's uncomfortable silence. Warren fidgeted, and Jess drummed his fingers on the cash register in time to the music from the bar. His eyes roamed the blank wall behind Warren's head. Uncomfortable silence seemed to be Jess' natural element.

Warren's patience waned first. "That a new shirt?" he asked.

"Yeah," Jess said, brightening. "You like it?"

"Yeah, it's nice. I like the lettering. Did all the bartenders get one?"

"Nah, I just had one made up, see how it'd look." Jess scowled down at the deco-styled white lettering arrayed over his left nipple, perky even beneath the black T-shirt.

"Yeah, it looks nice."

"Think I should have Joe get a bunch made up? We could all wear one, and we could sell 'em behind the bar."

"Sounds good. Joe likes little projects like that. He'll probably build a dressing room."

"And display racks," I said.

"Yeah," Warren said, "it might be the start of a whole new line, Bunkhouse Sportswear. 'Clothes that wear *you* out'."

"Yeah, right," Jess said. "Well, I better get back to my bar."

"So long," I called.

"Yeah," Jess said, "so long."

"I like the Bunkhouse Sportswear idea," I said when Jess had gone. "Trouble is, how much can you do with just black and blue?"

"People need something that goes with tattoos."

"You're right. There's a whole untapped market out there."

"A crying need. And black and blue's just for spring. Our fall line can be black on black."

"With leather trim."

"And fun furs. Gorilla coats and moose capes."

"No, you need something more sophisticated for today's urban homosexual."

"How about rat?"

"That's it!"

"I'll ask Joe if I can set out traps in the basement."

Warren's spirits had lifted enough that he managed to smile at the next few people who entered, though he nearly scared them out of the bar with a view of his teeth. After they paid and went in, Warren and I dressed them all in Bunkhouse Sportswear, from rat-

143

skin chaps to pigeon-feather boas. This was more like the old Warren, alert, dishing his customers to filth, but he soon tired and slumped back across the cash register.

"How's Charlie?" he asked.

"Oh, fine. I spoke to him tonight before I went out. My phone bill's going to be godzilla this month. At least he's coming up here next weekend. He asked for you, by the way. I said you were fine, but I'll alter the report when I talk to him next. Which will probably be tomorrow, since he can't figure out a train schedule by himself."

"You moving to New York?" Warren asked.

"Are you kidding? I have another year in my program here. But I may go down for the summer when school lets out. If we're still seeing each other by then."

"Sounds like you will be. Shit, I wish it was closing time."

"I don't even mind his being in New York most of the time," I continued. "At least I get my work done this way. It changes everything, even going out alone, when you know you've got somebody. I suppose I'll have to move down there when I get my degree, but I've got another year to worry about that."

"Teddy Gray's moving to California next month," Warren said.

"Yeah, that's when his new job starts, I heard. He's pretty excited about it."

"I'm going to drive out with him."

"Oh. Vacation?"

"No, I'm moving. Jess and I broke up."

I looked at him. "You're kidding," I finally managed.

"Nope. Last week. I moved out right after I got out of the hospital. I'm staying with Teddy Gray."

"Teddy Gray. Are you and he . . .?"

"Get serious. No, Jess is the one with the social life. He's been seeing this humpy little twenty-three year old named Kevin. You've probably seen him hanging over Jess's bar. I think the kid moved in right after I moved out."

"Shit," I said. "Was this building up a long time?"

"Well, I was fighting to hold on for a long time, but it still took me by surprise when I lost. He only came to visit me once in the hospital and stayed ten minutes and wouldn't even talk to me, and I knew that was it. I've moved out before, and he's always called me back. This time, he moved somebody else in."

"Maybe he's just getting back at you for moving out."

"No, it's been coming—and he's selling the boat."

"Oh-oh. Divorce court," I said. "I'm sorry."

"So am I."

I backed off for a moment to let Warren's words sink in and to escape his fetid breath. With the noise of the music and his difficulty speaking I had to lean close to hear him, and it had clearly been awhile since he'd been able to use a toothbrush. Warren was normally meticulous about himself, and his bad breath would have mortified him any other time. He sipped again at his straw, as if lubricating the metal assemblage in his mouth, while I tried to think of Warren and Jess as other than a couple. It wasn't easy; they had been a constant for so long.

"Well," I said, "at least he came out here to see how you were doing."

"He's gotten more thoughtful since I moved out. He wants to be friends."

"Friends?"

"Yeah, that's what he says."

"Hmmm. So it's California, huh?"

"Why not? I've never been, and I have to start over someplace."

"Why don't you stay here? At least you'll have your job and your friends."

"And all those reminders that I'm not twenty-three and humpy anymore."

"Right, you should look into one of those California retirement communities. Warren, Jess is the one who's getting middle-aged, not you. That's probably what all this is about anyway."

"Well, I can't just sit around watching him go home with hot young numbers every night. When it's not Kevin it's some other twink. He picks them up like fleas, working here."

"That's probably why he's working here. But why are you doing it?"

Warren's face hardened. "I need the money for California."

"If you'd drop this job, you wouldn't need California."

"I hate this town. I'm getting out."

"Okay, okay. When's Teddy leaving?"

"The sixth."

"You'll still have that contraption in your mouth."

"I'll bring the blender."

Bunkhouse patrons came and went, singly and in pairs. It was getting late, and the thin crowd was thinning further. Warren and I talked on with few interruptions, my chatting keeping a sleepy driver from running off the road. The conversation moved through blender recipes for puree of everything to further inspirations for Bunkhouse Sportswear and occasionally back to Jess or Charlie; although with me starting a relationship and Warren ending one, neither of us had much to say on that subject that the other wanted to hear.

Warren was edging closer to exhaustion. His eyes drooped nearly closed, and his mood swung from leaden to giddy and back again.

"I hope Teddy'll be ready to go home soon," he slurred.

A small flock of overcoiffed fashion queens let each other in the Bunkhouse door, probably refugees from Partners, the dressier bar across Copley Square. Their slacks were all neatly creased, and they shivered in tight little tailored jackets. Things must have been slow at Partners, too, for their customers to resort to the Bunkhouse this late.

"And they said fuzzy sweaters would never come back," Warren muttered.

"It's almost 1:30!" one of the bolder ones shrilled. "Do we have to pay?"

Warren examined his watch. "It's 1:13," he said, "and yes, you do."

"Well, that sucks!" Titters from the gallery.

"Sorry, boys," Warren said, "I don't make the rules."

A quick conference produced a handful of dollar bills.

"Wait till they see the pitiful crowd in there," Warren said when the vestibule was empty again. "They'll want their money back." Unable to rest his chin on his arms, he propped his hands against his temples and suspended his head over the cash register.

"Warren, I don't see why you're putting yourself through this. You couldn't need the money that bad. Why don't you just drop the door job and take it easy for a couple of weeks?"

He looked up at me and parted his lips over his aluminum snarl. "I wouldn't give him the satisfaction."

Lloyd Galvin's round, familiar face poked through the black door. "Hi, girlfriends," he called as he danced in. "Got room for some more trash in this tacky bar?"

"Anytime," Warren said, motioning away Lloyd's dollar. "How was Partners?"

"About like a funeral. Have the services started here yet?"

Warren smiled, and Lloyd froze. "Mother of God, what happened to you?"

"Busted jaw."

"No! You poor baby! Did it happen here? Tell me everything!"

Warren began the story mechanically but gradually warmed to the task, the effort of working his lips over his clamped jaws animating him a bit. Lloyd settled in for a good long listen, and I realized I hadn't been into the bar since I'd gotten the drinks long before.

"I'm going in for a minute," I said, feeling like someone freed from a hospital vigil by the arrival of a closer relative.

Warren waved to me without taking his attention from the rapt Lloyd, and I started away. A couple of people came in, I saw, but it was so late that Warren let them in free and went on with his war story, punctuated throughout with flashes of armor plate.

ROBERT FERRO

Robert Ferro's first novel, The Others, *Scribners, 1977, was a brilliant puzzle, a series of Chinese boxes, icy with distance, enigmatic and extremely controlled. The excerpt printed here, "The Aviary" from Ferro's novel in progress,* Marie Desir, *is almost the opposite.*

His subject is the attractive, still young, still aspiring solitary gay male who doesn't have a lover, and doesn't know why that is so. After limning aspects of this unfulfilled life, Ferro then presents us with an encounter between Max and a prospective mate—Carlos: an encounter that is untypical yet somehow representative and even explicatory about why Max is as he is: at the same time that it is sensual and pathetic.

Each of the chapters of this novel seems to center on an object as a symbol. In "The Aviary" the formal pattern of entrapment and release throughout the excerpt is held within the icon of the great birdcage at Stephen Foster's—a replica of one built in the last century on the Rothschild estate in England.

Ferro's earlier work has been in collaboration with his lover of many years, Michael Grumley: Atlantis, Autobiography of a Search *(Doubleday, 1970).*

THE AVIARY

Max is thirty-seven. He lives in New York City in an apartment infested with two kinds of coachroach: the first is large, fast and brazen; the second is small, easy to kill but numberless. He lives alone, is alone. In fact the first roaches were company. On occasion he talked to them, indulgently let them pass as if they were pets belonging to a neighbor. Now they wear his bug spray like cologne, his lethal sodium flouride like talc. They have dropped all discretion, do not wait for darkness, do not flee the light. Max feels powerless. He thinks they have too firmly planted their flag for Spain. The place is theirs.

He lives alone. It is a fact he repeats often to himself. It is perhaps his most common thought, that he—with his looks, his talents, his wishes—has no one. He still dreams of falling in love but no longer expects it. He is aware that his life, at the least, is half over. In two years, at thirty-nine, his bones will settle. The whole skeleton will shift like an old house. His hair will have further thinned, his gums receded, his lids drooped. His nose will not be as straight, there will be gray in his beard and in the hair on his chest. There will be lines everywhere, folds that hang, stretchmarks, disappointments. He will be old and alone, as he is now but old. People will no longer turn to look at him, will see nothing but themselves being seen. The game will have been over, and then long over, and then a memory.

He is aware, like Keats, that his life is a thing in water. The evidence of his existence disappears completely, immediately behind him.

Outside his window is an ailanthus tree. He has watched it grow in the past ten years from a sprig to a tall, fernlike fullness that relieves some of its ubiquitous banality. It is the roach of trees, in the way that the pigeon is the rat of birds. But the tree is green, clean, featherlike and fragrant. It has made the difference on countless afternoons. He lies on his bed and gazes into it. A wind up the alley ruffles it into shapes. His mind wanders. The tree thrives. Its hardiness and stature, together with a protected position between the large buildings, will assure it longevity. It will outlive Max. It will live a hundred years.

A voice teacher lives beneath him. In the summer, through the open window, he hears the beginning wail of "Summertime" over and over, different voices experiencing the same tortured giftlessness. Or there are ghostly exercises, bright high notes that die long falling deaths, Sisyphean scales, and short emotional triplets that seem, in ascending repetition, like vocal renderings of the perfect clitoral orgasm.

In the back, beyond the tree, there is other music. Drums — a huge chrome and vellum, big band set — sound as if they are being hurled down flights of stairs. A piano. A saxophone. And high up and reed thin, a flute presents the pure vocal ideal like a calm bird. It is all like the beginning of a disjointed rehearsal, for a performance which never occurs.

Several dogs belonging to the local supers live in the interstices of adjacent apartment houses. Two here are related, as the supers of the adjoining buildings are related. The dogs, father and son, hate each other. They face off, through a hurricane fence that divides their territories, and snarl and rasp themselves into a maddened stupor, arousing every other dog for blocks; the wild sound of wolves fighting over meat. At other times a graceful, apparently blooded Irish setter, directly under Max's window, has the habit of a single bark announcement of its presence at two-minute intervals. Max has been around to the other street, to talk to the doorman, to find out the setter's owner's name. It is the super's wife, Mrs. Capitalia. Max throws open the window. The morning light blinds him. Capitalia! he screams. Capitaalia! The setter looks up at him with a dumb red beauty. The face of another woman on a higher floor looks across at him, sees a naked man in a rage. The dog, not having made the connection, barks again. Max closes the window, switches the heavy curtains, falls back on the bed in the dark.

He has his friends. Carlton designs windows at Bergdorf's. Manuel cuts hair and makes seven hundred dollars a day modelling. Tom gives parties, knows everyone in the Village. Jack is a Transit cop, Walter sells tokens at 59th Street. Rick runs a pet shop and deals drugs. Winston and Richie are ballet dancers. David, who is called the Bishop, is studying to be an Episcopal minister. Jim and Larry are D.J.'s. Billy tends bar, Alec does the lights and Rafer busses, all in the same club. Matthew writes and acts. Gene paints. Bill, Tim, Ben, Sam and Paul, as far as Max knows, do nothing.

They have held themselves up to each other like Butterick patterns, to see what fits and what doesn't. They have compressed the developments of weeks into a few moments, with a series of carefully coded questions. A lifetime together has hung on the answers. Each time, and in a spirit of hope, Max has sought the complement of his mind and body, and failed in the effort thus far.

And each of his friends has his own list, like a list of romantic hopefuls that did not run well, and on which is also included Max, who writes and waits.

Waits tables, tends bar, passes trays, assembles hors d'oeuvres. At Bar Mitzvahs, cocktails, huge dinners at the Opera, small parties on the Eastside, bank openings, weddings, vernissages; he wears a white shirt and black bow tie, a black vest, black pants and shoes, over all of which is juxtaposed a long white apron. It is the classic sartorial statement of the servant. Or, if he has been assigned to the pantry, his costume is white, a professional, kitchen white, in case a guest should wander in on the trail of a returning waiter, back for another tray of butterfly shrimp and snow peas, scallop and avocado, minted chicken on endive, riddles wrapped in enigma, garnished with a mauve orchid on a bed of kale.

He prefers the pantry. Often he has looked out over the crowd, from the equivalent of the wings, and seen a friend or a table of friends among the guests. In the pantry he is safe from discovery. He can make his rent money in peace. He jokes with the waiters from a safe remove as they come in with empty, ravaged trays. They talk about sex and drugs and discos, about the guests, their habits, their clothes; about dreams and moods, the phases of the moon, about themselves. One of them comes in with the news that a famous guest is under the table, out cold. Another says, Sure, Talullah. Another says, Really, to himself quietly, everytime he enters the pantry. The chef answers any question he is asked with a slight inquisitive inflection, as if perhaps you might not have heard of candied yams? or of strawberries dipped in white chocolate? Max listens for this inflection and wonders how such an affectation ever took hold. Does it mean the chef thinks all replies are a matter of opinion and speculation? When Max asks how many guests are expected that night and the chef answers, four hundred? is he inviting Max to approve of the number, or to change it if he thinks four hundred is too many?

Among the waiters and pantrymen, everyone does something else. Most are actors, beautifully groomed, young and hopeful. Because of their dreams for themselves they see their circumstance in theatrical terms. It is a gig. At the end, when the guests have gone, they roll up their sleeves and put the place back together, as though striking a set.

Waits and writes. It is a combination that gives perspective to both endeavors, pinpointing each as an alternative to the other. As a pantryman everything he does is a distortion of his old pipedreams of being rich and glamorous. He is present at the experience but on the wrong side of the canapés. In his mind he is also the guest, the consumer, whose hand hovers over the proferred tray, reluctant to disturb the delicious symmetry, appreciative of the power to care about such a thing.

As a writer it is not so different. It is when working in the pantry, intensely involved in the trivia of feeding several hundred people, that he seems to think and feel most like a writer, when it seems clear that he wants the evening to go well in just the way he wants his life to go well.

He has written five books and published two. These events are classified in his mind as disappearing acts. He finds the terminology of magic to be useful and analogous to writing.

It seems that his standards for love have been raised to impossible, unattainable levels. He no longer insists on the perfect lover, although he believes such a man, such men, exist. But he has looked for him in so many men and found only parts of him, that now he looks only for the parts. It seems wiser to understand this, and to enjoy them as they are found — those traits, that quirk, that glance, this scent. These are clues to the man's presumed existence. As he comes upon them they are devoured.

The eyes, he knows, are dark, the look serious, benign, inquisitive, wise, melting; and then gone. It is an idea communicated in a glance.

Max has seen the man in someone else, in a boy he used to know but did not love then. A picture of the two of them documents this paradox. Max is standing by a bright blue swimming pool. He is looking at the camera. The boy is in the pool, looking up happily at Max. The love is like a third presence in the picture. It is a force which drifts across the photograph with the boy's gaze. It seems to come up out of the pool toward Max's figure like a weight, into which there is something in him that leans.

His past affairs have become his present friendships. Huge amounts of emotion have been transmuted into friendly affection, wine turned into water and stored in canteens. These friendships have startlingly intimate moments, alternating with long silences. It seems that what they all need and expect from each other — a little affection, a little concern, a little humor — is given out in doses, on demand. One will call with two tickets to the most inaccessible show on Broadway; another is in Bellevue with twenty-four stitches in his psyche. Another needs to convey the details of his father's death by cancer; another the hopelessness, the horror, the hideousness of his latest interior design installation. On occasion it is Max's turn. He calls in his markers with a long depressing complaint or confession. He is writing a story about a young man travelling through the Amazon jungle, moving from tribe to tribe as a visiting sexual deity. He struggles to define the connection between this and his life. His friends are the tribesmen. The drums announce him. In the anteroom of his imagination they strip off their street clothes, paint their bodies and enter his fantasies. He knows he is alone, and that just as there were limits to their love, there are limits to their affection and friendship. But the arrangement is familial, a benign conspiracy of the like-minded. The social affability for which they were all bred binds them together, as a sop to their profound romantic disappointments. They have passed together through many cardinal emotions — attraction, infatuation, love, jealousy, humiliation and rejection. And it has happened to each of them often enough to have made them realize that they, in this pattern, are part of each others' lives. To allow the spirals of condemnation and rejection to continue would in the end assure them of nothing but their own bedroom and loneliness. They are the remains of an army, once vast; their war a dream.

He wakes at four-thirty in the morning aware of the possibilities. At the moment two people encourage him to call and come over at odd hours. There are the baths, certain after-hour bars. He toys with the idea of breaking a pattern. But he was awakened at this hour, after ten hours of sleep, only because of earlier breakage. Is *breakage* the pattern? A police siren floats by, a long sliding wail to which, at the end, is appended the haunted, diminished howl of a dog in the courtyard. Max isn't going anywhere. No one is waiting. If ever, as a child, he woke in the middle of the night, there were comforts. He lay in a house filled with people. He had only to tap his fingertips on the floor for the dog to come over. Trapezoids of light would shift across the ceiling as a car passed outside. On the other side of town, in the silence beyond the crickets, an early freight train would clatter and move on. But here, now, the siren and dog say, nothing matters, go to sleep.

He finds that people in most of the contexts of his life seem to wish each other well. It is their intelligence, wit and heart he responds to, their equality with himself, rather than their beauty or flash or style—major points of sexual allure. Perhaps all these attributes together might comprise the perfect lover. In smaller fractions they at least provide him, minus the burdensome issue of love, with friends.

He thinks that they, the ones with whom he has had ongoing sexual, and friendly, relationships, and everyone else like them in New York, must constitute an odd, obsolescent social group, a kind of tributary which survives the river. They are like mistresses without marriage. Some of his friends have had lovers, with whom they have lived for years. In a divorce case Max would be cited as corespondent. Mistress of course was the wrong word, as was Master. In talking of this world, equivalents make poor bridges to the world of love between men and women. But then such divorces as occurred did so more simply. In Max's experience, his friends' marriages, if they were serious to begin with, went on quite smoothly.

He knows, for an instance, Stephen of Stephen Foster, two people who live together grandly on Park Avenue. To step through their front door is to enter an English country house. They are successful dealers of fine antiques, which they call lumber. Their lives are in it. Stephen Foster, their place sings. They give opulent evenings for thirty or forty men, here and there the occasional woman. Stephen calls them his Memorial Faggot Dinners. Max has attended many of them. Foster and he behave toward each other like Queen Alexandra and Mrs. Langtry.

There is an aviary at Stephen Foster's. A sunlit corner room has a walk-in cage filled with dozens of birds. Two albino quail keep the ground clean in a desultory fashion, like eccentric, foreign maids. A large green parrot won't talk; a canary sings although it's not supposed to. These are local legends. In smaller cages there are doves, finches, parakeets. A certain few of them fly about freely, like trusties. They drink at a fountain in the corner, pull matchsticks out of a glass holder, shit on everything. Max has seen the aviary at Waddeston, the Rothschild estate near London. He knows it lurks in the back of Stephen's mind because they saw it together and Stephen said then that he wanted one. Stephen understands the difference—this is a corner room on Park Avenue; that was as large as anything in a major zoo, with gorgeous exotics in gilded Victorian cages. The Rothschilds' weekend guests strolled out for a half hour after lunch. The ladies let their skirts drag over the immaculate marblechip path. Three or four keepers crushed their caps, answered questions, set white mice loose for the hawks. The ladies carried vestigial parasols to match their outrageous hats. It was late August and the leaves in the pedigreed trees were russet. Perhaps because of the birds in the cages, none were in the trees.

But usually when he discovers a married man, he withdraws, not for any damage he might do but because it is too obvious. Perhaps nothing comes of anything, but at the least he would like to start even.

He wonders if others expect to find what they want, as he does. Or do they only hope for it, and then settle for whatever arrangements they, like he, can make with one another. Do they really need to find someone, to love someone? Or will the search do? Is the obsession a man, or men? For they all seem to be willing to overlap, to double up, even to triple up and more. Rick, the pet shop owner, once told Max he was happiest in the midst of three simultaneous involvements, one important and two recreational—one pseudo marriage and two pseudo affairs. This sort of thing, together with a few nights out now and then, seemed to do for them all. Occasionally there was a real union; two men fell in love and meant it. When that happened they would disappear. They went to the country, or to mutual ground on the Upper West Side. They were no longer in the system. In a way they had been graduated.

Max would like to get out of it, to graduate too. He is thirty-nine, even if he looks younger. Is it his maturity, his savoir faire, his fame as an author or his skill in the pantry that will win him his mate?

A recent occasion on which Max thought he saw *the* man remains in his mind as a typical object lesson, of the sort which has hardened him to romantic expectation. He had met a friend in a bar downtown one afternoon. They had smoked some reefer and were standing at the bar talking when suddenly Max was hit, along with the grass, with what used to be called a thirty pound stare. There were the eyes, it seemed, in the face of the man; not rushing by in another life, or sliding quickly into some romantic reverie, but here in front of him — dark, wideset eyes that wouldn't look away, that seemed to have found, in Max, just what they sought. And Max said to himself, while trying to attend to his friend and at the same time return the man's look, that he would follow those eyes, tracking them all the way back to the man's mind, and that he would be patient until he got there.

A moment later they were talking. The man's name was Carlos. In this case, he was an upholsterer from Newark. It was necessary for each of them to repeat nearly everything they said to each other. Carlos spoke street talk, bar talk, you can't and you ain't. He had an extra maleness which could be the result of an additional YY chromosome or five or six years in jail. Carlos knew about his eyes, although he said he was raised to be embarrassed about them. They were too big, the lashes too curly and long. Women had teased him. Men had looked at him suspiciously all his life. But he used them. He turned them on Max, perhaps only imagining their effect. He turned them on and left them on, like lamps, and Max tried to see into them, through them, to see what Carlos was thinking or feeling; to see, in fact, if there were real thought and feeling behind them, or just the eyes.

Drugs as usual were something of a complication. Carlos said he had just taken some mescalin and for long moments the beauty was replaced by vacancy, as though the current had been cut in half, or even switched off. Then the eyes would surge, brighten and focus again; Carlos would right himself, straightening up and breathing deeply. He would reach out and take hold of Max by the arm or waist, each time making a kind of quantum move forward in the open demonstration of affection.

It was a mid-week, rainy afternoon. Everyone in the bar seemed content to stay where they were, perhaps until dinner, or until the rain stopped, or until they found someone they could love forever. Somebody's hat, a gray fedora, caught Carlos's attention and he reached out, snatched it and put it on. You look like a sharecropper, honey, the hat's owner said. But they love me in that hat, he went on, they love me. Listen, I'm not young and I get the boys. At the right moment I just pull out this thing I got and they mine. Ain't no foolin' around. Ain't no lie, honey. He seemed not to mind that Carlos had begun to pull and punch at his hat, even to put it between his teeth and chew on it. Carlos said quietly to Max, I used to have a hat like this. I used to block hats. He now rearranged it completely, rolling the brim, putting a triple crease across the crown with his teeth. The queen meanwhile kept talking, not to Max and Carlos but to everyone else. Last Call! he shouted suddenly, meaning the place was dead. When Carlos had finished reblocking the fedora he put it back on the queen's head. I can wear hats, honey, the queen said. I got a hat face. The hat now looked smart and crisp. All the flop had been pulled out of it. But the boys don't care about hats, honey. That ain't what they after.

The queen drifted off and Carlos went to the bar for drinks. While Max was alone a short man came over to him and said, I've been watching you for two hours. Aren't you two married yet? His shortness, together with his detail of ornament, of small utterances scaled down to blurbs, seemed to encode him as a ripe, variegated New York trick with a taste for the unusual. Well, my lover looks just like him, he said of Carlos. So gorgeous. My lover has more muscles. I saw you drop that other guy you was talking to. You got taste. He pronounced it tace. Max felt perched on a height. He turned his head and looked down. So when you going to get married? the little man asked again. We've been married for over an hour, Max replied. We're just trying to decide where to go on our honeymoon. The little man laughed, relieved that Max wasn't going to ignore or perhaps abuse him, and said, How about the Baths?

So romantic. Then Max laughed and Carlos returned with the drinks and when Max looked down again the man was gone, like a discrete maven of love. Let's get married, Max said into the dark chocolate centers of Carlos's eyes.

Oh man, he said. What you sayin? He leaned back and cocked his head and said again, What you sayin? Then he righted himself and put his beer on a ledge behind Max, a move which brought their faces together. You want to marry me? Carlos asked. Their faces were so close Max had to choose between the wideset eyes, as if he had already eaten one of them.

The queen in the gray fedora approached them again, with the timing and accuracy of a neighbor. Ummm-mmmm, this bar, honey; this town, this life, this planet! He whirled around, his hands splayed up in the air like a singer. A long, pure, high note, that slid perfectly over the song coming from the jukebox, slipped effortlessly from his throat, drowning the music, stopping conversation, and drawing the focus of the bar. The note continued, a clear, bell-like sound, like something up out of a well or down a tunnel, with, at the end, a short falling down, like a sigh. Some laughed or smiled; others had heard it before and went back to their conversations or cruising. The queen turned again to Max and Carlos, with a bright, charged look, and whispered so that only they could hear, Last Call!

They left and walked down to another bar along the river; the bar was empty. They sat in the front by the window. Carlos said, I ain't met anyone who put up with my shit as long as you. Max said it wan't so much to put up with. But they both thought it was time to go home, either together or separately. Carlos said, people got expectations, and Max asked him what he meant. About what they want out of me in bed. Max said, is there something they want that you don't want to give? I ain't got a big dick, Carlos said. Drugs or not, Max didn't think he should be held accountable for that, either the fact itself or any talk about it. Carlos looked out the window into the street. The announcement seemed to have made him morose. That's not important to me, Max said finally, thinking that while this was not perhaps strictly true, it was in this case. He thought that whatever was part of this man's beauty, it would be right. But what earthquakes of emotion could be expected along such a faultline? Carlos turned away from the window and looked at Max. I don't like flattery, he said. I looked it up. It means insincere. How about compliments? Max asked, and Carlos replied, I can deal with that. But I don't like it. Then in another shift he said quietly, my place is bad. I got a crazy Australian roommate. And roaches. Don't never take no one there. Max asked if that meant they were going there now, and Carlos said, If you like, if that's what you want.

It was a two and a half room walk-up with everything set down on the floor. There was one table, which itself held all the extraordinary objects in the room, like a kind of altar or a better place. The mattress was small, sheetless and thin. An open arch connected the two rooms; another lair, presumably the roommate's, had been arranged in a dark corner. It was empty. Carlos opened the oven door and lighted all the burners; also a joss stick and a candle that hung in a bracket on the wall. He snapped off the overhead neon ring and they turned to each other.

All the excitement in Max came from the fact that nothing separated them now, not convenience, place, people or chance. For a moment the idea of Carlos and him — untouched and unproved — filled him up. It seemed then that if they wanted to, they *could* get married, not because of all that they might be to each other, but because nothing, not an idea or a fear or a thing, had any power over them.

The surprise about his kiss was the softness of his lips. His tongue was big and moist, the kiss a drink. They undressed, helping each other, and lay down on the mattress. Max thought of surrender, of a return of anything Carlos might offer him. He thought of himself as little and intense, as if his body had been scaled down to something smaller than his brain.

These feelings brought in patience, even a reticence about what was to happen next. It seemed purer to draw away, to pause and consider. He lay back and looked up at the chipped ceiling. A joint would be nice, he said. Carlos went and searched among the odd things on the table. He returned with a thin joint and matches. He sat on the edge of the mattress and looked at Max. They looked at each other for a few minutes, until Max smiled. Then Carlos smiled and lighted the joint. After he had drawn on it a few times he handed it to Max and began fiddling with the matchbox. He rolled the cover back and forth into a thin tube, then unravelled it and rolled it again. When he has softened the paper, he split it apart so that he was left with a piece about an inch square. This he folded in half and rolled around the end of the joint, like an empty filter. It was like the hat blocking, a kind of home-craft, self taught, that filled the moments. He put the lighted end of the joint in his mouth and blew smoke in a thin stream into Max's. They smoked the grass down to the paper tip, not an ash wasted. On top of the mescalin, it seemed to make Carlos very high. He sat resting his arms on his knees and nodded his head back and forth. You going to fall out? Max asked. No, man, I ain't, Carlos said, and straightened up for a moment. But he was. The grass hit him like a sleeping pill, almost like an injection. He leaned over and slid along Max's chest, his lips parted, his eyes not completely closed. Within a moment his breathing had become deep and even.

Max watched him for awhile, feeling very high himself but judging the situation. Should he cover them both up and sleep too, or should he dress and leave? Should he reject the situation or use it? He touched Carlos's cheek, his lips. He stuck a finger in Carlos's mouth and felt the spongy tongue. Carlos didn't react. He breathed deeply, snored a little. He was gone, away, as if he had abandoned his body to Max. But Max felt he was unable to stop now, even if Carlos had. His head swam with excitement, his heart raced. He said out loud, Carlos. Carlos, I'm going to take it. Give it to me. He straightened the man's limbs, laying him flat on his back, kneeling between his legs. He kissed the flacid lips, nuzzled the neck, sucked the nipples and the limp cock; he buried his face in the crepey balls which smelled of fresh mushrooms. Through it all Carlos made no response, no sound except those of sleep. He was not there.

Or was he? Was he pretending? Was this what he wanted? Max stopped and looked down at him. Was it natural for all of this to be happening without a murmur of response, without so much as an involuntary twitch in reaction? Then a fresh wave of desire swept up and over him, so that the distinction of whether he was alone or not ceased to matter. Maybe Carlos needed to dream his way through this. But Max was going to fit himself into what was here, into what he had found. He thought that if their positions were reversed now, he would want Carlos to go ahead and do it. What he was about to take, had already been given.

He raised up Carlos' hips and put a pillow under them, then knelt over him and slipped smoothly inside. The silky muscle took him easily. Max wrapped his arms around the sleeping body and loved.

RICHARD HALL

The gay liberation movement and its literary adjunct is strikingly a young movement. We are mostly in our twenties and thirties, a few of us in our forties. That may explain why these age groups and their interests and concerns are so much in the forefront of so much gay and lesbian writing today. We seem to have an eye and ear for our present life, and when we set ourselves to historical writing, for our past too. Our future is still a blur. What will our lives be like when we are sixty? Seventy-five? Even fifty years old?

Richard Hall's powerful story, "A Touch of Fat," is about that unknown. Tom and Frady, lovers before, are reunited at post fifty in Puerto Rico, and the Lincolnesque Tom has changed: no longer a poet, but a businessman; no longer slim, but paunchy. Hall's tale moves with unrelenting psychological and physical realism, at the same time it is a lovely and romantic tribute to the love these men once passionately shared. If the story is disturbing, it is because most of us will find ourselves at some time in either Tom or Frady's position. Will we, I wonder, have their wisdom or grace?

Hall is a well known writer. He has done articles for The Village Voice *and* New Republic, *and is contributing editor and reviewer of books in* The Advocate. *His novel,* The Butterscotch Prince, *(1975) ought to be reissued. His plays are* The Love Match, *produced by The Glines 1977, and* The Prisoner of Love *1978, The Glines. His stories have appeared in* GPU NEWS, *and* Paragraph. *He was one of the two editors of Gayweek's excellent Arts and Letters section; and is currently writing a booklength study of the odd relationship between William and Henry James.*

A TOUCH OF FAT

It would soon be all right, Frady reminded himself as he strained to see over the crowd at Gate 18. Around him, hordes of Puerto Ricans, brilliant in multi-colored clothes, were chattering excitedly. He had never known people who talked so much. They nattered, they sang, they chirped. They did everything but stand still and listen. But that wasn't quite fair. Sometimes, when least expected, they did stand still, with the stillness of a lizard on a jungle leaf. That was equally disconcerting.

The loudspeaker boomed in Spanish and Frady's heart gave a little tug. The prospect of seeing Tom, of course. Seeing that familiar craggy face with the jutting chin, here in Suan Juan. It would be strange at first. But within minutes the strangeness would disappear and a fine familiarity would take its place. They would be instantly at home. Sometimes Frady thought that he and Tom carried home around with them, like two snails each with half a shell. Home was the place where they came together.

His recent troubles, he reflected, would evaporate. Wasn't that why he had urged Tom to spend Christmas here? Because Tom carried the remedies in his brown eyes, his quiet hands, his even voice?

The first passengers from Flight 63 filed past, pale from the northern cold. Frady's sense of homecoming increased. Tom was only a few steps away now. His sensory antennae had always been tuned to Tom. Once, at the very moment Tom was writing a letter to him from New Hampshire (he later found out) his own mind went into a spasm of receptivity and the window shade in his apartment in New York rolled up with a fierce splat. It was their private radio band sparking. When he had told Tom about this, Tom had smiled condescendingly — Frady and his psychokinesis! — but Frady hadn't been put off. He knew they got signals from each other on secret frequencies. He knew now, for example, that Tom would appear before he could count to ten. He closed his eyes.

"Hello Frady." He opened his eyes. Tom was at his side, smiling weakly and looking nonchalant. Important moments made Tom nonchalant unless he broke down and cried. Frady read his face as if it were a map to buried treasure. Then he reached out and hugged him tightly.

How well he knew that body! He imagined it again, not as he could feel it now — slightly saggy in the tits, the belly a little basketball, the hips lightly sheathed in fat — but as it had been twenty years ago when he had first glimpsed it. That had been in Tom's little apartment near Gramercy Park in New York. When they had stripped in the bedroom under a bare light-bulb dangling from a long cord, he had scarcely been able to draw breath at the sight of Tom nude, the wide bony shoulders, the triangle of black chest-hair, the square pectorals, the powerfully fleshed calves. But it was something else that had taken his breath away, that had convinced him that Tom (whose last name he had yet to learn) was the most beautiful man he had ever encountered. This something else was the gaunt boniness of Tom's face, the hollowness of his cheeks, the secret caverns of his collar-bone, the shadowy recesses of his pelvis. Tom, he had realized with a pang, was a scarecrow of bone and sinew. He might have been a half-starved Okie in the depths of the depression, caught for a tragic moment in the glare of Margaret Bourke-White's camera.

Later, after he and Tom had begun to live together, he had wondered at his taste for scarecrows, for Lincolnesque men, long-muscled and rifle-thin, and why that gaunt look signalled to him so deeply. But he had never been able to sort it out, never been able to trace it to some early impression or to some childish love. These men attracted him — he had known it when he was ten or twelve — but it wasn't until he met Tom Peniman in a bar on Eighth Street that he had realized the extent of his addiction. Sometimes, lying in bed with Tom in that first home they had shared, it seemed that all his life had been tending toward this time, and that whoever he was, wherever he had come from, could be summed up in his passion for the gaunt male lying next to him.

They were headed for the luggage area of the airport now, walking easily in step. Tom was talking about the flight from Los Angeles. Frady noticed that he had put on some more weight in the last year. His eyes seemed to have receded even more behind the bulge of his cheeks. His walk was more turned-out than before. Without looking, Frady could sense the extra fat around his hips and ass. But even as he registered this, he dismissed the knowledge as disloyal. Tom hadn't changed, not really. Under his extra flesh were the bones, the osteal fragments that spelled love. It was just a matter of getting through to them.

Tom was discussing the in-flight movie. He had seen it before, to his disappointment. As Frady listened, he recalled how Tom always talked — never shouting for attention, never raising his voice. He felt something inside him thaw out, something that had been frozen for a long time.

Frady chose the scenic route for the drive to the apartment. In the car, they caught up on people, places, events. Although they wrote each other every week, letters couldn't take the place of being together, hearing each other's voices. At one point, as they passed a crescent of beach, a wave soared up and broke into pieces a few yards away. "Look at that," Tom said in his flat voice, and it seemed to Frady that the surf had never been so beautiful, that he had never enjoyed it so much.

Tom settled into the second bedroom right away. The room became instantly messy. Messy and lived-in, Frady thought. It should have been that way right along. But he had kept it bare, impersonal. There had been a few guests from the States, a few island friends, but their traces had been quickly removed. Even the party he gave for his students at the end of the term, which had overflowed into this bedroom, hadn't disorganized it as Tom did. No one could appropriate space in his life in quite the same way. It had been like that from the very beginning.

A week after they had met, twenty years ago, Tom had moved in with him, giving up the little apartment on Gramercy Park and arriving at Frady's West Side apartment with the instinct of a homing pigeon. Frady had never shared so much of his life before. At first it was hard. Unlike Tom, who came from a large Iowa family, his own had been small and divided. His one sister, older than he, had been his bitter enemy for as long as he could remember. On the savage stomping grounds of childhood they had competed for everything—for love, attention, grades, friends, home-runs. Their childhoods had been scarred by a bitter mutual contempt. The causes were obscure, but not the result. He had avoided an intimate relationship with anyone his own age until he was thirty, until he met Tom Peniman in a Village bar and went home with him, overcoming his fear of intimacy, of rejection, of *family*, only slowly, over the months.

Tom, he had realized at once, wanted to become his family, wanted to extend their natural fit in bed to the rest of their lives. To sharing the medicine chest and doing laundry together. To drinking and quarrelling and wearing each other's clothes. To traveling and cooking and writing sonnets in alternate lines. This was all new to Frady. He had always protected his privacy, ever since the morning when he was five years old and had refused to share a bathtub with his sister, furious at the thought of sitting in *her* water, kicking and screaming until his mother had given in. Since then, the privacy had thickened around him like a fog, inside of which he moved, with all his deepest feelings veiled to view. Tom had punched a hole in that fog—he himself had been more than ready, of course—until it had evaporated altogether. Tom's simple assumption that Frady could share his life had made it possible to do so.

Tom was a poet. He had shown Frady a huge sheaf of poems on their first morning after. They seemed wonderfully fresh and new, with a kind of sweet innocence he would always associate with Tom. Tom, he realized after reading the poems, was not shored up with defenses like most people. He was without affectation or guile. "He has a good heart," he had once said to a friend. Of course, that was too simple. Over the months and years he would find Tom far more complex, with a dark side as well as a bright one. But under the shadows he always saw the sweetness. He believed in Tom's good heart the way he believed in his mother's love and in democracy. It made sense of the world. And he had never been betrayed.

They decided to have a swim before lunch. Tom squinted against the glare when they stepped outside. They had a race to the water, but Frady won easily. He was still slender and fast on his feet, his body (thanks to years of gymwork) sleek and full of tone. Tom, he could see, waddled as much as he ran, the extra flesh rippling around his stomach and hips. He tripped when he hit the water and pitched forward.

"Oh wow, I hit something," he said, coming up and blowing water.

"You went in like an old sea-cow," Frady yelled.

"Fuck you," Tom called back. Frady plunged into an oncoming wave. When he surfaced, Tom was heading toward the reef. Frady noted that he still swam well, his weight buoyed up by the water, his strokes slow and graceful.

Treading water, Frady glanced toward shore. A Chinese wall of condominiums ringed the beach. In front, spotting the sand, were hundreds of brown bodies. He knew those bodies. Many of them were exquisitely made. The sight forced into his mind something he had been dodging all day. He reached for it now, reassured by the nearness of Tom. Suppose he and Tom were to get together again! The thought caused a moment's panic, and he spun around in the water. Then the anxiety cleared and a vision sparkled brightly on the waves. Tonight. As they were getting ready for bed. A simple need. A simple act. They were better friends now than before—friends in a way they could not be when they lived together. Passion and jealousy had obscured the fineness of their feeling for each other, the fit of their minds, their spirits. Why not convert the friendship back into something physical?

He thought about the power of Tom's presence. He was always strengthened by it, purified. Tom's sweetness called out his own. He was, quite simply, a better person when Tom was around. His pettiness, his spite—all the unpleasant sides of his personality, dissipated in Tom's bright sunshine. Couldn't that be part of his life again permanently? He thought about the bleakness of things since he had turned fifty a few months ago. Wouldn't that be wiped out too?

He floated on his back and stared at the sky. What was it the physicists said when their theories were especially apt? He searched for the word. *Elegant.* That was it. Reconverting their friendship into passion would be . . . *elegant.*

He turned over and let a monster wave carry him to shore.

Frady watched Tom carefully over dinner. He had fixed a Puerto Rican meal, taken from *Cocina Criolla.* On the plates were arroz con pollo, fried bananas and chayote. Tom, who had slept all afternoon, was looking refreshed. Some of the lines cut into his cheeks and chin had begun to soften. In a few days, Frady knew, he would look much younger. Tom wore a flowered Hawaiian shirt which glowed in the candlelight.

"Remember that first Thanksgiving on 88th Street?" Frady asked.

Tom nodded.

"It was the most beautiful meal I'd ever had."

"It was okay."

"Okay!" Frady was outraged. The old memories hadn't excited Tom tonight. He had spent most of the meal reminiscing, but Tom had added little. He decided to give it another try.

"After we set the table you said, 'Let's just stand here and admire it, it looks like a Norman Rockwell painting.' "

Tom grimaced. "I always hated Norman Rockwell." He pushed the food around on his plate. He hadn't eaten much. Too starchy probably, Frady thought. "What are we going to do tonight?" Tom asked.

"I thought we'd stay home and take it easy."

Tom took a sip of wine. "We've been home all day." He knitted his brows. "Why don't we go to the casino?" He looked up, his brown eyes alight. "Hey, I haven't been to a casino in a long time."

Frady thought distastefully of the hotels, which would be filled with tourists in cruisewear. But Tom was on his feet, peering out the window. "Which is better, El San Juan or the Hilton?"

"They're all the same," Frady said petulantly, but Tom didn't seem to notice his tone.

"Dress up, baby," he crowed in a voice Frady had never heard before, "I'm gonna make us some house money!"

He turned around. Frady blinked rapidly. Tom's face seemed to have taken on a new shape. It had broadened, fattened. It was almost as round and fat as a basketball. Frady blinked some more, trying to chase the image away. Maybe it was a trick of the candlelight. He looked away, then back. There. That was better. The roundness seemed not to have disappeared exactly, but . . . condensed. Yes, there was the face he knew so well. Gaunt, cavernous. He stared hard, fixing it, in case the basketball look came back again.

Tom started to clear the table. "That was good, Frady, but I just wasn't hungry, I guess."

Frady knew the signs. Tom would fix himself a large salad in an hour and top it off with some dried prunes and a box of fig newtons. Luckily, he had laid in the necessary supplies. He sighed and got up. The casino seemed unavoidable.

Tom was in high spirits as they walked toward the hotel, bouncing along the pavement, pointing to the palms, the prostitutes, the cars packed with Puerto Rican teen-agers. Suddenly he started to sing. "*Asturias, patria querida . . . Asturias, de mis amores . . .*" The melody surged through Frady. It was a song they had learned in Mallorca, in the tiny mountain village where they had lived for six months. Someone had taught it to them in the village café, where they had been drinking Fundador after a day spent visiting the monastery where Chopin had lived with George Sand.

"God," he said, "I haven't heard that in years."

"Haven't sung it in years," Tom replied. He went into the second verse—he had an amazing memory for lyrics—and some Puerto Ricans in a passing car let out a whoop. "*Hola!*" Tom cheered, waving back.

Frady felt drenched with nostalgia. Mallorca! Could it have been eighteen years ago? They had taken up residence in a handsome house with blue shutters, surrounded by the sound of sheep bells and the silvery flutter of olive groves. They had made love almost constantly in the upstairs bedroom.

"Here we are!" Tom's yelp interrupted his reverie. The hotel lobby loomed in front of them. Its furniture seemed designed for a race of giants. Tom speeded up. "Next time you come out to California I'll take you to Las Vegas," he called back over his shoulder.

Frady snickered. Las Vegas wasn't high on his list of desirable experiences. "I'd rather go back to Ensenada," he replied. They passed two bouncers at the door to the casino.

"There's nothing to do in Ensenada," Tom announced just before disappearing into the crowd.

Frady watched him go, thinking about the little village where they had lived in Mallorca. There hadn't been much to do there either. No movies, no concerts, no casinos. They didn't even have a radio. What had they done all day? He searched his memory. They had looked at the vines and flowers. Tom had worked on his poems. He had learned Spanish guitar. They had taken long hikes over the stony soil. They had invited their neighbors for tea. They had made love. Was that all?

He saw Tom in the distance, at a blackjack table. He seemed to have bought some chips already. The unpleasant notion inserted itself into Frady's mind that Tom had changed. That he wasn't the exact person he had always been. The old Tom had hated plastic environments like this. He'd pass up a casino for a poetry reading any day. And there he was, chatting with a burly croupier and watching the drop of the cards as if he were Nick the Greek. It was very puzzling.

Frady drifted over to the slot machines. He liked to watch the players. They were mostly elderly women holding plastic glasses full of quarters, which they fed into the machines with a drugged air. He wondered if his own life would end up that way — an idle search for the excitement that sex and friendship and a career could no longer provide. He shuddered at the thought. And then, without warning, the bleakness of the past few months hit him again. Instinctively, as despair spread through him, he sifted through the crowd, looking for Tom. Where was he?

Frady moved to get a better view across the room? *Where was he?* There he was, at the roulette table, standing behind a woman with red hair. Frady watched him accept two black chips from her and lay them on the cloth. The woman laughed and offered Tom a cigarette. Frady watched numbly as Tom took it. The two put their heads together for a light.

And then, by a strange alteration, it seemed to Frady that Tom had grown shorter and fatter. At the same time, his hairline moved upward, although it was possible his face had slipped downward instead. Then it struck him that the short fat man across the room was someone he had never seen before. The confusion made him slightly dizzy. He felt as if a crack had opened in the world, a huge crack that might never be closed if he didn't move carefully in the next few seconds. He moved rapidly across the room.

"Tom." Tom, his eyes on the roulette wheel, didn't turn around. Frady pinched his arm. "I'm leaving," he said. The ball had settled into a groove but the wheel was spinning too fast to read the number. "I'm going home," Frady said.

Suddenly Tom let out a cry. "We won!" He threw his arms around the woman with red hair, who shrieked. Tom turned around. His eyes were glazed. "We won!" he cried again, but he seemed to be addressing everybody, not just Frady.

Frady left the casino without actually deciding to do so. His feet simply carried him out the door. The air around him was thick with betrayal. His last sight of Tom was as he placed another bet on the green cloth. He looked, Frady thought, like a shoe salesman who had just sold an especially expensive pair of shoes.

Frady drifted along the pavement, vaguely aware of the sound of the surf on his left, of a tree-frog striking its tiny marimba across the street. A huge emptiness seemed to have blown into his chest. Several times he had to stop walking to fight the sensation of falling through it. If he didn't have Tom, what did he have? Could he survive?

When he reached his corner and turned toward the apartment, he shook his head briskly. He had to get control of himself. It was absurd to be so dependent on Tom. That suffocating dependence had been the reason for their break-up in the first place. They had almost smothered each other to death. What was it he had written in his diary during that last unhappy year? "Together we make one person, and that's the problem." Wasn't he doing the same thing now? Being childish and jealous and possessive? Of course Tom had changed. You change in order to survive. Tom was no longer the young poet. How much poetry is left at fifty?

By the time he reached the door to his apartment he felt a little better. It was a case of facing facts. His wrinkles were facts. His slow sexual reflexes were facts. Time and change and the end of illusion were facts.

But even as he reminded himself of these things, an image formed in his mind — or rather, a series of images complete to the tiniest detail. It had been on the ship that took them from New York to Mallorca. One night he had gone to bed early, tired of the endless card-games and boozing. It seemed he had slept only a few hours when he heard Tom's voice breaking into his sleep. "Frady, Frady, wake up!" The voice was flushed, excited. "You have to come on deck!" Tom had kept shaking him until Frady got up and followed him through the deserted passage to the deck. He had followed Tom's slender, muscular figure to the bow and there Tom had pointed to a dim shape on the port side. It was a land-mass, faintly illuminated by dawn. "Look," Tom's breath was warm in his ear, "Africa!"

And he had looked at the dark shape as images and associations thundered in his head. "I stayed up all night," Tom murmured, "I was afraid I'd miss it."

And then, quite without thinking, they had reached out and taken hands, heedless of who might be watching, as the ship throbbed under them and Africa took shape in the dawn. Tom's hand had been warm and papery, but Frady had sensed the wild pulse beating, had understood Tom's feelings because they were as important as his own. And he had known that this moment would always stay with them, that some part of them would always be on the deck of this ship, holding hands while Africa grew large in the dawn and the morning star winked out.

Later, they had gone to sleep in the single lower bunk of their cabin, entwined together, neither wanting to spend the rest of the night alone.

Now, standing in the middle of his living room, Frady asked himself if the man who had stayed awake all night for a first glimpse of Africa could ever be a stranger. Could ever change, deeply and truly. He knew the answer to that as surely as he knew anything in the world.

Tom didn't come back until almost two. Frady had dozed off on the couch after fixing himself a rum-and-tonic. When he heard the downstairs bell, he woke up and moved to the buzzer. Tom stepped from the elevator with a fuzzy air. He and Isabel had won almost a thousand dollars. They had been drinking Remy-Martin in the hotel bar.

Frady waited while Tom went to the bathroom, then into the bedroom. When he heard the bed squeak as Tom sat down, he went in. Without speaking, he began to unbutton Tom's shirt.

"What're you doing?" Tom's speech was slurred.

Frady found himself suddenly nervous. "I thought . . . I thought I'd rest with you a bit." He paused, then more softly, "Like old times."

He felt, rather than saw, Tom studying him.

"Just for a few minutes," he whispered, feeling like a liar.

Tom stood up and disrobed slowly. Frady moved onto the bed, stretching out against the wall. He had always slept on the inside of any bed with Tom. It made him feel safe.

Tom was down to his boxer shorts. Frady could see that the skin on his stomach was shiny and tight over the bulge. Briefly he thought of a pregnant woman.

Tom's weight on the bed made Frady tilt toward him. He started to roll downhill, then grabbed the far edge of the mattress and hoisted himself back. Tom settled himself on his back. Frady waited a moment, then dropped one arm lightly across Tom's chest. "This feels so good," he breathed. Tom grunted and put his arm over his eyes.

"I was thinking . . ." Frady paused. Tom grunted again. "I was thinking we haven't given ourselves a chance in years." His hand, automatically, had started rubbing Tom's chest, pulling at the triangular patch of hair which, he had noticed earlier in the day, was not quite gray. He moved to Tom's left nipple. It was the size of a small grape and had always been amazingly sensitive. Tom twitched briefly. Frady watched Tom's other arm — not the one over his eyes — move down to the groin and start a regular rhythm.

His heart beating rapidly, Frady slipped out of his underwear. Tom turned toward him. Their mouths searched and found each other's. As they kissed, Frady felt an easing through his whole body. It seemed that he had traveled for years and only now come home. Tom's arms encircled him. The sense of homecoming increased.

Tom started to vibrate his body against Frady's. *Jiggle, jiggle, jiggle* went Tom's body. Frady could hear the slap of Tom's stomach as it hit his own. He pushed lightly against Tom's heavy form. This was not exactly what he had in mind. Tom's stomach heaved and quivered some more. *Jiggle, jiggle, jiggle.* Frady pushed away a little harder. The slapping sound grew louder. It seemed to have nothing to do with sex. Frady suddenly had the feeling he was being buried in a hill of flesh. At the same time he was aware that the tingling in his own groin had stopped. Nothing was happening down there. "Oh Christ," he said out loud.

The jiggling stopped. "What's the matter?"

"I don't know."

"Well let's go."

"I don't like that."

"Like what?"

"Rubbing bellies."

There was a silence and he could hear Tom's raspy breathing. "You started this whole thing," he mumbled.

"I'm sorry. I . . . just . . ."

A sound came out of Tom, half-way between a snort and a bellow and he tightened his grip around Frady's middle. At the same time he hoisted himself up. Frady felt Tom's body slide over his. He suddenly had the feeling he was at the bottom of a vegetable bin. *Jiggle, jiggle, jiggle.* It had started again. Frady had a wild urge to shove Tom off and leap out of bed. But then, by a powerful effort of will, he mastered the urge. Instead, he decided to think about something else. Mallorca. Of course, Mallorca! The upstairs bedroom where they had kissed and grappled and hugged the night away. He kept his mind trained on this, not hearing the slapping noises, not feeling the thumps of Tom's body, as he remembered Tom's long lean muscles, the bones that clicked under the skin, the orgasms that slid out of them in tongues of fire.

The jiggling wasn't getting any faster. What was going on? In the old days it never took Tom long to come. And Frady's back was beginning to hurt. He'd end up at the orthopedist again if he wasn't careful. Still, he didn't want to be selfish . . .

He twisted his mind back to the bedroom in Mallorca. But it seemed to have slid away, disappeared completely. He was here, now, with the dead sound of Tom's thumping in his ears.

He waited. Time seemed to have stopped. The thumping went on. Tom's breathing got heavier, raspier. He waited some more.

"Tom," he whispered. There was no answer. "Can you come?"

There was still no answer and suddenly he couldn't bear another second of it. He pushed Tom hard. The heavy body fell to one side.

"I can't do it any more," he growled.

"Whaddya mean?" Tom's voice was faint, almost sleepy.

"I just can't. Can not." He sat up. Across the hall his own bedroom glowed in the dark.

"I was almost there," Tom moaned.

Frady scrambled out of bed. "No you weren't. You were miles away." He was surprised at the coldness of his voice.

Tom twisted onto his back. He seemed totally inert, like a sack of grain. Frady, looking down at him, wondered how he had ever thought they could get together. And then their failure in bed seemed to grow in size and darkness until it cast a pall over everything between them. He felt himself moving away from the figure on the bed. There was no link, no bridge. Tom had changed, he had changed. He was living in the past, but there was nothing there. The old fantasies were finished. He was alone. He would have to face everything alone . . .

Suddenly he realized that Tom was crying. He turned. Tom's face was bright with tears. "Don't cry," he said. But the tears kept flowing. "Tom," he pleaded. "Tom."

Tom lay there, not speaking. The tears ran down his face and dripped on the sheet. He made no effort to wipe them away. And then Frady, with a wrench, realized that Tom was crying for both of them. His tears bathed them both. The realization came to him in a flood of joy. Tom might have given up poetry and taken up gambling, he might be fat and fifty, he might be finished with nostalgia and illusion . . . but his heart was the same. It was still good. And if that was so, there was nothing to be afraid of. The world still made sense.

His last sight was of Tom lying in bed, weeping and jerking off.

They didn't talk much in the morning. Frady felt raw, as if a wound had opened in the night. At the same time, everything seemed very vivid — the furniture, the food, the sea and sky. He knew it must be the same for Tom.

About noon they decided to go for a swim. On the way, they talked of unimportant things, but Frady found himself getting worked up even about these. As they headed across the sand for the water, Tom said nonchalantly, "I knew you had that in mind as soon as I got off the plane."

Frady froze. "You what?"

Tom chuckled. "Fucking. I knew you had it in mind."

"How did you know? I didn't even know myself."

"Just did." Tom paused and knitted his brows. "I had the feeling it wouldn't work."

"You sneaky bastard, why didn't you say something?"

Tom shrugged. "I figured we would just see what happened." His voice was mild. "Just . . . let go." He searched Frady's face and Frady knew he could read everything there. A delicious calm took possession of him. They still understood each other perfectly. There was nothing they might not say or do together. They might even —

he giggled slightly — repeat last night's fiasco. It would still be okay. It would always be okay.

"Bet I can beat you in," Tom said suddenly. He lunged toward the water. Frady chased after him, the sand hot under his feet, the fat familiar body just ahead rippling with love.

A TRUE LIKENESS
LESBIAN AND GAY WRITING TODAY

POETRY
JAMES SCHUYLER

Although James Schuyler is chronologically a generation apart from most of the writers in this anthology, his first book of poems did not appear until 1966; late for his age, and fortunate for his readers, who encountered perfect pieces of his art. In the seventies, he published two more books of poetry, The Crystal Lithium *and* Hymn to Life *which contained his deceptively loosest work. The Crystal Lithium won the National Book Award and contained three poems herein reprinted, which I've always used in my lectures on lesbian and gay poetry, including "Letter Poem #3" with which I usually end those lectures, calling it one of the loveliest love poems in our language.*

Schuyler's most recent book of poems, The Morning of the Poem, *and especially its fifty page title poem, represents another step foward in the confessional mode, made famous by Robert Lowell, Plath, Sexton and Berryman. As a poet myself, I'm in awe of its suppleness, range of emotions and ideas, and its lucidly balanced command of language. As a homosexual I'm astounded by Schuyler's seemingly effortless revelations of the richness and interrelatedness of the gay experience in one poet's life. Two other poems from that book "This Dark Apartment" and "Korean Mums," also display that delicate balance between the grace of the employed form and the naked beauty of the content.*

Other books by Schuyler are "Freely Espousing," and three novels: Alfred and Guinevere, What's For Dinner? *and* A Nest of Ninnies *with John Ashberry.*

STEAMING TIES:

Steaming ties, cutting rue
when I'm alone it's hard
at times to know how unalone
I am, loved by you. We phone.
A heavy talk of real estate, you
own land, I don't. Once did.

Sold it for a trip
Italy, France, two years:
bye bye, Arkansas homestead.
Still and all on this radiant
September leaf light day
the leaves lit it seems or
seeming is from insides,
lovely inwardness of leaves
that dapple themselves with shade,
and all, and still I have a
place to lay my head
in you, oh, anywhere:
I'm not body bigot but
sometimes even yet or now, I
mean, I forget for a few
sad minutes how unalone I
am, steaming ties you gave
me, ties are, yes even ties
are silk and real. Your
voice to me is silk and rustles.
We will meet, soon, not
soon enough. I remember I'm
unalone, you are with me,
salty sneezes off Atlantic
Ocean, there, where you are
here, in my heat and head
you blend in softly bright
September: you are moonrise
you are pain, you're mine
and I am yours, steaming
out silk ties, they bind.

WATCHING YOU

Watching you sleep
a thing you do so well
no shove no push
on the sliding face
of sleep as on
the deep a sea bird
of a grand wingspread
trusts what it knows

and I who rumple crumple
and mash (snore) amble
and ankle about wide
awake, wanting to fold,
loving to watch sleep
embodied in you my
warm machine that draws
me back to bed
and you who turn
all toward me
to love and seduce
me back to sleep "You
said 9:30, now it's
10:" you just
don't seem to care
cold coffee (sugar
no milk) about time.
you never do, never
get roiled the way
I do "Should I nag
you or shut up? If
you say, I will"
always be
glad to return to
that warm turning
to me in that
tenderest moment
of my nights,
and more, my days.

POEM
LETTER NO. 3

The night is quiet
as a kettle drum
the bull frog basses
tuning up. After
swimming, after sup-
per, a Tarzan movie,
dishes, a smoke. One
planet and I
wish. No need

of words. Just
you, or rather,
us. The stars tonight
in pale dark space
are clover flowers
in a lawn the expanding
Universe in which
we love it is
our home. So many
galaxies, and you my
bright particular,
my star, my sun, my
other self, my bet-
ter half, my one

JOAN LARKIN

I first heard Joan Larkin's poetry at a poetry reading we shared at Bernard Baruch college in 1978. I remember thinking, what a beautiful, engagé, intelligent woman. Then, why haven't I heard this wonderful poetry before? Joan read selections from her book, Housework, *and a series of other poems addressed to her brother.*

One of the great strengths of the confessional school of poetry (Plath, Lowell, Sexton, Berryman, etc.) was their ability to make their lives, their problems, the reader's. Intensity of language and emotion was their method. Their weakness, of course, was the same turned inside out—overly private poems about completely private worlds; lack of contact with the outside world and its problems; the overintensification of what might be a minor emotion.

The Larkin poems reprinted here partake of all the strengths of the confessional mode, and do so with a restraint and almost classical perfection of tone, image and language. "The plainest everyday things are dangerous," Joan Larkin writes in "Cautionary," and her idea that we are trapped by our perception of ourselves and others roles and lives is a common thread throughout her work. In another poem, Larkin writes "the heart, naked, is beating/need   need   need," and this second theme informs her work, giving it compassion and scope.

Joan Larkin is co-publisher of the Out and Out Press, a small lesbian press in Brooklyn, New York; she co-edited Amazon Poetry, *published by Out and Out. Her book* Housework *was published in 1977.*

HOUSEWORK
for M. W.

Through this window, thin rivers
glaze a steep roof. Rain: a church of rain,
a sky—opaque pearl,
branches gemmed with rain,
houses made of rain.

I am in the kitchen
killing flies against the cabinets
with a rolled-up magazine,
no Buddhist—
I live by insisting on my hatreds.

I hate these flies.
With a restless wounding buzz
they settle on the fruit,
the wall—again, again
invading my house of rain.

Their feelers, like hard black hairs,
test the air, or my gaze.
I find I am praying
Stand still for me
I'll devil the life out of you.

The human swarm comes in
with wet leaves on their sticky boots.
They settle on me with their needs; I am not nice.
Outside, headlights of dark cars are winding the street.
The mirror over the sink will do me in.

At five o'clock, rain done with, in darkness
the houses gather. In the livingrooms
Batman bluely flickers; the children all shut up,
all but an angry baby or a husband
the suburb is wreathed in wet leaves.

I forget what I wanted. Was it old music
laying gold-leaf on the evening?
lamplight sweetening the carpet?
like honey from Crete? A dream of/ door to Egypt?
Something to do with the life force.

December turns the sky to metal,
the leaves to gutter-paper.
Leak stopped, the bedroom ceiling starts to dry.
Its skin of paint is split and curling downward.
There is a fly in this house that will not die.

CAUTIONARY

Be quick
Watch out for the mirror
with the border of tin fruits.
Watch out for the worm spoons
from a set of wedding silver.
Do not listen to the music
in the wooden piano—
it has a use for you.

The sink will try to seduce you.
the clock   the clock
will try to wear you away.
The bed will not let you rest
will not let you wake up.

You are in danger
of a bloody rag
a doll with something missing
an unflushed toilet.

The plainest everyday things
are dangerous:
the clear drip of the faucet
the fire under the kettle
the hum of the refrigerator.

Take what you need
but hurry.
Do not stop to listen in the hallway.

There have been many before you.
Few have come back.

STORY

Once I took a mouth
into my kitchen —
a little, pretty one,
but it got bigger
in the warm room
and filled my whole
house up. It got
loud then, and its big lips
were fringed with black hair.

It ate out of my hand.
It made me cry.
It made me come.
But what disgusting noises —
I came to hate it.

It fastened on my tit
and would not let
me alone. I loathed
the sound of it sucking.

I had to hack it off,
finally, with a knife,
also to cut off part
of my body: I became
hideous. The lips bled,
and where the drops fell
in the kitchen, the bedroom,
there budded up
hundreds of baby mouths.

WORK SONG

I have been sitting
on this one's lap
a long time, fingering
his gray business
suit: a long time,
smelling the piss
in its sour threads.

He smokes.   He smiles
as he strokes my breasts.
I concentrate on hairs,
on cuffs, the red
gleam of his ring.
His thing is stiff.
He licks his lip.

Dear uncledaddy.
tell me how you like
your kitchen, your silk mesh,
your anything —
let me know when
you're ready,
what you'll give me.

He gives me what
I ask for, he says
I have it pretty easy.
But I'm tired.
I've been sitting
on this one now
for a long time.

THIRDS
for Kate

I move lovers
in & out
of this house
like rented pianos:
heavy, temporary,
taking space —
away from you
as you see it —
each discord
rubbing the air
of the apartment
raw.

The tenets
of their faith
in me
are black
& white
as keys
I press —
sexual —
against,
longing
for my own
song.

I am what they call
promising. Still
sometimes I think I'd kill

my half
finished body —
quit
playing
on violent hope
& be done
with this un-
easy music
except for you.

Clear tone,
can't you come
out
simple
tonic
like the red baby
who came howling
into my mess
clean
sudden
complete —
to be sustained.

DIRECT ADDRESS
for S.T.

You said
"I am afraid
 I want to be a woman" —

I think it only fair to warn you
it is not what you think
trailing your skirts,
brow-pencil, night cream —
these aren't the feminine
or any softnesses you were denied
but some extreme costume of the heat.
Steve, you wanted to be a queen.

I think it only fair to warn you
the heart is sexless.

It lies undressed in the dark,
and under the silk
of the single earring of gold,
the many-sexed apparel,
the heart, naked, is beating
need   need   need.

SOME UNSAID THINGS

I was not going to say
how you lay with me

nor where your hands went
& left their light impressions

nor whose face was white
as a splash of moonlight

nor who spilled the wine
nor whose blood stained the sheet

nor which one of us wept
to set the dark bed rocking

nor what you took me for
nor what I took you for

nor how your fingertips
in me were roots

light roots torn leaves put down—
nor what you tore from me

nor what confusion came
of our twin names

nor will I say whose body
opened, sucked, whispered

like the ocean, unbalancing
what had seemed a safe postion.

STOP

I hate it when you
fill my glass up
without asking me.

I always liked
a little
on a plate
in a cup

an egg
with space around it
an orange
with a knife
next to it

a cup
with space above
the coffee

discrete colors
orange   pewter   black

the porcelain glaze on the china
the blue napkin.

I want to keep things
separate. I hate it
when you break my egg.
I hate when you assume
I want cream
or the shade down
or touch, or looks
of kindness.

I want nothing
to lose
its cutting   edge
nothing to run together.

You had better
stop pouring yourself
into my glass.

JOE CADY

I had known Joe Cady for a while before I discovered he was a poet, or read any of his work. We exchanged a few poems, then a few more were published in Out *and* Magnus, *and I heard Cady read others at The Glines.*

Cady's poetry ought to be required reading for younger gays and lesbians — especially those that came out (like myself) easily, unexpectedly, deliberately, delightedly. The nine poems included here form an autobiographical sequence according to the poet. The pain of the past and of the present become fused in the poetry, transformed from object lesson to warning to signifier of an individual's experience — without in any way losing their more general appeal. Other themes besides the pain and suffering in being different early emerge — the heterosexual life as a fantasy alternative; and how one partner's pain — and past — become both lover's present and truth.

The sequence, "Destruction," printed here is one of the most powerful gay poems I know of — terrifying in its relentless long-lined elegant revelation of the heart of darkness and inherent violence that lies in wait in so many relationships.

Some of these poems appeared in The American Poetry Review. *Cady teaches gay literature courses at the New School; and is currently a psychotherapist. He has taught literature at Rutgers University, and is now working on, a critical study of gay American literature of the 19th & 20th centuries.*

EARLY INSPIRATION

I won the schoolwork prize again that year.
The chief nun weighed me at the ceremony.
They skinned me in the alley after —
smart ass, smarty fat ass, get smarty fat ass!

There.
I have built my own country.
Perfect kingdom, masterpiece —
Save Me!

GRADUATION FROM THE POORHOUSE: IN 1952

The principal, Sister Mary Robert,
has just awarded me the diploma
for General Excellence from St. Matthew's Grammar School,
commanding "Go to Sacred Heart High School in Yonkers,"
when a passionate and lovely voice cries, "Joe! Joe!"

It is Elizabeth Taylor, just as she looked
when she discovered Montgomery Clift
in the game room of her family's mansion
during the part at the beginning of "A Place in the Sun"!

She runs toward me now down the aisle
in her white formal gown like a beam of pure light
and sweeps me from the principal, proclaiming:
"This is not the road your life need take — I love you!
"I will drive you away in my white convertible
"to the country club, to the secluded lake
"where we will splash each other and I
"will fold your head to my full rich breasts!"

"Oh, I will get you a job with a future in my father's factory,
"just as I did all these things for Montgomery Clift!
"Only now, unlike his fate, there will
"be no lonely town girl you must drown,
"no capture, no imprisonment!
"Now the cost of rising above your place
"will not be lying, murder and the sentence of death!"

COMING OUT

O what
        to do!
I'm new
        at this and have
no style!

O for the craft, the magnitude,
of ugly Socrates,
whose words alone sparked half the men in Athens
to scout him in the streets
                      and drove
fair confident desirable Alcibiades
                              to potions
and to drink!

Perhaps a confidential wink
                      at the locker-room mirror,

   managing to dry
                    my hair when you do?
Or maybe bumping
                    you on the track,
apologies, discussion,
                       how my stomach ached
watching you
                force all those sit-ups?

Once we rode
              down together
in the jammed elevator.
                      Outside the cage
you blazed
round the corner of a hall,
                         I fell
onto Twenty-third Street —

                         O the dark winds!

STARTING 1973: WHAT TO DO NOW THAT PEACE HAS BEEN ANNOUNCED

At the end of January you again will see
the man you'd been wanting to meet for months
and at last you'll go up and say you'd like to meet him.

This man will go home with you later from the bar
after saying that he hardly ever goes home with anyone anymore.
You will tell him he is beautiful;
he will tell you you are beautiful;
you will sleep side by side every night for two months.

Then at Easter this lover
will knock you breathless and leave you:
he will say that he never felt joy in the relationship;
he will tell you he can no longer hold in his violence.

DESTRUCTION

1.
You said that your relationship with your former lover
almost destroyed you,
you loved him fiercely and lusted after him terribly,
he was the most beautiful man you had ever seen,
and each time you opened yourself to him
he closed off whatever feelings he had
and pushed you away.
So you shut him out in turn,
and whenever this happened
he came back,
and you gave way to your feelings again,
and he turned away again,
and the repetition of this pattern almost destroyed you.

2.
When you and your lover went back to the leather bar
where a friend had introduced you two years before,
you were trying to force a final reconciliation.
And even that time it wasn't working,
despite the dark bar and no matter how hard you pleaded,
so you asked him if he'd go outside for a walk with you,
and he followed you in the same lackadaisical and noncommittal way
that he had whenever he left your house in the morning
and you weren't sure when you'd see him again.

You led him under the highway across from the bar,
where you thought you wouldn't be seen because of the shadows,
and in your cracking voice you accused him of being dishonest
while you darted your finger back and forth at his chest.
Then he said he'd come back but couldn't promise you anything.
You stepped away for a second, dropped your head in your hands,
then turned back wailing and quickly began to beat him,
driving and driving him down to the ground
until you thought there wasn't a shred of him left there at all.

3.
You reached across the bed and held onto me tightly
and told me you were just getting over
a two-year affair that almost destroyed you,

and I said you didn't have to tell me about it if you didn't want to
because I knew it didn't have anything to do with me,
and you said it did have something to do with me
because you had something to do with me,
and you said you had wanted to talk to me before,
but had been afraid, and that you'd like to stay now,
and I said I was glad I finally went up to you in the bar,
and that I didn't feel afraid, and that I'd like you to stay,
and in the morning I got up and made coffee for both of us,
and you sat stretched out on the other end of the couch from me
and warned me not to get too close to you
because of what had happened before.

AFTER HEARING HETEROSEXUAL POETS IN OCTOBER 1974: WHAT IT SEEMS LIKE TO WRITE A MALE HOMOSEXUAL LOVE POEM NOW
for Joseph Chaikin

It is to be without the staple references
   of male heterosexual poets.

It is to be without a wife whose beauty and faithfulness
   can be mentioned convivially to audiences at readings.
It is to be without a son whose discovery of the world
   can be turned into a parable of the loss of innocence
   that demonstrates our wonder and sorrow
It is to be without a exhaustive history of mistresses,
   whose delicious parts can be listed as marks of our lustiness
   or whose riddle can be claimed as the source of our pain.

It is to cut the ties of such familiar images,
to start again at the first cries of speech,
over and over, inventing our voices,
until our unheard-of testimony
transfroms the understanding of reality irrevocably.

New language
in amazement
from this plain statement:
I am a man; you are a man; I love you.

DESPAIR OF MEN

The four-thirty whistle from the mill.
The empty men would climb the hill and stop
for one beer, yeah, another, just one more.
They'd shout, turn still, then wait, then stare away.
My mother, minding time again, would make me call
the bar to get my father home for supper now.

Now this is a bar that holds only men,
on a Sunday afternoon in early spring.
With clipped beards and moustaches, and in clothes
of construction workers, soldiers and cowboys,
they stand still or lean
away from each other
and when they flick their eyes back from him
they gaze into a far distance, not stirring
as the rising, warming air outside
and as their longing for each other's grasp,
if only they would give way, would have it.

It comes to summer weekends, beaches. Yes, it has to.
Oh you beautiful bodies of men, you, rippling and flexing!
Oh, you flash your lush buttocks in the packed cups of trunks!
Hope! Hope that your bodies are beautiful, bodies!

BACK AND FORTH

Believe this happened?

On New Year's night,
the new decade's first,
my former lover
came for supper. How I saw
him shine. He brought
wine. He said,
"Nice to be here again."

Still early when he left.
The dishes.
Done.
I turned to poems

without expecting it,
I took down Yeats
and the Chinese.
Yeats! Master!
Passionate cries
from the old country!
The Chinese, then.

Suppose Li Po and Tu Fu were
lovers? I opened
any page instead
and found
an unknown poet, poem,
of the eleventh century:
Huang T'ing-chien,
"Buffalo Boy."

That village in the distance.
There Ch'ang-an welcomed
"many guests of fame and gain."
Their treasures faded.
"Not so with you,"
herdsman on an ox.
You and your flute.
Across the fields
winds take your music
to the village, standing, still,
you passing.

Believe this, happened.
Changing life its mark.

IN AND OUT

1.

As in the summer just before ninth grade
I dreamed that Marilyn Caldwell would,
I dreamed the girl, so shining, blond,
her beauty through her veil so pure and breathtaking,
proceeds along the aisle to me and only me,
ready at the altar rail to take her
hand in marriage, to part only at death.

To be the trusted, the revered, insurance man
of classic small New England towns,
who's home at six o'clock and always
comes in through the kitchen door,
my wife who waits (devotion to our union),
my boy home from the team, my girl, the scouts.

2.

My lover stirs. Again today
he will rehearse
their company, passing all
tradition in the theater,
all actions free
from standard scenes and structure,
each generated wholly from
outside. In sleep his face
is smooth and blessed and happy,
uncannily resembling
the expression of the baby
in the picture on the cover
of *Birth Without Violence*.

CHUCK ORTLEB

Although he is best known as the publisher of Christopher Street Magazine and the author, with illustrator Rick Fiala, of several extremely popular gay cartoon books, beginning with "And God Bless Uncle Harry," *Chuck Ortleb is also a distinguished poet.*

His long poem, "Militerotics" included here, first published in Mouth of the Dragon, *was singled out for an award by the Small Press Association: it remains one of the most powerful gay political poems I know, dealing as it does with the idea that "force and sexuality/go together," and with the grim realization that "On the last day of the world/there will be one of these (political) beatings."*

Ortleb's poetry has a variety of subjects and moods. But all of it is viewed and written from the perspective of an extreme — almost scientifically precise — detachment, which should not be confused with cynicism. The poet's views of love and other relationships, though strongly bound by guiding images ("An Affair,' Gilbert and Lucien,") partake of a rare clear-eyed objectivity. His other poems are political without being polemical, hopeful without being fantasy ridden, and often blackly humorous, without sarcasm, especially in "Primal Liberation."

I'm astonished that this is the first time Ortleb's poems are available in permanent form. They ought to be better known.

GILBERT AND LUCIEN

(For Pierre Blaise)
France, 1944 or 1974

I am a French boy.
Name: Lucien
Age: 17
Race: horny

String the codpieces of Rouen
across what I say.
I am not truthful.
I am sexual.
We all choke on the seventeenness
of farmboys.
I have swallowed my own cum
once in an experiment.
The experiment did not fail.

One day, outside of Lyon
I am hunting for rabbits.
I come upon a boy
bathing in the Rhone.

What do I do?
I try to calm down.

But it is only Gilbert, soon to be
my friend.
Gilbet, I thought I was hunting for rabbits.
I was looking for you.

I am a French boy.
Name: Gilbert
Age: 18
Income: I make love for a living and eat
         garbage.
Penis size: Everyone has always said enough.

Gilbert, what can I tell you of my schooling
except that in the picaresque vacuum
you go from silence to silence
without adventures.

Lucien, my family's barn is
not far from here.
There the two of us can
talk wet, sticky
women talk
man to man.
Do you want to be a man, Lucien?
Have they also sent you to the showers?

Gilbert, you seem incurably alive,
meeting you is like . . .
being at the end of a war.

Lucien, open the barn door.
Close it.
See how the barn bursts with homosexuality.
Even the cows watch us in peace.
Their milk is gay.

Gilbert, when I grow up
you can be
in my credit card.

Lucien, come over here to the corner
of the barn. I must whisper something.
France is still occupied.
The Nazi heterosexuals have not left.
We should seize power, Lucien,
and dance the first tango
in Paris
above our peers.

Gilbert, I like your sense of
humor.
You have eaten
much bread and much cheese.
Gilbert, my mother is a masseuse
in the underground.
I sometimes go down into the
cellar to
feel myself.
Is it autism, Gilbert?

You had to get ready for me
somehow, Lucien.
I've got some wine
buried over here.
Please hold me
and drink too much.

Gilbert, let's open a dilapidated hotel
together and always be
naked.
Help me into the foreplay.

Lucien, let me kiss you 5,896 times.
They can never stand exactitude in
this sort of thing.

Gilbert, let's love without hesitating
to make things clear.
This is the wettest
dream of all.

Lucien, let's not leave the barn.

Out there, straight boys are
sitting around in tree houses
trying to make poems
out of the bleeding of
their sex lives.

Gilbert, once at a station
my father held a man's head
under water
until he named his leader.
And then some more.

Lucien, I have made love to you.
That's how I like
to get my information.

CHAMINADE

An all-male prep school, 1965

We all began novels at desperate moments,
interrupted vacations to buy notebooks,
gave up our childhood on the soccer field
to walk back to the dormitory to begin to write
novels, neglected plants, and love affairs
to write about plants and love affairs
or we were so close to life that
we began writing novels about novels
or we needed someone in our arms so much
that we took to literary criticism,
and on warm days among growing boys
things were written twenty-five times
before they were spontaneous, and always
late into the night there had to be a torrential
group writing, automatic, associated
in order to develop great journalistic
loneliness, and they would find us in closets
or under the dormitory beds in the morning
pen in hand, quivering, abrupt in the
world, not sure of our bodies, closing
chapter two and already pushing a theme.

TO ALL THE DOCTORS

Doctor, naked in your ajaxed stirrups,
tell me, do you like remote, almost arrogant prostates?
Just how medical is your soul?
Do you know why each sentence feels this way?

B—, C, C—, A.
The moments vanish into each other.
Probe where it starts.
I'll spread for you.

Here in the almost arms
of your equipment
you are surgery.
I am neighborhood.

Already you know how much
I love him. Can you tell that I
scream at him
for two hours
without losing the hardon?
And still beside the bed
I keep a gun
in case one of us
should leave.

But now, the prostate.
Check the prostate. How's the kid?
The last doctor said
it gave off a keen, almost innocent light.

PRIMAL LIBERATION

Nobody is listening to anybody's advice on sex
and God saw that it was good.
Women making it with German shepherds on cruisers,
amputees beating each other off into cigarette wrappers
the rich uncorking the diamond dildo
the sea captain advertising for the mermaid
the mermaid lubricating her
long memorable tail off the coast of Missouri.

The eighth time that night
they employed the crucifix.

Nobody cares who sees your body.
The telescope pulled affectionately from the peanut butter.
The acrobat taking off his bandages.
The plastic surgeon rimming the eyes of a mask
the small boy coming out of the closet to give his
book report
a string pulled from the mouth of one candle to another.

The ninth time that night they employed
a sleek trim line telephone.

Nobody cares what you do with your body.
The petite telephone booth slides, with
a little grease, into the casket, the nail
with proper technique, can be screwed into the apple.
The librarian goes neatly on top of the janitor.
The hottest message can be pressed harder and harder
into paper until paper makes a sound of release
and you could hold me tighter.

AN AFFAIR

I make love
to you in a bakery.
You put twelve cookies in a bag.
When I return home
I eat ten.
Two are left for tomorrow.
Like my eyes.
I make separate entries
in my diary.
One for the love
and one for the cookies.

You phone me.
We talk about the cookies.
We are going to last
as long as the cookies.

THE RECONCILIATION

There had always been rules
about the end of the day in
his family. "You must never
go to bed angry at your mother."
So at dusk there was a rush for
reconciliation. The father had to
forgive the son, the son the daughter,
and the daughter in her pink pajamas,
the mother. That's what it was
like after a long hard day of hating.
Actually, behind it was the fear that
God would attack like a mad dog in the dark,
that the mad dog would be waiting there
at the door in the morning
for the pretty little boy
who hadn't kissed his mom goodnight.

Later, the little boy who escaped the
dog went on to more handsome things
with a lessened metaphysical threat.
The way he danced and dressed and
who he loved became modern and Greek.
But not everything in a boy changes
Lovers were always the bread of his life.
His moods and his sheets were always some shade of blue.
He kept a lover's chair by the window at dusk.
It always remained a good time and
a good place to forgive and invent.

MEN

When I look at the
   faces of men
I imagine
the temperature of their love.

The feats their bodies perform
twisted hot
just before coming.

I imagine the kitchen
in which they would look good
doing the simple things.

Years from now
I will not make
love to a man

until I see him
pare an apple
sitting next to the fire

where he is also burning.

MILITEROTICS

Sexuality grows out of the barrel of a gun
                              — Homage to Jancso

In Vietnam
eels live in the water
until they are stuffed
into the vaginas of the opposition.
Do not think of the women.
Think of the eel:
bloodstained, hungry,
staring out of
the cunt
having completed
a political journey.

In Chile the opposition
dream from cattle cribs
that they have not been
castrated
and forced to eat
their own erections.

As young boys
they stripped each other
naked, tied each other up
in their basements

and then the beatings began.
The beatings have not ended.
On the last day of the world
there will be one of these beatings.

Normandy was erotic.
Pearl Harbor was erotic.
Hiroshima was erotic,
but too quick, like
premature ejaculation.

Let's play animals and
guards, someone says
in the echo of time,
in the holocaustic maleness.

Chile,
Cuba,
Lawrence, Kansas,
Dallas, Texas
force and sexuality
go together
like men with men
on horses,
like whips with marriages.
Force seeks sexuality,
sexuality seeks
out force.
There is all you need to know.

How well you coordinate
it all
almost symphonically.
You speak, cry,
pull out your hair
and hemorrhage at the
same time.

II

What do you do in a room
full of torturers but
begin the show.

I seek
the perfect solitude of
having a jail full of
naked men to throw
into the sea
one at a time
or to retain one
for sleepless nights,
spontaneous pummelling.

I must find a way
to fuck you that
begins and ends
with the words
yes, sir.

To love: to promise
a prisoner that you will be even
worse to him
tomorrow.
To say it mellifluously.

You can
encompass all of a man's
sperm
through electric shock
and cattle prod.
Sometimes during initiations
in Kansas, naked 18-year-olds
are taken from the locker rooms,
stuffed into Volkswagons
and driven into cornfields
for good old-fashioned
gang rapes.

Even the Mafia is erotic:
to be in a
sauna with
your father and
to be asked
how you want a
specific man destroyed.
In or out of his underwear.

III
Orders:

Order a wife to go down
on her son in front of her son's teachers.
Order a mother to masturbate
her baby in front of her mother.
Order a mother to castrate her
political teenage son with a
potato knife.
Order mothers to stick sharpened
pencils up your daughters' asses.
Order that all communication be
translated into sexual terms.
Order that all men must be fucked
ten times a day by their fathers.
Order that all pain be suspected
of having sexual origin.
Order that all shitting be done
in open-air theaters with Greek choruses.

Build
museums of mutilated
freaks to demonstrate
the male sensibility.

Reward civil artists
for humiliation captured
in rococo
and Baroque.

Panorama of problems.
Panorama of naked men.
Whether to starve them
before you humiliate them
or humiliate them
before you starve them.
Generals,
consult management experts.

When a young girl is
stripped and tied to a pole
in an alley

let the artists
capture
that confused look in the
face of the gang
the look of
what to do first.

IV

This is the do not be bitter
part of history,
the part the church sponsors,
the part where they line them up
and make them fuck each other
and then punish them and
ridicule them for fucking each
other and then make them do it
again . . . not in circles, but in
rich spirals, forever and ever
in a vertical movement
into heaven.

When a father beats
his son behind the barn
he must take off his belt
and from then on
it's lust.
In the cries of the son,
nude where he lays,
nations form.

V

Juan Mirabel.
You ask what turns men on.
You do, Juan Mirabel.
When your dress is
torn from your thighs
they flay your skin
and bounce your head
in the stadium
in soccer
the national sport of Chile.
But if you save up a little money

for a weapon,
if you tell
another man
to take off
his clothes and
you are holding
a gun . . .
you are a political genius.

John Doe.
You ask what turns men on.
You do, John Doe.
When, in a small
Dallas County jail
they have the power
to strip you down
and examine the folds
of your ass
for nuclear weapons
nightly after dinners
with their wives
when they're burping,
when it's more fun
than stretching.

John Doe, Juan Mirabel,
if they let you wear
pajamas,
if they do not
immediately
change your name,
If they give you
your knuckle for
your last toothbrush
the day you die,
bite into bone,
John Doe and Juan Mirabel.
You turn men on.
You always will.

JUDY GRAHN

When St. Martins Press recently republished the collected poetry of Judy Grahn, with an introduction by Adrienne Rich, they returned to print one of the most popular books of lesbian poetry of our time. Originally published in 1975 by Diana Press, the volume contains "Edward the Dyke, and other Poems," "A Common Woman," "A Woman is Talking to Death," and "She Who."

Judy Grahn is not afraid to label herself — she is proud to have earned the names lesbian, dyke, woman, common woman in her life and in her writing. Her poetry covers a wide range of subjects and uses a variety of techniques, but they all revolve around being an aware and defiantly different woman in a male dominated society. Some of the poems are fables, some love lyrics, others portraits, some openly political rally cries. Others such as "Edward the Dyke" are hilarious exaggerations of how women are psychologically battered by the establishment that are both funny and terrifying, fantastic and all too real. One poem, the book length, A Woman is Talking to Death, is a comprehensive, harrowing, questioning, demanding, angry, tender masterpiece. Its repetitions become incantory, its power irresistible, its message striking and undeniable.

Judy Grahn selected the poems printed here from The Work of A Common Woman, reprinted with permission from St. Martins Press, and she also included an unpublished poem, "Natural Lovers," from her work in progress A Chronicle of Queens. Of her selection, Judy writes: "I have noticed how rarely lesbian or women's anthologies touch the direct, descriptive, explicit subject of sex, in utter contrast to gay (or even straight) men's anthologies — and it's beginning to make me mad. And even though hundreds of women memorized "In the place where," because it was the first lesbian sex poem they'd ever been allowed to hear, it has never been reprinted except in occasional underground newsletters. I feel censored in this regard and I wish you would keep this in mind when you make your selections, maybe ask other lesbians if they feel similarly?"

I certainly agree with Judy Grahn on this matter: readers interested ought to turn to selected poems by Pat Kuras and Susan Belew in this anthology, and to Emily Sisley's novella, "Margot's Novel," which I believe is a beginning in righting the balance.

in the place where
her breasts come together
two thumbs' width of
channel ride my
eyes to anchor
hands to angle
in the place where
her legs come together
I said "you smell like the
ocean" and lay down my tongue
beside the dark tooth edge
of sleeping

"swim" she told me and I
did, I did
 * *
If you lose your lover
rain hurt you. Blackbirds
brood over the sky trees
burn down everywhere brown
rabbits run under
car wheels. should your
body cry? to feel such
blue and empty bed dont
bother. if you lose your
lover comb hair go here
or there get another
 * *
the harvest spider
flowers on my wall
ornately
legs stretched long and
easy as a young queen
in the park
he knows his trick
will come and meanwhile
he's not asking

A HISTORY OF LESBIANISM

How they came into the world,
the women-loving women
came in three by three
and four by four
the women-loving women
came in ten by ten
and ten by ten again
until there were more
than you could count

    they took care of each other
    the best they knew how
    and of each other's children
    if they had any.

How they lived in the world,
the women-loving women
learned as much as they were allowed
and walked and wore their clothes
the way they liked
whenever they could. They did whatever
they knew to be happy or free
and worked and worked and worked.
The women-loving women
in America were called dykes
and some liked it
and some did not.

    they made love to each other
    the best they knew how
    and for the best of reasons.

How they went out of the world,
the women-loving women
went out one by one
having withstood greater and lesser
trials, and much hatred
from other people, they went out
one by one, each having tried
in her own way to overthrow
the rule of men over women,
they tried it one by one
and hundred by hundred,
until each came in her own way
to end of her life
and died.

    The subject of lesbianism
    is very ordinary; it's the question
    of male domination that makes everybody
    angry.

        *   *

The many minnows are fishes that live in a stream,
and greedybeak is a bird that lives on the land
and comes down to the edge of the stream where he
sticks his head under the water and eats the
many minnows. After a long time of this greedybeak

had ate up all but 47 of the many minnows and they
were tired of it so the next time he approached
their stream they had a plan. They thrust all of their
silver scales and fins out as far as they would
go, and all in the same direction. The sun's rays
glinted off the silver scales and fins, and when
greedybeak looked down he saw nothing but his
own reflection. "There's another greedybeak down
there with MY fishes" he screamed and dove
straight into the water, in a rage. The 47
remaining many minnows promptly ate him up
and turned him into many more many minnows.

A GEOLOGY LESSON

Here, the sea strains to climb up on the land
and the wind blows dust in a single direction.
The trees bend themselves all one way
and volcanoes explode often.
Why is this? Many years back
a woman of strong purpose
passed through this section
and everything else tried to follow.

*   *

The most blonde woman in the world
one day threw off her skin
her hair, threw off her hair, declaring
"Whomsoever chooses to love me
chooses to love a bald woman
with bleeding pores."
Those who came then as her lovers
were small hard-boiled spiders
with dark eyes and an excellent
knowledge of weaving.
They spun her blood into long strands,
and altogether wove millions of red
webs, webs red in the afternoon sun.
"Now" she said, "Now I am expertly loved,
and now I am beautiful."

Carol and
her crescent wrench
work bench
wooden fence
wide stance
Carol and her
pipe wrench
pipe smoke
pipe line
high climb
smoke eyes
chicken wire
Carol and her
hack saw
well worn
torn back
bad spine
never-mind
timberline
clear mind
Carol and her
hard glance
stiff dance
clean pants
bad ass
lumberjack's
wood ax
Carol and her
big son
shot gun
lot done
not done
never bored
do more
do less
try to rest
Carol and her
new lands
small hands
big plans
Carol and her
long time
out shine

worm gear
warm beer
quick tears
don't stare
Carol is another
queer
chickadee
like me, but Carol does
everything
better
if you let her.

    * *

Love rode 1500 miles on a grey
hound bus & climbed in my window
one night to surprise
both of us.
the pleasure of that sleepy
shock has lasted a decade
now or more because she is
always still doing it and I am
always still pleased. I do indeed like
aggressive women
who come half a continent
just for me; I am not saying that patience
is virtuous, Love
like anybody else, comes to those who
wait actively
and leave their window open.

    * *

My name is Judith, meaning
She Who is Praised
I do not want to be called praised
I want to be called The Power of Love.

if Love means protect then whenever I do not
defend you
I cannot call my name Love.
if Love means rebirth then when I see us
dead on our feet
I cannot call my name Love.
if Love means provide & I cannot

provide for you
why would you call my name Love?

do not mistake my breasts
for mounds of potatoes
or my belly for a great roast duck.
do not take my lips for a streak of luck
nor my neck for an appletree,
do not believe my eyes are a warm swarm of bees;
do not get Love mixed up with me.

Don't misunderstand my hands
for a church with a steeple,
open the fingers & out come the people;
nor take my feet to be acres of solid brown earth
or anything else of inifinite worth
to you, my brawny turtledove;
do not get me mixed up with Love.

not until we have ground we call our own
to stand on
& weapons of our own in hand
& some kind of friends around us
will anyone ever call our name Love,
& then when we do will all call ourselves
grand, muscley names:
the Protection of Love,
the Provision of Love & the
Power of Love.
until then, my sweethearts,
let us speak simply of
romance, which is so much
easier and so much less
than any of us deserve.

NATURAL LOVERS

Surely it is the ocean
we make love to
in each other.
Surely it is her influence
swelling out our pockets

with pulse blood, and
her desiring tides that pour,
that slide in waves, each
formed, like feelings,
by the one before.

Surely it is the ocean
moving us as she is moved
by her own lover, the moon—
strung so far out
over her, on the chain
between two forces,
eternally swayed,
arching and pulling,
yearning to return and
yet compelled away.

Surely it is their
unfulfilled attraction
we fall into
when we fall together,
rocked in our own salty waters
all the more magnetic,
all the more wet
for what those two vast
natural lovers want
and cannot get.

WALTA BORAWSKI

Walta Borawski is one of that large and talented group of Boston lesbians and gay writers that has included Paul Monette, Sal Farinella, Rudy Kikel, Pat Kuras, Charles Shively, et al. The literary centers of Boston's gay life have been The Glad Day Bookshop, the Fag Rag *collective,* and Gay Community News; *the two magazines viewed by many in the national gay community as intensely political — even radical.*

So, naturally, one would expect to find one of Boston's most prolific and popular gay poets to be rigidly political — if not completely doctrinaire, right? Wrong! Borawski is too good and too interesting a poet for that. His politics seem to be so internalized they are expressed naturally, in the very subject matter of his work, as in the poems included here, "Power of One," "Live Free and Die," and "Some of Us Wear Pink Triangles." But Borawski has more to say than repeating what we all know — he has a distinctive personality to express; likes, dislikes, ironies, moments of self-questioning. He is a gay man who is not afraid to say he likes promiscuous sex and s/m or Barbra Streisand, that he has read Judy Garland's biography and sometimes wears outrageous clothing, that he'll be whom he wants, thank you, even if that means being inside the mind and heart of one of his long dead idols — as he displays in his very fine long prose poem — "I am not Billie Holiday."

Borawski's work has appeared in many places. These poems are from his new book, Discipline and Compulsive Behavior. *"Dead Languages" appeared in* Gay Community News, *Vol. 5 #4,* "Pygmalion, L.I." *in* Bachy 16, Winter 1980, *"Surprising Kisses," in* Mouth of the Dragon, *Vol. 2 #1.*

POWER OF ONE

I am the sole homosexual
in Wilton, New Hampshire, & I

was imported only this afternoon.
Rafts of whirligigs scatter

as I approach by canoe; cut-
worms devour potatoes,

raccoons split wood houses,
scoop, eat, birds inside,

are hunted & shot in turn
by black dogs, & hunters.

Mining insects leave striations
'cross leaves of water lilies,

beavers topple trees, water
rises, raises mosquitoes, fleas.

Grey, white, black, yellow
birches dwarf blueberries;

no safe spot, no domain. Hurricane David yanks branches

from fruit trees. Japanese
beetles make lettuce artless lace,

porcupines pierce the tongues
of hunters' dogs — all because

there's a faggot in New Hampshire.

LIVE FREE OR DIE

Here in New Hampshire the ghost
of a gay man who never knew love

stops me in the meadow, leads me
by web-chain to his lean-to, rot

& mice dung. Points to my penis,
wants me to piss on his rusted

bed springs. lay naked down on
wet coils.

My own bed has its own stains.
Spotless he walks before me,

points out the *bottled gentian:*
not poisonous, but purplish-blue,

lovelier than Venetian glass;

genetically programmed
never to open.

SOME OF US ARE STRETCHED TIGHTER THAN OTHERS

He says all the birds are flying
south this year, & I

am too intense to sleep with.
It's warmer, that's why they

go, kissing me is
kissing February, it stretches you

out, & then sticks in the tongue,
the tongue, the icicle tongue.

     I
only wanted warmth myself,
didn't feel like flying

for it; & these eyes —
my mother's side of the family

has them. These feathers —
how I've plucked for them!
— & you
want things easy, you

want to fly without
greasing up the engine
without
twisting up the rubber
band.

INDEXING JUDY GARLAND'S LIFE:
A Found Poem, from Gerold Frank's Bio.

Birth
childhood
stage debut
training
changes name

death of father
early love affairs
drug use
poetry

remarriage of mother
in love with Artie Shaw
romance with David Rose
marriage with Rose
health problems

divorce from Rose
in love with Joe Mankiewicz
psychological problems
psychiatric treatment

weight problem
marriage with Minnelli
birth of Liza
drug dependence

suicide attempts
[pp. 230, 281, 299, 360,
402, 427, 525, 534, 541].
suspended by MGM
financial problems
contract terminated

relationship with Luft
separation & divorce from Minnelli
marriage with Luft
birth of Lorna

death of mother
loss of Oscar
birth of Joey
drinking habits
TV debut

conflicts with Luft
reunited
battle of custody for children
illness (overdose) in Londo~

219

divorce from Luft
quarrel with sisters
TV series

legal problems
marriage with Herron
marriage with Mickey Deans
death
funeral

PERVERSITY

I know that my holding onto
a book of poems by Ezra Pound
separates Sylvia Plath
from Adrienne Rich
on one shelf in America
but I keep it there.

I know that lust feelings
for my lover's boyfriend
are illicit — not even smart;
but I do like the man, I do
like the man, I do, & I never
was much good at *platonic*.

Many men women & children
would call me, Christians
would call me, shrinks &
my mother & right wingers
everywhere would call me
perverse but very likely
for the wrong reasons.

CIRCLES MIGHT LEAD TO RECTANGULAR BEDS, STRAIGHT LINES DON'T

*O yes — I too come here
merely to watch sculls
skim the river:* Had I

told him *that*—not
I'm looking for a man,
& you're . . .

certainly a man.

THE SKY OVER CAMBRIDGE
is bluer than Oz! How
he'd have preferred that

to: *You look like a runner.*
But he did. & bolt he did,

he ran. Had I invited him
to play frisbee
we'd still be in bed.

I AM NOT BILLIE HOLIDAY,
BUT I LOOK GOOD IN MY DRESS
& MY RUNNING SHOES

It is very smoky in here. Billie Holiday is singing "You Turned the Tables on Me," proverbial pin-drop. I am looking for someone. I jangle my bracelets, he might be blind. Very smoky in here. I will come back to this.

* * *

At work Alison's father has died. I turn right from the elevator, the door closes, I turn further right; Alison is there, standing, shorter than me but eye-to-eye. "Are you okay?", I am this inarticulate. *"Are you okay?"* It could come from either of us; they could be any words.

* * *

Sometimes I stand in the living room between the speakers & pretend I'm Billie Holiday singing "These Foolish Things Remind Me of You." It doesn't take much range, though this is a limitation I do not share with her, I cannot be her, this is why I do this duet in the living room, alone. I find it increasingly hard, not being Billie Holiday. No-voiced, I don't know what to do with all these songs.

* * *

Sometimes I am Barbra Streisand. It is a very integral part of my survival, why & how I am still here, being, now & then, Barbra Streisand. I steel myself up on heels, I make chiffon into armor, I send every word of displeasure disappointment &/or hurt out to attack. I'm unable to forgive, today. I stand alone. From observation I know this is very impressive, when the stance is enhanced by talent. I cannot sing, I can only bring someone else's intelligence & fury & phrasing & weight to the words. I am a mimic. But I copy the greats. This is not pride, it is description. It's deception too. I will come back to this.

* * *

The fish tank is comforting. Life has even more limitations. I commiserate. This is how we survive work: We experience together alone Sunday to Monday — or whatever they label the opposite ends of our dream-non-dream excursions. *Would I stay in a warm bed. Would I prefer to be in arms. Would I choose to be alone over a second cup of tea, a second cigarette.* That is Monday. By Tuesday I am strong on commiseration. No one did well at work yesterday: the smoking room was filled all morning, the coffee ran out before noon; elongated faces settled in any number of corners, no longer a rectangular room: faces confronting regiment. We are a disciplined lot. I do not consider myself a disciplined individual. I do leave the house Monday mornings. But if I meet a face I am not ready to meet I will dart down a sidestreet, take a mad inefficient route to work, smoke a cigarette in a churchyard, arrive late, anything, anything, to keep the barrier, I am not out of the dream yet. I was Billie Holiday eight hours ago, I stood alone between speakers, between inverted obelisk black jet earrings, I smelled the orchid behind my ear, I felt my silk dress, *from the inside,* I felt this rustle, I heard this drum, I moved my notes like a saxophone, like a cello, leave me alone now.

* * *

Eleven people were crushed & otherwise battered to death on their way into a rock concert last night, the Who in Cincinnati went on. Where would the energy of 18,000 expectants go if the music, if the show, did not go on? I imagine being on acid, being stepped to death, I imagine being in a crowd, the word *Stop* suddenly lost from my vocabulary, the word *Help* being beyond my understanding.

* * *

When I am making love, when I am having sex & there is pain or there is nonenjoyment or my mood goes red to dark gray I stop the action, I pull away. I have never had to slap a hand. If I wanted the tit-clamps off, if I wanted the symmetrical pain stopped, they were off, it stopped, I went on. I have never had to deal with mob lack of mentality. In Fenway orgies, fucked suddenly too often, too eagerly, I have pulled my pants up, I have walked away. I have never heard the Who. I love the rhythms of rock & of fucking. I love the abruptness of *Stop*, and potential of *Help*.

* * *

On tv last night, a nationwide show, a man behind Christ's name subtly strung together homosexuality, a negative aspect of witchcraft, & the dismemberment of teenage bodies. He said Keynesian economics, developed by a homosexual, is responsible for our slipping economy. My friends & I did not laugh. I suspect there were many watching who did not take it so seriously, who did not know it was insidious, surreal, that this middle-aged Howdy Doody playing dumb & naive wants very badly to put me & my kind in concentration camps. I always wear running shoes, even though boots go better with my leather jacket, sandals better with my flowing shirts. I fear wearing color. I've cut my hair. I leave my earrings in a soapstone box, I hide that behind books. I consider myself only marginally eccentric, totally within an endangered species. *Survival* is a word I have never felt cozy with. This is why I listen not to the Who, who keep on, after all, rocking, but to Billie Holiday; this is why I smoke cigarettes & sing against midnight & try so very hard to become her.

4-7 December 79

DEAD LANGUAGES

He didn't remember my name,
this letter-sweatered man

with six hundred & fifty pages
toward his doctoral degree
in long-dead tongues. I
remembered his, I've a knack
for simpler bits of life:
three letters, one syllable,
two vowels, rhymes with bee.
I said it on departure, stung.
He could muster only dusty words,
a prospectus on the day, its
matriculated absence of me.
It was 6:30 a.m., the sky
was showing us a clear trick
or two, without words.

SOME OF US WEAR PINK TRIANGLES
(for Rudy Kikel)

At the Lesbian & Gay Pride March we
strode through main streets shouting
"Two/four/six/eight: Gay is just
as good as straight." Their hundreds
looked at our thousands. Some threw
insults, some supported. Most were
silent. We were noisy inside the
shelter of numbers. Balloons flew
into the face of the sky, forcing
all to see: *We are everywhere.*

At a dinner party in Somerville,
eight of us sit talking about music,
gay politics, gay literature, gay
love. In the conversation's first
lull we hear it: First come wolf
whistles, then: "Hey! Why don't
you guys look out? Lots of beautiful
guys on the sidewalk down here. You
talking about Anita Bryant up there?
You drinking any orange juice? Hey —
play us some more Beethoven." We

look at each other, trying to find

words. Rudy talks of gays beat up
after tying to throw a gay-straight
party. Kenny's been hit by a beer
bottle the night before. He'd had
his arm about a man. We all have
our stories. Then: THUD! —
Patrick hears it, I hear it, something's
been thrown against the house. Twice
more it happens, & laughter, & whistles,

& then: "Goodnight, guys. See ya
tomorrow." Already we've been moving
from windows, & changing
the subject. But there's no room
for music now, & literature seems

removed. No matter how real Henry James
can make a character, *we* have to deal with
characters in the street, we have to
get from here to there & worry about
survival between Ball & Harvard squares.

Once Bruce told me he'd try gay sex, only
he'd never want to be branded *homosexual*.
I used to laugh.

3. PYGMALION, L.I.

This poem is for Howie, who told me I've
a lovely ass, & fine-featured face; then
stood me in front of a full-length mirror
to say:

"Now look at your pants — they're
very New York, sure, but
they don't show
your body; & this shirt — great
plaid, but
with that hairy chest you
should always have at least
three buttons doing
absolutely nothing — even in

this weather. Those longjohns
have to go! Now
look at this hair — too much of it,
& *Loving Care* could color that gray;
never say *dye* — it's got
bad connotations. That beard — that
beard! I feel a fine face
under it — no wrinkles at all; just
a moustache would do you fine.
The glasses are awful, but
what glasses aren't? Have you
tried contacts?"

    This poem
is for Howie, who showed me
his cat Rebekah, though he
had to run through nine rooms
naked to find her — past his
mother, sixty-six & asleep somewhere
in that split-level home.
       Howie,
who cuts hair for his living &
has lived on Long Island too long.

SURPRISING KISSES
FOR MALCOLM

You were my first S&M man, you
showed me the ropes, though we
had to imagine them, in the dormitory
at St. Mark's Baths.
     *"Don't move
one wrist from the other,"* you
ordered, *"Now lick me all over."*

    And like a tired
or drunk ballerina my tongue
twirled, passion without form,
taking your pleasure moans
for applause, & flowers.

     Now & then
I'd *plié* at your closed
mouth, lick your clipped beard &
tight lips;
    now & then, on cues
very much your own you'd
open your mouth, & give mine
surprising kisses: how odd,
how more desirable these
than those given freely,
in uncategorized love, as if kisses
are just commodities, obeying
supply & demand.

     Later you
worried that my hair, wet all the while
from whirlpool & sauna, steambath & love-
sweat, would catch me a cold. You offered me
taxi fare home. Surprising concern,
surprising kisses: but like men
of less choreographed fantasy you
said *Goodbye,* & *Good knowing you,* & I
danced uptown unbound.

JON BRACKER

"So this is it, to be alive," Jon Bracker writes in his poem, "Letter to My Ex-Therapist,"—and the poems printed here have that unusual degree of sunny optimism about life, even at its worst moments. Bracker isn't a Pollyanna, however Californian he is—he is an evoker of life's gifts—whether they be showers of new t-shirts, or a new love, or a lovely little fantasy about the mother and father of American poetry (Dickinson and Whitman) being friends.

Perhaps Bracker's fullest statement on homosexuality is his poem, "The Opposites of Straight," where one by one all of the advantages of heterosexuality are effortlessly replaced. To all those readers who find writing about current gay life to be depressing, please read and re-read Jon Bracker.

Bracker's biography is as follows:

"Jon Bracker is the author of two chapbooks of poetry, Constellations of Clover, Prickly Pear Press, 1973, and Duplicate Keys, Thorp Springs Press, 1977; he is the editor of the selected poems of Christopher Morley, University of Pennsylvania Press, 1965, and co-author of a study of Morley's writings, Twayne Press, 1977. His poems have appeared in Gay Literature, The Mouth of the Dragon, Writer's Digest, College English, The English Journal, and numerous little magazines. He lives in San Francisco, where he enjoys teaching college English to U.S. Navy personnel for Chapman College. An essay on the poems of Windield Townley Scott by Bracker recently appeared in Gregg Kuzma's A Book of Rereadings in Recent American Poetry, Best Cellar Press, 1979."

THE OPPOSITES OF STRAIGHT

Curving, bending.

Not: queer, crooked, wayward, out-of-joint,
gnarled, wizened, bandy, bowed,
crippled, snaking, knock-kneed, askew,
maimed, deviating, knurled, —

but antlers
disclosed by
lightning,

the dragonfly, his zigzag hovering,
twigs rafted on a stream,
the tacking advent of swans toward hand-held offerings.
The ins-and-outs of hummingbirds. Pigeons' progress. Some
bills, legs, unfolding wings (and the unfolded legs of cats),
the necks of birds (the darter's thrust, the heron's
upward toss to order fish); how sandpipers spirt
onto blotting sand.

The investigatory spider's light approach.
Ligament, filament.
Eyelid, -brow and -lash. The wrists.
Now-pulsing blood through arteries.
Pastern, fetlock, hoof. Rootlets. And trees.
The raindrop's slow concessive downpane path. Paths.
Peaks. Eagles'
outings.

All burgeonings: the sweet pea tendril's grasp; unsmooth
viny wood from which the wistaria-blossoms grape;
petunia seedlings, their green slight shoulder-pads fronding
into strength. Worm-tunnelings. The in-
direction of an ant. Gartersnakes' naive appearances. Dark
skittery flies. Grasshopper-leaps.
grasshopper-flights.

The prickly meadowgrass, the manly weeds to stretch and laugh out on
beneath the sheer and unpolemic sky sky-blue and gay.

LOVE POEM

Some had cantering hair
the best of them blonde

or a dent above the lips
God's little finger
poised to make

or a space discovered
between rib cage and loins
exact for a face to rest into
upside down, after kissing

the liked one's head
on the mattress on the floor,
the body rag-dolled on the bed,

I inventorying the person
slowly, without passion,
from forehead over the lips
down shoulders the neck.

But though I remember such details
encountered forever

you have supplied me with no such splendors
subtle or strong.

I am disturbed
after all these times together: today

everything overheard is forcibly, unexpectedly
about to change into something entirely unclear:

something is coming

and as always
from the quarter least expected.

I LIKE THAT BROWN ONE A LOT

Shelley's skylark, Keats' nightingale,
Herrick's roses, Burns' daisy,
William Carlos Williams' pompommed slippers, —
to these I would add
T-shirts.

It is time we paid homage
to what we feel comfortable in,
what makes us cheerful,
what we give each other
as pleasant gifts.

Lauding their colors faded or bright,
their inscriptions witty or coarse,
their clean or grubby sloppiness
or their second-skin newness,
their pictures transforming chests and breasts
into contemporary Louvres, I state
they brighten every day
and ask that they be included
in the annals of verse
as something
loved.

A friend insists yellow is best
but I have no favorite,
unless it is
flesh-colored.
            (The color doesn't matter,)
it is their clingingness,
making torsoes
figureheads, our bodies ships,
assertive, sailing forth. . . .
(Armadas in the shopping malls!)

   Thank you, Nan, for the egg-yolk-yellow extra-large
   from Texas with armadillos folk dancing,
   I have washed it gently again;
   and John for the black one
   with *Writer's Digest* and the fist
   wielding a fountain-pen: I feel
   ready to meet Gertrude Stein
   in that.

Life is a picnic without ants
when we are flat on grass
and looking about for where to lay my head and hand
I see your sunny heart,
T-shirted

or any time you stride into a room
T-shirt first,
smile definitely second.

ONE-NIGHT STAND

We came and then there was
each's afterholding of the quieting other.

Now, you lie on your back so still
you seem to hardly breathe. I ask
if you are all right and you reply
with an oh yes you cannot say without smiling.

On my side, head level with yours, undisturbed
when you are not moved by my kiss on your check,
I consider how you look and simply wait.

AFTER BEING TALKED TO BY A FRIEND

Buckled for what appeared to be life
behind the shield of defencelessness,
he neither won nor lost the daily skirmishes.

Now, this went on for thirty-seven years
of believing himself an appealing little boy —
until he learned how men respond to muted cries.

And then this person I have been acquainted with
who had before not seemed to understand
saw all the nothing he possessed to lose.

Downing the drink he thinking went to bed.
And then I hope he woke and poseless strode
naked into the naked fray

and saw the thronged combatants turn and smile.

LETTER TO MY EX-THERAPIST

Dear David,
                I hope you are happy: I'm emotional.
Blushing, smiling, weeping, I roll through the days
like a peeled tomato: whole and red and raw;
squeeze me, I burst. Feelingly I respond
to happenings I cause. Like an eyeball
beneath a contact lens in a San Francisco wind,
I am forever irritated. Horny, I cannot resolve
do I want sex or to write a poem, or both? I drink
little coffee now that I get high on mornings.
Feel like running, see rainbows.
Haven't the foggiest what I am doing
but read myself like a best-seller, unwilling
to put down my life or stop turning the pages.
Each season so far smells like Spring this year.

So this is it, to be alive!
                        Constantly like Whitman now,
"I discover myself on the verge of a usual mistake," —
wanting, needing, and telling the human so! I wonder

where it will end: in the suburbs with charge accounts?
Me wearing a tie? Am I to discover
contentment and be content with that? Seems so.
                                                  Only,
it *was* easier walking past the lighted windows, greeting
the occasional cat
all those years. . .

Why, this is the sort of life
I would wish on my best friend,
not me. Well, David,
we'll see.

TWO

Among the very few
(we would never try it, say,
with Hawthorne and Melville)
we first-name you:
Emily, Walt.

As though
you were brother and sister.

Or neighbors
in some imaginary town between Amherst and Camden, —
    Emily sending quince jelly, once;
    Walt unsuccessfully proposing
        an evening at the opera.

Ignorant of the other's cottaged life,
    Emily you studied the bobolink in his pear tree,
    Walt you loved the lilac budding near her barn.

But you two never chatted over the pickets,
being not forward in that way
especially when not encouraged,
unaware how
long after proper citizens fell asleep
the other also sat
before a kitchen or bedroom window
looking out.

Solitaries, you continued in the morning
(going forth in search of necessities,
a basket of for-sale *Leaves of Grass* on your arm;
or baking pumpkin bread, your dimity sleeve rolled up,
flour freckling your dark wrist)
Mr. Whitman, Miss Dickinson, —

and at night wrote by steadily flickering candle-flames.

GOING HOME

Small butterflies the color and texture of cigarette-paper
hither and thither zipping at the outdoor swimming pool
over close-cut grass from sun to shade
around the orange or aqua or white plastic recliners
signify nothing

and the wheelbarrow brimming with
bright yellow popcorn-like blossoms
raked from where they fell
onto the major's yard
is meaningless

(although I am happy to have seen them both), —
but the thought of you I cannot embrace for four days yet
is as exciting, steadying, and hope-bestowing

as any stand of the pale-blue wheels of the chickory
cooly blazing along an American roadside,

comrade Orion's presence above any country,

of the existence, serviceably covered
with what looks like gift-wrap
and protected by plastic sheeting, of *Bolts of Melody, New Poems
of Emily Dickinson* in this one-room air-conditioned
in the Philippines.

KERRIC HARVEY

Kerric Harvey is one of the new writers I'm proud to be able to introduce to readers of A True Likeness. She read about the Sea Horse Press in an interview I gave for the Washington D.C. Blade. She had moved there from Montreal where many of her poems were written, and where many of them are set. She has been giving readings of her work in various audiences with excellent response. I'm happy she did contact me and send me her work.

I find these poems beautifully crafted and realized with intensity, humor and shades of delicacy that I can only call in the best sense of the word feminine. The long poem about prom night, is something I only realized after I had read it that I always wanted to know from a woman's point of view. Kerric Harvey's other poems are love letters written with Japanese brush strokes of strong imagery and restrained passion.

ST VALENTINE'S DAY

Come with me to lie on the beach that we make with our own white
   bellies.
Your eyes will be moonstones
and I will be silver against you.
Long and shiny in the dark.
Island nights
are the best for loving.
You smell of silver and   your burn too brightly.

I will remember this   brightness
when dawns are slow   and grey
   in the city.

BIRDS ARE THE BEST THINGS

I always saw the geese
winging shadows of russet gold on a river that ran warm
in the fall.
Black-tipped, flaming in the sunset.
And I have been remembering how they felt
brushing their feathers on my closed eyelids.
We told ourselves we were rowing then,
slipping swift silent through six o'clock magic.
The white boat the soul of a ghost, the legend of winning.
It was our cradle and our mother
as we stroked her in ever-stronger pulls, silent oh so silent

the day we rowed in silence.
And all of us rooted there in that smooth-moving rocket
that arrow of our arms
that full stretch of our legs, our painfully cavernous hearts,
all of us
knew that we could not fool ourselves again:
we may wear the dust of the land that births us,
but full as much as the crimson-winged sun
are we the children of the geese.
kneeling in the dusk.
I smell fertility.
No one has been here before
who has not been born of my salt-rimmed tears.
I am the Universe
and spring came early the year
I touched the razor to my own throat.

AT THE START

I am the Universe.
I have a sword in my right hand and
blue fire streaming from my eyes and
an itch between my legs.
There is water in my bowels.

I turned once to catch a shadow
and faced a mirror in a cave.
Time held its breath:
I could see it quivering in the corner of my own mad whirling eye
blink blink stare
into the star-studded dark.

I am the Universe
and I turn slowly on the dreams of my memory.
There is a taste of salt on the back of my tongue
and blood on my fingertips.
There are no more virgins.
There is only the waiting
to start. To pray.

VIRGINIA BEACH BLUES

Rain in the summertime
and the heavyset breathing of God crossing his legs
at the stairs of the 55th Street Beach.

I hear the echo of that old July like a bad Bruce Springsteen song.
Oh lover I remember you.
You loom over my brain like sullen dough
refusing to rise.
Summer you are too fertile for even the fecund poet.
You smell in my nostrils like wet earth,
like smoking smouldering lightening,
hanging over the limp wet sand an unspoken profanity.
You stink of unfinished lovemaking.

Alone and unfinished in the sand
I think and I wonder
if chastity
is the last voice in the crowd.

THE PASSION FLOWER
Ottawa, October the 7th, 1978

Today we took the morning bus back
back into envelopes and letters and photo albums,
and shyly you showed me your
child-life,
grown small and dense, as shy child-lives do.

I saw the mother's window,
where she loved you and watched you when you did not know or care.
I felt the wind kiss your playground hair.
Ghosts of other October mornings and I learned to love more fiercely
the lines in your young face.

Down by the rust-rimmed northern river
we walked in fallen leaves and our feet left prints
on the wet palms of each other's pasts.
This gold and reddening autumn
the river runs full and strong
and I wrap my cordouroy coat more tightly around my thoughts.

We walk on in tweed and silence,
and the hours grow gently on our twi-lit shoulders.
And I do not know how to tell this child now so grown
that the breath of my life will warm her rivers past and future.
So lonely is
a loving red red red red rose.

PROM NIGHT WAS A COMEDY IN ONE LEGAL ACT BUT FOUR NASTY SCENES.

So it's started. Play-acting in face powder and perfume.

"I have a hard time putting things into words"
he always said, so "dance with me."
Forget the glint of the mirror ball
the glint in the teeth of a California girl smile
the glint of eyes watching in the adolescent dark.
All you have to do, he said, is smile.

Two o'clock in the morning and we're moving in the
dark closeness of after-dinner after-dance.
Another basement bash. Mashing lips in the lawn furniture
Who lives here anyway?
Just-friends and not-quite-lovers and
everything is triplicate. He and she and she for me,
and a night, another night to remember.

Moving windows flash by the car, and the traffic light stares
an accusing red. It's come to this.
The hardest part of it, my sister said,
is when he turns off the radio
and there is only you and him and the car
and the late night expectations.

Approach the door.
Suspended on the steps
whirl in the moment of spinning indecision.
This is what you remember when you think back
lying thin and cool in a tent:
The glittering night and the polyester dress
pressing hotly against your thighs.

The glistening of your face:
They are not right when they say you'll grow out of it.

Click. Blink the porch lights in forgiveness, and
in apology.

Drinking milk in the kitchen.
The sticky wilted stockings
and the cold leftovers.
I wonder what life was like at home tonight?
All lights are out
and there is the whisper of the enveloping night
and there is the peek of morning around the corner
and there is the voice of the clock
tick ticking
another one down.

So
next day early cold morning.
The long line of the road
and the secret thoughts flittering.
The morning-after blues.
The remembered beat of the blood
in unnamed places:
Hands on the wheel
and whoever was it that told me
the first time is always the worst?

BLIND MAN'S BLUFF

The record is thin there
where you've played it a hundred times over
(it's over)
brittle fragile breakable, and frail:
if it's time to love then it's record time and it's time to turn it
over.

This music is
not man's pretty petty melodies and whistles,
but the classical sound of some one's fingernails scraping the wrong side
of the grave.

You still will not sing.
Well, I'd rather have a rockingchair,
and the warmth of my feet propped on the quilt of your bed.
I told you
I will be the needle
and ring from you the sounds between quiet people.
Sit with me and share a room of yellow Stepember light.

We will be very very still.

The record spins down and around and
the end of it
comes again.
The awful click at the end of the song is the loudest click there is:
In the heavy finality of the sudden silence
you begin softly to rain.

CHRISTMAS ISSUE POETRY

Snow dancing down,
a Montreal chuckle in the December lamplight.
The cold draws a heat to your cheeks,
and quickens my steps going home.

I would bring Christmas home to you,
piled high in my arms, and giftwrapped like a loving lie.
I would knock on your door, and stand in the dark,
waiting for our breath to meet under winter's silent sky.
I would draw you out of your candlelit cuddy
and roll you around in the star sprinkled snow banks,
breathing into your veins the magic you have woven
in between the words of my unspoken self.
But, snow dancing down;
a December memory in the Montreal lamplight.
Windsor Station smells cold in the dark —
we stamp our feet.
Only your eyelashes tremble.
    You are samller,
             smaller
                      smaller still
                                and then you are
                                          away.

When you open your door, come Christmas Eve,
there is a brush of my heart
in every gentle drift of
snow dancing down.

TODAY

Today
time stretches out
whitely before me
pulling myself ahead of me.
The memory is now.

You are strong and translucent
   standing thrown against the winter glass
   of cold Canadian sunlight.
   Your head is the rich black silk
   of my heart.
Watch the squirrels
nestling their nutty treasures against the coming of the snow.
They chatter through the silent.

Today
I learned the treasure-thing
of quiet.

DAN DIAMOND

Dan Diamond's poetry was first shown to me by Ian Young, whose protege he was. Later, I read some excellent new poems by Diamond, in a chapbook called Gay Bards, X-Press, 1979, one of which, "Sportsman" about the relationship between a gay and straight brother, I use in my own lectures on gay poetry. Nevertheless, I was hardly prepared for the eleven poem sequence "True Gesture," Dan submitted for this anthology, which represents a real step forward in Diamond's work, and for gay poetry.

Diamond dedicates the sequence to Isadora Duncan, the great founder of modern dance and "spiritual directress of the twentieth century." Duncan appears in each one of the poems—as guide, role model, artistic conscience, romantic counsellor, muse, icon of our times, and finally, as victim of philistinism. In short, she becomes if not the subject of each poem, then what Rilke meant by its gesture—i.e., that action which by its very existence allows us to understand life.

Diamond calls the sequence "Dreampoems" and this allows him to assemble a large portion of the modern poet's vocabulary and usage: thematic materials, images and metaphors; he even brings in historical personages such as Scriabin and Singer. The poems are moving, touching, frightening, amusing, sly, confusing —just like dreams or nightmares.

I'm pleased to introduce Diamond's "True Gesture" to readers of this anthology.

TRUE GESTURE
Dreampoems

for Isadora Duncan, spiritual directress of the twentieth century.

CALIFORNIA GIRL

The wind from the ocean and the hot summer air
I ran into kept my hair up on end.
My legs were pumping. My feet sank slightly
into the hard damp sand the waves packed down.

Running felt wonderful, like there was only
me there. But my father and my cousin Don
sat on a beachtowel some way ahead,
while a lone surfer paddled out past the breakers.

From the transistor radio I carried
came a current hit. "I've been all around

this great big world and I've seen all kinds
of girls." I kept running tirelessly.

The surfer latched onto a wave, maneuvering
the surfboard gracefully with her feet.

I was getting pretty close to my father.
He was fondling a softball. My cousin,
who looked just like me except for a crewcut,
was playing with green plastic soldiers,
building bunkers and forts in the sand.
He used real pieces of barbed wire as defenses
and maneuvered toy troops through these barriers.

Impelling myself against the sea breeze
made me ecstatic. I really got into my radio.
"But I just can't wait to get back to the states
back to the cutest girls in the world."

The surfer neared shore as I ran up
to the beachtowel. My father looked annoyed.
"Shit," he said, "is that the way a boy runs?
You look just like a pansy." I couldn't speak.
I just stood there and watched my cousin
twist barbed wire into a pair of bracelets.

Just then the surfer walked up. "Excuse me,"
she said, "my name is Isadora Duncan.
For many years as a dancer I've studied the movement
of this ocean looking for the secrets of gesture.
I have learned beings must make gestures natural
to themselves, not imitate the movements of others."

Isadora grabbed my arm and we ran into the surging waves.
My cousin almost caught us as we cleared the breakers
but we paddled the surfboard faster and pulled ahead.

My radio bounced up off the smooth fiberglass
playing, "I wish they all could be California girls,"
and splashed into the ocean. I turned and saw
my cousin still doggedly pursuing us. I guessed
he would always be.

MEETING FOR COFFEE

In a cafe beyond a nameless courtyard,
hand-lettered manuscripts aflame in the fireplace,
(the illuminated first letters torn away
and used by the waiter for mopping off tables),
Isadora removed her cape and sat in the chair
I had pulled out for her. We exchanged greetings
as I sat down across from her and Isadora said
"now what's the trouble?"

"Oh Isadora," I said, "my living with him
is like an insect trying to live with a snake.
It's like being a rock half covered with molten lava
and half covered with cold seawater."
Isadora was spooning sugar into her coffee. "Our love
is a room which gets so hot we take off all our clothes
and then so cold we put on sweaters and cover ourselves
with blankets, but nothing is warm enough."

Isadora had dropped five teaspoons of sugar
into her steaming cup. "Go on," she said, watching me.
"Our fights are violent, our making up is passionate
and involved. We distract each other from our work.
Things are either wonderful or horrible.
I can't stand this intensity!"

"Well, if what you want is just something sweet,"
said Isadora, "drink this and tell me how you like it."
She slid her cup in front of me, sat back
and adjusted a fold of her toga.

THE DIAMONDS

Glittering in snowflake clusters, a diamond necklace
Isadora held, surprised and amused, a gift
from Mr. Singer. Isadora laughed,
the sound of crystal champagne glasses breaking.
"I never wear jewelry," she said. "It is false adornment.
The human body has all the beauty required."

Embarrassed, I concealed my ring while I continued
to fold Isadora's purple cloak, placing it
alongside her other costumes in a steamer trunk.
It was the alexandrite ring you gave me saying,
"The stone changes colors often, like your eyes."
Isadora sold her diamond necklace and purchased
simple white cotton tunics for the little girls
in her school. Mr. Singer couldn't understand
her disregard for diamonds. They had never failed
to impress his lovers.

Where are you now?
I admire my ring daily, failing
to live up to Isadora's standards.
She can't even brow-beat me into removing it.
Where are you now?
Yesterday I was mugged by a man in the hallway
of my apartment building. He forcibly removed the ring
from my finger. Then, seeing my expression,
(loss of the ring a final loss of you)
he said, "keep it."
Where are you now?

THE ABDUCTION FROM THE PARTHENON

I watched Isadora meditate in the moonlight.
She stood near one huge pillar, hands folded
Across her breasts. "I will find a dance worthy
of the Parthenon," she had said.

Suddenly a black cloth was thrown over my head.
Blinded, I tried to struggle, but my arms
were held firmly in place. I felt myself lifted
and carried. I tried to call out, but a large hand
landed over my mouth.

I came to in a very dark room. I reached out
and felt the damp rough cement walls
of what seemed to be an unfinished basement.
The only illumination was an old electric heater
tucked into an unused fireplace.

An emaciated derelict appeared from somewhere.
"I'm the super of this building," he said.

"Building?"

"Well, it's not an ordinary building." He smiled.
His eaten and drooping face surrounded perfect teeth.
"You might say this room is the underworld
of the underworld." He laughed, choked, hiccoughed.

"I'm Hades," he said, "I brought you here to rape you."
He came slowly at me. "Haven't you got the story
a little mixed up?" I asked. "What about Persephone?"

"I was just giving into family pressure," he said,
approaching until he stood in front of me. I
remained paralyzed where I sat on a plaid sofabed.
Scabrous hands reached out for me, the red glow
of the heater grill reflected in his well-buffed nails.

Suddenly I was jerked upward, attached to a rope
someone was reeling in. When vision cleared,
I saw Isadora leaning slightly forward,
arms arched in silent exhaltation,
as classic as the pillar she stood near.

"I've found the dance," she cried, "a dance worthy
of the Parthenon."

"It has certainly uplifted my spirit," I said,
awed and breathless.

AT SCRIABIN'S DISCO

I'd gone to great lengths to prevent it,
but somehow Isadora found out I was working
as a go-go boy in Scriabin's Disco.

Improvising an updated Watusi, I looked up
and there she was. "You can't do this," she said,
pulling me down from my spot-lit cubicle.
"The rent has to be paid soon," I replied.

Impeccable in a grey silk Armani suit, Scriabin
emerged from the manager's office. A bushy mustache
almost completely hid a bandaid on his lower lip.
"Isadora, what an unexpected pleasure," he said,
"I see you've caught the light show."

"Hello Alexander," replied Isador," so this
is where your dreams have led you."

"I knew you wouldn't approve," said Scriabin.
An argument ensued. I heard Isadora use phrases such as
"jazzy music," "dancing from the hips," and "sell-out."
They were interrupted by a phone which began to ring
in Scriabin's office.

"Just remember, Isadora, we were both born
before our time. I wanted a little recognition now.
Anyway, this is my last week. I'm going bankrupt.
There won't be any money in this kind of thing
for another seventy years."

He went into his office and after one backward look,
during which he mumbled "before our time"
over and over again, closed the door on us.

"Bankrupt," I said, "now I have to find another new job."
"No you don't," said Isadora, "I got you a position
helping out at Frau Wagner's tupperware party."

THE MONKEY-PEOPLE

It was your dream!
You were the one always having dreams
about monkey-people, not me.

Wearing velvets and brocades like guests
at a rennaissance feast, joyful crowds of monkey-people
danced along the winding roads of Central Park.

One of them gave me a chimpanzee smile
and scampered over on all fours with a shiny apple
and a bright banana. They were singing in a language
sounding like balloons struck with bicycle spokes.

But this was surely your dream!
I never dreamt about monkey-people!

A monkey-person held the leash of a Pekinese.
A monkey-family picnicked. Two monkey-lovers
leaned forward and French-kissed.
Monkey-kids threw a frisbee.

But this was your dream!
No. No, it wasn't, it was my dream after all,
for there is Isadora dancing on the Bethesda Fountain
in a scarf the light green of tarnished bronze.

I ran toward her, calling her name and she turned.
Tears lined her face like crystals rainbowing the sunlight.
"They won't let me stop dancing," she cried.
"They're demanding I teach them how, but they can't.
Just look!" The monkey-people hopped around
like cartoon gorillas.

I turned and you were beside me.
Was this your dream or mine?
Were we having the same dream?

"Isadora," we shouted, "come down, stop dancing!
Rest! No one can ever duplicate you!" Suddenly
the monkey-people had us surrounded, no longer friends.
They chattered menacingly and bared long sharp teeth.

From your horrified expression I knew you
thought the same thing I did. Neither your dream
nor mine, this dream wasn't Isadora's either.
It wasn't a dream at all.

The monkey-people held us back, snickering as they
tortured Isadora. They bound her to a styrofoam
Doric column and surrounded her with forty-nine
sewing machines pumping at full speed.

We both covered our ears. So did the monkey-people.
Isadora tried covering hers, but coils of rope
held her arms at the wrists.

BERATED AT THE BEACH

"Isadora and I were walking on a cement pathway.
It zigzagged through sand dunes. Wild reeds
and marshy plants grew in the cracks.

We rounded a curve and were confronted
by a puddle of thick red liquid. It stretched
to the right and left as far as we could see,
but was only about five feet across.

We tiptoed over the warm sticky cement,
holding our beachtowels and picnic baskets
up out of the vermilion pool.

We heard an angry cry from behind. We turned
and saw a big grey truck. Two men wearing
'Sanitation department' overalls stood
beside it.

One of the men was you.

The other kept on yelling at us in Russian
as he tossed a bottle of 'Stolichnaya'
into the back of the truck. He kept playing
with a length of rope around his neck.

Then you both picked up long black hoses.
Strong shots of water diluted the clotting red
around our feet.

You pointed at us and shouted,
"can't you see you're walking on blood?
What's the matter with you? Don't you know
it's unhealthy to walk on blood?"

SLEEPING WITH YOU

Exhausted when I returned from Macy's,
"I'm going to lie down for awhile," I told you.

"Isadora has called for you several times,"
you said a bit derisively.

"If she phones again, you can wake me up."
I went in and stretched out stiffly on my bed.
Soon I was falling asleep.

Dimly, I heard the doorbell. You answered it.
The Segal lock clicked as you opened the door.
I heard you say, "oh, he's right in there.
Just go ahead in, I think he's asleep by now."

I opened my eyes as a stranger entered the room.
"Hello," he said. "I'm sorry, I don't remember
where I met you," I replied.

The stranger stood at my bedside. "I don't know
who you are," I said. Lunging, he grabbed me
around the neck and squeezed hard.

I tried to struggle, to throw him off,
but he was too strong. Nothing was near enough
for me to kick so you'd hear the noise.
The bedside phone rang.

I concentrated, drawing on all the energy left me.
If I could just reach the phone. . . .

I screamed and woke up. I was next to you
in your bed. The phone was ringing.

"What's wrong," you asked. "Did you have a nightmare?"
I was silent as I answered the phone. It was Isadora.
I started to tell her about my dream, but she
interrupted me.

"I just did a tarot reading for you," she said.
"Beware of weak lovers who expose you to the aggression
of unknown enemies."

KARMIC SYMBIOSIS

Isadora's spirit rented a motorcar
and drove from place to place for decades.
Eventually it was reborn in the form
of a chestnut tree. Yearly it bloomed,
developed round brown fruit
encased in prickly green skin,
shed its leaves.

My spirit followed winter, figure skating
wherever it found a frozen waterway.
It was reborn a poison oak, a vine
growing out from around Isadora's roots,
finding footholds in her rough bark.

A nearby glacier retreated, leaving a lake
from which Isadora and I drew water
through long roots.

Smokestacks bearing 'Old Glory' emerged
from the lake. German Shepherds in scuba gear
swam out of the water and urinated on us.
Children in JFK teeshirts docked pontoon boats
and sprayed us with defoliants. An old honored
tortoise crawled from the lake and published
bad reviews. Two human-headed bats invaded
Isadora's branches. The male sank saffron fangs
into the female's throat and slurped. They
strapped on 'souvenir of Miami Beach' waterskis
and a speedboat towed them away.

Isadora and I tried to ignore all this.
We were concentrating on growth, on expanding
and adding to our intricate root system.
Daily, our need for water grew.

Maliciously, the lake planned more assaults,
but already it was drying up.

THE DIFFERENCE BETWEEN PRETTY AND BEAUTIFUL IS TOO GREAT

The difference between pretty and beautiful
is too great," said Isadora, as she dropped
one more peony-red scarf over a lampshade,
adding, "I can't bear white light."
I couldn't figure out what she meant.

I brought you in to meet her, holding your hand,
and she said, "the difference between pretty
and beautiful is too great." Did she mean
we weren't an attractive couple? Did she mean it
for me, or for you? Was she being purposely vague?
Was she referring to us at all? Or even
to the white light?

I opened my mouth to ask, just as she moved away
down a long silk-papered hall, hung with huge
gilt-edged portraits of someone important's ancestors.
She dropped scarf after scarf on little lamps
along the wall. She reached the end, turned,
and yelled, "the difference between pretty
and beautiful is too great!"

I didn't know what she meant, but I think you did.
I haven't seen you since.

DIAGNOSIS

I dreamed I died. First I was very ill
with fatty lumps all over my body
which looked like port wine cheddar cheese
and then I died. My family called an ambulance.
I was taken to a mortuary.

Before they could embalm me, they said,
they would have to get all the air
out of my body. They laid me down on the stage
of a theatre. All my relatives attended,
my mother and sister wearing dark cocktail hats
with small veils and jaunty feathers.

Two attendants in white side-buttoned shirts
twisted my arms and legs all around
and sat on my chest in a dance of squeezing.
The spectators applauded the steps appreciatively.

Isadora sat in the back row arguing with an usher
who claimed she was improperly dressed
(in what he termed her 'nightgown')
for an air eliminating ceremony.

The two attendants lifted me and placed me
in a coffin. They came at me with needled hoses.

But all the pummeling had brought on
one of my asthma attacks. My breath rasped
in the quiet theatre.

Isadora rushed onto the stage and said,
"can't you see he's having an asthma attack.
You must reconsider the burial of this person."

After minutes of haranging, Isadora convinced
the coroner I was still alive.

My relatives quietly filed out of velour seats.
I heard my Aunt Louise saying, "that Duncan woman
is a perfect harpy."

RUDY KIKEL

Contemporary poets have openly and easily appropriated the forms and structures of Japanese Haiku, Chinese lyrics, ancient Greek odes and epodes, symbolist French and modern European poetry, and have enriched their work by doing so. Less frequently encountered is the sonnet sequence, developed in fourteenth century Italy and culminating in the great Elizabethan sonnet series of Spenser, Sidney and Shakespeare. In our century only a few poets have done such series, among them notably, Auden, Roethke and Robert Lowell.

Both Auden and Lowell are influences on "Local Visions" Rudy Kikel's sonnet sequence party published here. Lowell for the form—fourteen unrhymed lines—Auden for the tone: urbane, anxious, sometimes objective and amused, always involved. "Local Visions" is a very contemporary gay male poem about how a relationship begins, continues, begins to unravel and ends. Its figures are those of contemporary gay life: poppers, bars, brunches, back rooms, the bushes. Its metaphors are more varied: from the entrapment imagery of "Theme and Violation," to the healing of "Combat Veterans," and the temporary impotence of "Intrusive Withdrawal," which Kikel wittily personifies as a "she." Wit, of the most modern kind in poetry, is the key to appreciating Kikel's very real emotions held within his elegantly made fabrication.

Rudy Kikel's poetry has appeared in American Review, Fag Rag, Ploughshares, Small Moon, Christopher Street, The Boston Review of Arts. *Kikel lives in Boston, not far from the scene of Lowell's autobiographical poem, "91 Revere Street."*

From LOCAL VISIONS

Our Inhaler

At first I was suspicious, when in the heat
of our getting into each other
you would call for "Amy." I wondered
who it was you wanted, me or her.
But when you kept coming back for both
of us, I realized that losing you
to her was also a way of keeping you
for myself. And so I learned to doll her up,
to keep her butt end moist and ready
for us both under her long silver gown.
Now at the bedside she sits tight,
waiting for her critical enlistment,
the bright lady, who keeps together men
who much prefer to sleep with other men.

GIVING WAY

After our busy day, I post you,
as Rilke says, at the gate of my solitude.
You call, request another date — a movie,
the coffeehouse, anything not to be
alone — and then, of course, again the bed.
Your gate, it seems, is swinging wide.
When I beg off, you remind me of
the rival of mine you'd love to see
assume my performing self. Are you
obliging me, punishing me, or both?
I approve, encourage you to make
the call. Is that my punishment of you?
I don't know. Only, this was not
what Rilke meant by guarding solitudes.

SWIMMING LESSONS

My friend the Cambridge poet and his lover,
who insist on making regular visits
to each other, believe in wading through
the seaweed they brush up against in their
relationship. At present, that is shoaled,
and for days my worried friend has been
reworking the revision of a line
in his adaptation of a poem
by Villon. I am pouring off sonnets
before breakfast, after lunch, from buckets-
ful of words you, whom I sometimes see
and cannot coax into conversation,
are sending me from Charlestown, where
you swim easily in someone else's arms.

OUR SHILL

You reared her to immanence in the minds
of her first small coterie, your over-
hearing colleagues: "Hello Sue, this is Mike,
I'm calling from work." But it was through me,
after I hadn't heard from you in weeks,

that she broke into Boston's underground
press, where she broadcast her pathetic
appeal: ". . . I miss you, please call. Sue."
She's gone now. Telling your roomates
all about us sent her up in smoke.
Or does she play a part in our present
history, too, though changed, our legendary
Phoenix lady, who scorning sleight of hand
now bids us lay our cards on the table?

LOCAL VISIONS

Dallying all last year with pretty
girls and the idea of "going straight," I didn't
consider ours a serious affair, until
by toddling off to bed with a close friend
of mine and his friend, you opened my eyes
to violent greens and reds. I hear less,
too, this year, about your Floridian
dream of gold coast lobster fishery.
I guess we're holding on, and giving one
definition to Auden's definition of love
(staring not in each other's eyes but in the same
direction) by taking turns in the window
bent-wood rocker and scanning pant-
legs passing on Charles Street, Boston, Mass.

THEME AND VIOLATIONS

Noticing you beautifully breaking the law
by sitting cross-ankled on the esplanade
wall, I exposed myself indecently
in public response to nature's purest call.
Lawlesly, I loitered on the bridge
you crossed over headed for the bushes,
where I lewdly and lasciviously laid
both hands on your most private parts.
We arrested our attentions immediately,
each sentencing the other heavily to
from one night to unnumbered years of lively
love-making in his own enclosing arms,
with the penalty added of an early parole
in the case, only, of too much control.

JAMMING

The snow has got your car stuck in it
and us both in a new experience. Three
evenings running, you return from work
to my arms and my apartment. There is an evening
we do not make love, a morning we do;
there are periodical readings in separate rooms;
there is a listless evening with the TV on.
Delighted, we admit we feel like married men.
Every few minutes at breakfast, you take up
the spider plant stripling from its watery nest
to see how its roots are growing strong.
I have been paging through Kate Chopin
and wonder if having once "awakened" to
domestic notions, we always waken from them.

COMBAT VETERANS

You've been briefly away; I had my wen
removed yesterday. Solicitous ex-Navy medic,
you volunteer bandages, sponges, alcohol baths,
and I repeat what it is so hard for me
to know I really mean: "I missed you."
You respond: "I missed you, too."
Again, my scepticism gets the better of me:
"You're saying that because I just did."
Then you remind me that about feelings
you don't say what you aren't sure you feel.
Cynical about America after your Viet Nam stint,
you still believe unbelievably in love.
Boston based but battle scarred, I seem
to need all your basic healing training.

INTRUSIVE WITHDRAWAL

Suddenly there she was between us on the bed,
the one third party and broken-off
relation I would least like to see share
in our menage. Tight-lipped and glaring,
she waits for me to do the introducing,

own up to an old association,
and with hanging head advise you not to be
surprised by her occasional visitations.
Her message conveyed, you and I lock
eyes in mutual frustration, and wonder without
provoking her into a prolonged stay
how delicately to hint to my spinster lady
Impotence that she slip out this once
as unobtrusively as she just slipped in.

DIPPING IN

Fearful all week, I bring us armored
with five close friends to the new bar.
It's worse than I had imagined: a labyrinthine
sea of writhing bodies and melting glances.
Returned from tending to a sinking stomach,
I find my shield dissolved and you in flowing
discourse with an old beau. There is no
alternative except immersion: vodka gimlets
and fluid eye-and-foot movements of our own,
broken by attempts focused on finding our friends.
Next morning, we agree we had a good time
and should go again. I venture a suggestion,
"Maybe we should go alone," and am much relieved
when you think I mean without friends.

SOLITARY STEPPING

You were going "out." Out, I find out
this morning, means tripping into the bars
without me. Recounting your adventures of the night
before, your phone voice is rife with dark
insinuations about seductive friends
who in my absence made their erotic intentions
known to you, I brought this situation
on myself, I presume, recently having treated you
to a private showing of what constituted
perhaps the last piece of secret knowledge
I had closeted off from you, the physique slides
from my photographic *belle époque*. Adam
playing devil's advocate to your Eve, am I paying
the price of having you fully know me?

CAPTIVATING RISK

You seem disturbed that first exposure to it
should have proved her flattery attractive.
Having had my fling with her and for some time
been expecting this fascination of yours,
I am less surprised. How should she not delight
with all those boozy hydra heads equipped
with glassy eyes that when one is young and cute
like you swivel and mirror every move.
Of course, responding to her, you take a chance
on her finding you a lively addition to
a growing body, an admirable new piece
of head cut from another group of adventurers,
and once our monster lady bar life
has appended you, any severance is painful.

JIGGS AND MAGGIE

I swallowed your Saturday night story
about staying in Cambridge to nurse a cold.
By accident, we come across you brazenly
Sunday-breakfasting on Beacon Hill.
I know your explanations are not meant
to be believed, but nothing I say seems
to involve our friend in teasing laughter
at your louche behavior. Is he jealous of us,
or have I failed to strike the right note
of unromantic mimicry? Why have my appeals
to appreciate your new defections always
embarrassed friends, members after all
of the family we have chosen one way
or another not to exclude from our affair?

MY AUTONOMY

My repeated efforts to bury this brain
child of mine, preventing communication
even of her suffocation anxiety, her dream
of destruction, made her turn to plotting.
Blithely I went on opening everything up —

coffers, closets, couches — in recognition
of your undisputed needs. Finally,
she had had enough of fuming, and not
without some dark complicity from you, who
naturally must have missed the increase
of tension she supplied to our menage,
set her plans in motion, managing to cut
through the penetration power line
of the humpbacked beast who hogged our bed.

PAT KURAS

These poems appeared in Sea Horse Press's P.O. Box, and as with all unsolicited mss, I opened it up and flipped through at random and began to read just anywhere. I ended up reading all of the poems and re-read them again before I left the post office. I recall thinking how similar this lesbian woman's life and thoughts and problems were to mine.

These poems are about love; in the old sense of the word "about," i.e. on or around, before, after, in reflection, and in resentment. In "Escapist," Kuras writes — "Like a Monet landscape you/ blur before my eyes," and this sense of how little we know and can know those we love is an underlying theme of Kuras' poetry. Her style is simple, direct, uncomplicated by larger mythologies, events of history, or politics so typical of much contemporary women's poetry. Kuras seems to have cut her work down to the bone of its intention. As though proving step by logical step how her life and attitudes became what they are.

Her biography is as follows:

"Pat M. Kuras was born two minutes after midnight, on Sept. 30, 1954. She attended parochial school, and since high school graduation, has worked in various blue-collar jobs. She has been a contributing writer to Gay Community News *for many years, and more recently, her poetry has appeared in* Mouth of The Dragon.*"*

HYDRA

We meet in smoke-filled bars and
compare notes on our respective ex-lovers.
Yours wanted you to be something you were not,
while mine didn't want me at all.
What is wrong with us?
We rant and rave on how our ex-lovers were,
yes, such assholes,
but we continue to love them just the same.
Someday the anger may subside,
but for now, it is a great
rollicking monster that
rears its ugly head
always too often and,
like a hydra, decapitating
it would only encourage
more hurting heads to spring in its place.
We meet in smoke-filled bars to
compare notes on our ex-lovers;
slowly, we are groping along,
learning to love again.

CRUSH
This poem is dedicated to all my
ex- and would-be lovers.

I have made love to fat lesbians before.
I have mooned over straight, blue-eyed, blonde-haired women.
I have tagged behind politically-correct dykes who
        have found my romantic advances to be
        oppressive and grossly incorrect.
I've had crushes on brown-eyed Jewish girls.
I have chased upwardly-mobile lesbians who
        wore doubleknits and always combed their hair.
I have been trampled by women who demand control and enjoy
        crushing those who have crushes on them.
If my heart had teeth, I'd say those teeth have been kicked in
        many times; but
despite the beatings my heart has taken,
        it always goes back.

LOVE-MAKING AS A HOLY WOMAN/LIFE-SAVING ART

I   I bleed sadness in your kitchen; you mop up the flow.
    Crippled and shaken by my emotions and head, I fill your arms;
    a crumbling creature, I feel capable of doing,
    wanting, needing only one thing right: to love.
    You respond easily.

II The bed is narrow enough to insure closeness.
    We tumble, roll, stroke, suck.
    I get my licks in.
    We join hands to one another's
    respective cunts   rubbing, shaking,
    probing, sweet suction squeaking;
    coming doesn't matter, getting there
    is more fun.

III We dissolve in tickles and smiles,
    little girl/dyke giggles,
    warm, soft, holding.
    Did I remember to say thank you?
    My mother would be so proud.

HOMECOMING

You return on a dusk flight, prior to a night that
promises to be heavy w/ stars. Bat-like,
I'm blinded by the glare of airport fluorescence;
I stay near the walls, familiar w/ their
cool aloofness.
                        I am a flower of differing
                        germination & geography; like
                        willows that dip to kiss the
                        ground, I falter in the background.
I look for proper gates & allow a
corridor to swallow me. People tote
Samsonites & buzz around me w/ the
urgency of fast flight. They swell
at safety points. I pass thru the
scanning arch — unblipped.
I walk to the appropriate gate &
sit in an orange plastic chair. I watch
silver planes plop perfectly to ground & slide along
runways. It does not matter to me that it will take
a machine in the form of a cock w/ wings to return
you to me. The process is
so long. A plane rolls
towards me. (Its
windows are like many
eyes.) As I wait, I
wonder from which eye
you watch me.

THIS POEM IS HOT

lately when i masturbate i
dream of you   and when i

have pleased myself   i   bring
my hand close to

my face and   imagine
that waft of cunt   is

from you   you are
here with me   the odor transcends

i pretend i am
not alone   and i have

pleased you
rather than myself

ESCAPIST

Like a Monet landscape you
blur before my eyes.
Whether it be a
faulty prescription, tears or
too much vodka, you
fade from my view, make
yourself scarce, withdraw
into your shroud of
solitude, evading
my touch.

ANTAEUS

all day long it is impossible
not to notice you

fists jammed in pockets you
saunter around like one of

the neighborhood toughs from my
childhood   in your smugness i know you

will not let me touch you
you sap strength by rooting yourself in

my adoration for you
ardent

fertilizing agent i
remain your life's source

BINK NOLL

Below is a biographical data sheet for Bink Noll. None of it, I think, is adequate preparation for the published long poem that also follows: "The Signification of the Phallus," one of the most sophisticated and original longer poems in gay literature, and a clear sign of its enormous range.

This poem is contemporary satire at its most multilayered. First, of course, is its trick of parodying Stevens' "Thirteen Ways of Looking at a Blackbird." Next is its epigrammatic wit and pointed observation on a great deal of human nature and especially attitudes toward sex. The poet goes on to ring a great many bells in Penisology: as food, as a source of humor, as object of questionable value, as wearing apparel, as a source of a multitude of emotions. Surely we've all wondered about the great destroyed or still hidden gay poems of the past — this contemporary classic might have been written by a latter day Byron or Pope.

Bink Noll is professor of English at Beloit College where he is also Poet in Residence. His poems have appeared in The Atlantic, The Saturday Review, Poetry, The Yale Review, The Nation, The Chicago Tribune. *A lecturer in poetry, during 1967-68, he served as Resident Fellow in Creative Writing at Princeton University, and was on the editorial board of the* Beloit Poetry Journal.

His first book of poems was The Center of the Circle, *1962 Harcourt, Brace and World; in 1967, Harcourt published his second book,* The Feast. *He recently completed a new book,* The House, *poems unified by their domestic theme. Portions of "Signification of the Phallus," appeared in* The American Literary Review, *Vol. 1, #4.*

"THE SIGNIFICATION OF THE PHALLUS"
(title of the eighth chapter
in *Ecrits*, by Jacques Lacan)

1   ADAM NAMES HIS EQUIPMENT
    the parade: "abalone and Atlantic conger
                   rhinoceros and prehistoric gar
                   pike, wasp, cuckoo, mole
                   the cobra dancing, the puzzling tortoise
                   giant sea worm, Egyptian crocodile.
                   These approximate its nature."

    the hunt: "to stalk, chase, attack, bring down
                   and kill a boar, a ram, a stag
                   and any big cat, any fleet big wild male
                   stands for genital rigidity,
                   more efficacious if done with a club.
                   But best is by hand, limb from limb.
                   I imagine Hercules. I imagine Mr. America."

                   For the fun of it, Adam hangs his hat on it.

2   **PRIMATE URGE A:** to see, inspect, compare
or *Á LA RECHERCHE DE LA PINE*

    Lifelong as hunger.
    Rather, lifelong as meals
    that at the end of the month
    have blurred together like last month's news.

    Still, the search after one's *beau ideal*
    set since early fascination with Daddy's
    and the boy next door's
    and the swimming instructor's.

    Still, the roving on the street,
    at night places, in the office
    bringing it home, inspecting it.
    The heart skips a salacious beat

    and measures it against one's standard.
    The trophy fades. The heart wanders on.
    From every crotch promise glimmers.
    Ignis fatuus. There is no relief.

3   **THE MAN ON THE OPPOSITE SEAT**

    wears no underwear,
    one hot-weather layer over his manly thing.
    Better looking this — easier — than
    iconography of codpiece
    or jockstrap fetish.
    One's head has been turned.

    One layer of loose tissue
    to delineate the landscape,
    to suggest
            ah ! the thickets
            ah ! the pendancies.

    He stretches. His pants tighten.
    His case is by no means ordinary.

In the minutes before he leaves
one's eye stores erogenous truth
in the eye's archives, then saddens
when his bravery of form
has walked away with the possessor.

4   PRIMATE URGE B: to touch, feel, fondle
or THE MIRACLE OF ERECTION

    small, tranquil muzzle
    bunny in its nest
    mere pillow
    doeskin to the touch
on fondling feels
rouzing motions the way Samson did
and breaks the surface of its mindless sleep.

By divine mechanics it responds
to the fondler's hand and grows a handful.

Without its captain's high permission
it grows the bone in its rubbery pod
and stands
and has its heft and springiness admired,
a captain in its own right.

It takes the initiative, issues commands.

5   GOOD ENOUGH TO EAT

Weiswurst instead of the vulgate "hot dog"
Cornichon instead of "pickle"
Quenelle for "dumpling" and
Fig to improve on "banana."

The thing fresh, like trout
caught, filleted
and cooked on the shore where it was caught.

Shrimp on a bed of curly endive.

Lobster tail

Morsel of veal

Morel

Chocolate truffle

A parfait

Raspberries

6   HE CARRIES IT WITHOUT URGENCY

He stands and looks down.
He unveils it as if it were
a surprise — porcelain
          or a gold ingot.
It hoists into full view.

He sees:
        the earliest idea for a lever
        a sign cantilevered, swinging
        a pleasure craft bobbing on the lake
        a zeppelin in the stranger's dream.

He envies it its apparent calm.

7   STUCK ON HIMSELF

A rarity in his own hand, a twin
to the ideal image in his fancy.
And his hand around it a second rarity:
a flute and the player of the flute.
It plays "Pretty little thing
      pretty little thing
      pretty little thing."
Otherwise deaf, he who
waits for the ducks to be still,
then masturbates above the dirty reflection.
Men whisper redundant promises

from the bosky path. For the solipsist
is just as beautiful as he thinks he is.

"Then he just stood there in front of me
and I kept staring at him. The only thing
I could think of was turkey neck and
turkey gizzard and I felt very depressed." (Plath)

8   IN THE ROLE OF SPOUSE

The phallus exhibits staying power,
the way being on hand to dry
one another's dishes proves.
It is the place where lust intersects love,
one instrument to make marriage happy
like the deferential voice
or the conjugal kiss.
It has become a member of the family.

Familiar as
    the doorbell
    the cat on the piano bench
    the interior of the kitchen
    shared opinions
    the smell of their own room
    the heating pad

the comfort of the long haul
that no one outside
can tell the secrets of.

9   THE POISON OF ROMANCE

O boy, the full orchestral setting
for satyriasis, the Heathcliff model,
a rogue elephant come in from the wilds,
all stress and tempest,
obsessed by a loner's view of orgasm.
Stung by that idea, veins
like rivers on a map,
it takes itself with red-faced self-importance

that yowls to have its way,
pillages,
victimizes its true love,
throws a last tantrum
and dies of 19th Century apoplexy.

10   THE QUESTION OF BIG

is a question of sufficiency,
of salience, of scale
that makes the male nude impossible

either in the classic sculptor's
squeamish loops and scrollwork
so his hero shrinks to infancy

or the salami that jumps from
the crazed pornographic mind
and regains sanity
in the gags of burlesque.

But in the order of nature
the Real Thing is big enough
to be made love to —
ready and useful,
handsome because it is both,
and feasible. It fits, for
"the phallus is the privileged signifier
of the mark in which the role
of the logos
is joined with the advent of desire." (Lacan)

Anyway, it desires.
The years do not change
its engorged shape and size.
Nor does age wither its dreams.

11   FUNK

No one would kiss you now, little pig.
Toil-worn. Flaccid. Sticky. You snooze

not in the image of god the father,
strong as Liederkrantz, contaminated.
A fly finds you out, kisses you,
finds you still adorable
as you do yourself, if you'd admit it,
sniffing your own effluvium,
evidence of a recent feast.

12   THE BEAUTY

is that of Plato's abstract chair
where the chair in fact seats somebody,
the same as nose when the nose sniffs
or the apposable thumb when it pinches.

Its beauty is achieved while the thing
gathers up into its own nature
and performs. For three minutes the man
does nothing else than to bear his emblem.

Its beauty is most intense
in the seconds when pleasure is most intense,
when it bursts into bloom, so to speak,
is assuaged, is the simple sum of maleness,
       is the perfect pornograph.

13   ONE DOZEN FURTHER SIMILITUDES

the head	supported on the spinal column
the king	sure about the homage of all his vassals
the battleship	riding on its anchor chain, and anchor
the delphinium	made possible by its woody caudex
the belfry	reaching down into its footings
the machinery	that marks the mineshaft
the fireplug	culminating the mains
the blade	joined usefully to the handle

    the clarinet   centered in the shimmer of notes
    the erotic phrase rooted in the throat

    the smile   stemming from lechery
    the sail   balanced against the singing keel

14 OF PARIAN MARBLE

or bronze
or wood
or wood covered with leather
damaged from wear and tear
long as a colossus' thumb
ithyphallic
but repaired for the occasion
hung with gaudy garlands—
trillium, fleur de lis, anemone—
parching at noonday like the men
who braided them giddily
while they chanted
whatever chants were in style
that millenia
on that continent
wearing whatever garments
or nothing at all,
who've had no more sense
than you would expect
to drink in this rocky heat.
Still, the men are doing right by it.
Their adoration is why they understand
the creature between their legs.
It is holy. It is wild.
They improve their relations with it.

15 WASHING UP

The suds, the heat, the slippery rub
so rose-cheeked Hygeia is served
where lust and aesthetic cravings meet.
Here, soft as pussywillow.

Ah, that conundrum born anew
and born every time you glance.

Wild surmise has it that
the first priest of all was
the best hung caveman.

And today the phallus — rinsed like this,
as chaste as Venus wading
from her annual bath
in the fathering foam —

remains as much the subject now as then
of unbroken theorizing
and object of shameless stares,
the cynosure plump and resting

to all appearances harmless,
itself shameless
and the cause of half man's woe.

16 THE NUN VIEWS IT

from the starting train.
In an abandoned doorway
a man without a name rotates.
Without pretense
    — the blush, the downcast eyes —
she takes it in.
She sees and does not quite know
what she has seen
    a tuber
    a fossil fish
    her notion of rape dazzlingly embodied
    a wondrous caterpillar
    une petite icon . . .

not like the soft examples
she has looked at in museums
but this one
in ambush and naughty,
enough to take your breath away.
The material cause of all our lives.

She's glad she didn't faint.

IAN YOUNG

Ian Young is another one of those writers who are known in a variety of contexts having to do with gay literature. He is the publisher of Toronto's Catalyst Press, which has published such authors as Judith Crewe, Oswell Blakiston, E. A. Lacey and Tom Meyers, among others. He was a contributing writer for Gay Sunshine, and still is with Body Politic, where he writes a column on small press books. He has edited two collections — Crossing Press' Male Muse, a classic gay poetry book, and the upcoming On the Line, of gay male short stories. He recently also edited Little Caesar #13, a volume given over to overlooked and underrated writers of our time. Young has contributed articles on subjects as diverse as Man-Boy Love, S/M, and Japanese Poetry, for many magazines; and is currently updating his ground breaking and invaluable bibliography of gay male literature.

Young appears here as a poet, a role he has assumed from the first. His wide range, his extremely economical style, and his lyrical abilities applied to gay subject matter have made his body of poetry much quoted and anthologized. For readers of his most recent book, Common or Garden Gods, 1976, the selections of new poems included in this anthology will be both familiar and surprising. The firm control, the precision of language and emotion are as present as in that fine collection — the references to the classical Chinese and Greek poets still evoked. But the subjects of several poems are different: or at least perceived differently — with an intensity and ruthlessness absent from the almost Mandarin sentiments of his earlier work. It will be intriguing to see how much further in this vein Young will continue to go, and still retain the clarity and balance that make his work so fine.

THE ONE TIME TOM SAW BILL ON THE STREET

He turned around in the road
he hooked his thumb in his belt
he remembered a tune
he forgot the words
he forgot to blow his nose
he opened his mouth
he remembered he had tight pants on
he tried to think of something witty to say
he felt lucky
he felt silly
he felt hot
he imagined himself a flatterer
a hero
a friend
a companion
a savage

a boot-boy
a slave
He imagined himself grinned at
told to get lost
taken to dinner
ignored
fallen for
lived with
asked the time
fondled in public
carried away
frowned at
grown old with
remembered in a will
spoken to
invited to a movie
given a light
given a talking to
given a good spanking
given a new name
given some blue sand in a mysterious bottle
given a hug
attended to
written about
featured on the front page
featured in the want ads
featured in the marriage announcements
featured in the obituaries
thought prissy
thought lewd
thought boring
compared to somebody's brother
compared to a girl
compared to a blond kid
compared to a baseball player
compared to a pink cloud vanishing behind a building
He touched a pocket
he blushed
he swaggered
he thought of his room
he thought of his name
he thought of his cowboy boots
he thought of introducing himself

he thought of his name again
he got confused
he pursed his lips in a whistle but didn't whistle
he opened his mouth
he unbuckled his jeans
he drifted away
he leaned against a wall
he closed his eyes
he breathed

The moment ended.

A NOSEGAY FOR JAMIE

A nosegay is a collection of blossoms gathered together for
their fragrances. This poetic nosegay was suggested by
"The Poetic Friends Nosegay," an anthology of gay poems
by Quakers edited by Steven Kirkman and David Murphy, who
suggest there the fragrances (meanings) of the different
flowers.
The poems themselves are all inspired by Jamie Perry,
whose bouquet this is.

STRAWBERRY BLOSSOM
(foresight)

I walked past
the magic shop,
stopped,
retraced my steps

then saw you
exploring the same occult shelves
your glance
catching my need for you

We met
by magic

TULIP
(dedication of love)

You said:
"I have
such a craving for you. . ."

I smiled,
about to quip something,
and then:

". . . I mean,
I love you"

ROSE
(love)

And you
open for me

To be
held by this warm
red flower

through daylight and dark

BLUE VIOLET
(faithfulness)

Tonight,
waiting for you,
I sleep lightly

on your side of the bed

HONEYSUCKLE
(bonds of love)

Would you,
I wondered,

ask for those
bonds of love?

You begged:

Strung up by the wrists,
nipples sore,
bottom spanked,
eyes bright,
cock ready to burst.

It's I who am bound,
slave to your need,
to your trust,

found by you

SWEET PEA
(delicate pleasures)

Two months after,
you had the few dollars
to buy me my birthday music

We listen together,
eyes gazing into each other, no need
to look away

Your small hand
touches the grey in my beard

That and those flowers,
what other gift could there be?

FIRST SNOW

Where the owl's voice calls
or a few half-wild geese
the lake keeps
sound over water

a night full of snow
the first snow
fills the air

It's not enough to hear your
voice now
in this swirling whiteness I
can't see the night I'm in

It
calls again   clear now
to who?   to who?
as I turn home

Snow blows from drifts
the first snow
filling your name

IN DARK SPRING RAIN

In dark spring rain
or a chilly shore
I found a shell
from the ocean floor

I held it
still all about
it was your distant voice
I heard call out

In summer sun
in the empty air
there was no-one, no-one
yet I saw you there

running, running
toward me again
on a chilly shore
in fine spring rain

The fallen leaves
piled red by the hedge

the clothes you dropped
by our window ledge

The empty hall
the cup by the stair
in the slanting sun
and empty air

A ticking fire
and skittering mice
in the roof for warmth
in a world of ice

Was it your footsteps
coming near
through halls of deepening snow
at the end of the year

Wherever I watch
or listen or dream
your absence troubles
things as they seem

A FALLEN ANGEL ANSWERING TO THE NAME OF JOE

sprawled on a couch
such long legs

can it be true?

(dropped
from a great height
into my dream)

STRAW MAN'S BLUES
for Jonathan Williams on his 50th birthday

At 17,
    going to se
        Sleepy John Estes

at the Half Beat
(or was it the Blue Note?)

      They
carried him in like
   a straw man &
flopped him on a kitchen
      chair, he
   used a pencil for a
      capo,
snoozed
   slumped over
till someone
     poked a rib &

    (as though a gust
skedaddled through a skeleton
      making the bones
  dance) he

    dandled the music
on both knees,
   both eyebrows, all three
      elbows, &
made us all

    remember.

DRACULA DIES A THOUSAND DEATHS
(from the words of Christopher Lee)

"Being struck by lightning was the least of my discomforts"

Dying as Dracula
was worse than having a tooth out—

bullets, daggers, paperknives, stakes,
darts and lances were imbedded in me.

Poison, heart failure and old age
attacked me from within.

I was drowned,
asphyxiated, incinerated.

I was struck by lightning.
I became dust — red, green, or sooty.

The worst was the time they discovered that vampires
cannot abide hawthornes.
I crashed through a snarl of hawthorne bushes
with a crown of thorns on my head.

I tore through a tangle of spikes two inches long,
shedding blood like a lawn sprinkler.

I died.   I rose from the grave,
I staggered through fog.

I hurtled about with a cross driven through me,
uttering unearthly cries.

I was struck by lightning.
I became dust.

Again and again I died.
Fog, frost, light,
attack me from within.

Leaves and roots are imbedded in me.
My blood falls like rain through the air.
I rise from the grave, I am struck by daggers,
I scream. . .

Each time, dying as Dracula is worse.
Each time,
it moves me further from death.

Something claims me from within.
Each time, it frightens me more.

Each time, something stops dying in me.

ABSENCE MAKES THE HEART GROW FONDER
A Valentine for Gavin

I dreamed I came into your room and saw you again for the first time after three years.

We were both naked.

You had long hair.

Your ankles were shackled, with a loose chain between them and you had a thin leash of soft brown leather around your balls.

You were very tanned and a trickle of sweat ran down your temple onto your cheek.

Your mouth was slightly open.

I fastened your hands behind your back with handcuffs.

I noticed you were uncircumcized and wondered how that could be.

Your foreskin was tight over the head of your swelling cock.

I reached down and began to gently masturbate you with my cupped hand.

In a second or two your cock started pumping a flow of warm come onto my belly, cock and pubic hair, for what felt like minutes.

It was like warm milk on my skin.

I dropped to my knees.

Your cock was pulsing and warm in my mouth as I gulped down what seemed an endless stream of your hot piss.

Then you turned around and pushed your smooth ass into my face.

I pulled your ass-cheeks apart and worked my tongue into your asshole.

I pushed you onto the bed and gripped the back of your neck in my teeth.

When I mounted you, the come soaking my belly made your buttocks
slippery and sticky.

I pushed my cock into you with one thrust and shot my load deep into
your ass.

All the time we held each other in a wet, hungry kiss.

I had you across my lap with your hardon against mine and my hand on
your warm ass ready to give you a hot, hard spanking when I woke up,
with a hardon, my body curled around my friend's.

He was asleep.

I masturbated and came all over his naked ass which was not golden
and ripe-looking like yours but pale and thin and delicate.

I smeared the come onto my cock and fucked him.

He moaned and hugged the pillow.

I wanted to spank his ass till he cried.

I wanted to come and come and never stop.

A YOUNG POET SITS IN BED WITH A COLD

He aches.
The decade draws to an end,
not violent enough, he thinks,
for the guys he hangs out with.
Each week he grows less like them
(He is not getting any younger).
His thoughts

drift, his ivory eyes
slide a glance to the open window.
Clots of light roll across his arms and
loud music grates out of the radio,
some group or other.
He pictures the lead singer,

a real bastard
whose ass he'd like

to suck.
He opens his mouth. Nods, nods:
a body rehearsing its dismemberment.

WOULD I?

If
I knew I had fifteen minutes —
no more — till my last breath,

would I embrace the friend beside me
and end it all in passionate ecstatic struggle,
my lips locked on his mouth,
my cock up his ass,
or my face buried in his thighs with
his boot in my crotch,

or would I dash around madly
trying to put my papers in order
for a neat, carefully annotated,
posthumous volume?

STANDING AND KNEELING FIGURES

his eyes are closed
parts of his nakedness glow
with the pleasure inflicted

his mouth is open
his face shines
with ecstasy and light

he is kneeling
leaning into darkness
his elbows pinned behind him
resemble wings

there is a slight pressure
from the gloved hand
above the head

without it he would faint
or levitate

the curve of his white back
glistens with dew

the black hand's mate
brushes where narrow wrists
nuzzle at steel boundaries

the earth
and the standing figure
anchor him

his mouth and hands are open
his eyes shine with nakedness
he would levitate
with ecstasy and light

a deep uneven breathing
as though an angel
trapped inside one lung
gasped for infinity

"take it slowly now"
the sound of keys
turning in silver locks"

"take it slowly now
unfold your white wings
and fly"

PHOTOGRAPHY

What is it? This person with a black box, yourself,
waiting to make a border around what occurs,
to keep it, small and absolute,
between the stiff covers of a book.
Friend or lover,
laughing group, party camp or public building,
no matter what the subject, there is always
something erotic about it.

This lens, poking erect into another's world,
invading his being, his glance perhaps resisting
or coy, pretending to resist.
That image of the other, threaded
into the metal works and etched
invisibly on virgin film.
A mutual penetration.
The soft, firm pressure of the finger
on the shutter's cold
consummates. A click.
Conception takes itself.
Then the development in a dark place, closed,
uninterrupted, warm.
In soft, red light, the stillness of heavy air,
you can hear the body and
the picture, an utterly new thing, ascends,
in fluid with amniotic scent,
the womb's fluid.
Gradually it emerges.
Tongs, forceps, guide it to the surface,
to the world,
surprising always, no matter how expected,
pictorial flesh
resolving into black and white.
Then it is washed. The soft, slopping sounds.
The dark warmth is still.
With both hands
you lift the image up and gaze and gaze
into your own longing, that will outlive you.

SUSAN BELEW

Susan Belew is another poet I am pleased to be introducing to readers. Her work came to me through a friend, and I immediately sensed an individual voice, an adoration of our language, and some already well-developed forms and themes. I must say, I was surprised when I finally met Susan: her cherubic good looks seemed so contrary to the strong passions and dark visions of her poetry.

The nine poems included here were written out of the lesbian urban experience, and it is the city as a jungle, and its various denizens — psychopaths, sychophants and poseurs that runs through Belew's work like a dangerous vein. The perils of relationships — and how difficult it is to give up even a part of oneself to another, is a second theme that concerns Belew — and which I find refreshingly honest, amidst all the rhetoric of lesbian spokespersons who are often ready to put down male relationships as the only violent or problematic ones in the gay world. A quick scan of the titles of some poems here — "Cats-Claws," Selfish Tendencies," Bad Girl of the drive-In," show that Susan Belew, like all good poets, is more interested in the truth than any political stance. Balancing these works are poems such as "Catalyst" and "Restoration" — paeans to the unending power of discovery in love.

CATALYST

It should have been dark —
    there were no lights or candles.
    But as your body covered mine
    our fingers slid past
    flesh and formalities.
    Magic lights and colors dancingly blazed
    and blazenly danced through the room
    and my skin.
    They call this sin?

We courted and cavorted,
    building again and again,
    dispelling the nonsense of a required end.
    Somewhere in that festival of you and I
    feelings bloomed in colors and shapes
    no master has yet to comprehend.

It might be imagined that you were the catalyst
    required to unlock these hidden zeniths.
    You were, but —
    I had never taken time to truly
    want,

trust,
or seek.
Why should I?
You had yet to arrive.

SIDEWALK CAFE

He's there in the sidewalk cafe —
    posed with pen and paper,
    his coffee,
    and that casually neglected
    look of elegance.
He has no words
    or letter to write.
    No, it's the romance
    of the image
    he's courting tonight.

BAD GIRL OF THE DRIVE-IN

That monster of adolescent love and lust
    sometimes manages to pry you
    from the others.
She isn't polite
    having waited for her own
    hot drive-in nights —
    the ones where your lips and hands
    are the first to find
    her back seat breast.

SELFISH TENDENCIES

Poets who offer you gifts
    wrapped in words of love
    are the greediest of them all.
    They hope to steal into
    your fantasies
    by retelling their own.
    Aiming to slide their visions

into your thoughts
and through your fingers,
until your body aches
for the release of its own song.

FLESH MONGER

Oh, but you are slow with me —
    not loving patience,
    but exquisite greed,
    that drives you deeper and
    closer.
Exposing more of us both
    to the other
    and ourselves.

RESTORATION

Smooth
    and so softly
    you strip away the cloth
    of fears that I'd lived in
    for eternities.
    Sitting so closely to my skin
    My eyes had forgotten
    the textures of my true flesh.

JUNGLE II

A hot lady lives
    behind your eyes.
    Her panther's voice
    purring an invitation
    to draw nearer.
Nearer to receive
    those stroking licks
    that return us to the jungle
    she seeks tonight.
Living among the civilized
    makes her restless for

nights mixed from the smells of
wet earth, closing flowers,
and a closely, distant fire.
Her throat and skin flexing —
anticipating sounding the cry
of our arrival.
Anxious to untether the
creature forever kept polite —
lest the strength of her cries
intrude into the City's night.

CAT CLAWS

There are times
    when frustration holds court.
    Etiquette requires
    silent observance,
    damnable correctness,
    understanding,
    respecting your needs.
Maturity bears birthmarked responsibility,
    graciously accepting:
    your sidetracks, your moods,
    your space.
    Still, a nasty hiss inside
    refused them any name
    but unnecessary whims.
Oh, yes!
    View and think me
    an ever-giving, compassionate lover.
    But know, I also carry
    a howling heathen inside,
    who does not speak
    nor care to learn
    any language that includes fairness.

#1 LOCAL

There is a man —
    a black man

      an older black man.
      His face has followed me all day.
It is a black face
      an older black face.
      One no longer reflecting beauty —
      only anger now.

We sometimes ride the same train.
      I try not to,
      it is a disquieting face.
      One I will see again.
My train, always too full and warm
      to call comfortable.
      But the car fills with
      carnival sounds only travelers make.
      Diversion promising a quickened trip to
      my home
      my time
      my love.
His ride allows no clowns
      no secrets
      no adventure.
      His eyes blinded to theatrical costumes —
      cruising courtships go unnoticed.
      He remains apart from the silent celebration
      of smiles given the young man
      finally grown enough
      to reach suspended stirrups.
He permits no excursions —
      only the parasitic growth
      of overcrowding warmth.
      He does not like this train
      this time
      these people.
      Disliking even his growing anger.

One day I will know his name.
      Captioned beneath his newsprinted photograph
      reporting no word of his life
      or thoughts.
      Only the anger
      and its eruption.

He will have grown too warm
> too uncomfortable.
> Destroying some spurious celebration
> in his dance of anger
> grown too well
> too nurtured
> too ripe.
When that time has arrived
> his anger will grin
> as the long-readied scythe is wielded.
> His rotted blooming coming
> too soon
> too late.
> Vistas met, the zenith spent
> ramifications anesthetized.
> Only the newsprint
> and momentary flutter will remain.

For now
> I try not to share his train.
> I do not want, ever,
> to know that face
> too well.

AARON SHURIN

I knew of Aaron Shurin's poems for years from their publication in Mouth of the Dragon *and* Gay Sunshine, *and their inclusion in various anthologies.*

Aaron Shurin is a San Franciscan, a shaman of poetry who uses verse to invoke as much as to evoke or explain. Although his work is unique in its structure and language and imagery, Shurin's literary forebears seem to be Creely and Bly, other wizards of the emotion transmogrified into the substance of language. The experience of moments of sudden self awareness, and the fears and joys and consequences attendant on them are the stuff of these poems, which are from Shurin's new book published in 1980.

Shurin writes of himself:

"I was born in 1947, in midtown Manhattan, grew up in Texas, L.A., Berkeley, Boston, and in San Francisco since 1974. My first book, The Night Sun, *was published in 1976, followed by little* Toot Suite *(1978) and* Giving Up the Ghost *(1980). In 1979, I wrote and performed a play in S.F. entitled* Line Drawing.

I believe poetry is an event that takes place in the body, and so all human intimacies are appropriate to it. Anything that curls around the tongue and passes over the lips has body language; I say it comes from the Poetry Gland. I love the tactility of language and delight in the sound and texture of the American alphabet, mmm."

RECURRING

Dreamplace so forbidden
    you can't escape NEEDING to go to
the mens
        room. stall after stall
a labyrinth
of urinals. Men pose
everywhere in attitudes of enticement
                          some
    doing it are they doing it?
You wander through
   dazed   excited   afraid.
                        This maze
you've stumbled into once-again is

OCCUPIED
              "j-j-just wanna piss"
you hold cock in hand & lie

AMY COMES OUT

Hooded, a canopy of
slow realization:
                      am I
this am I this am I really?
                            Something palpable
in the brain puts pressure on, bites
the veins.

Every cloud has a face
in this scenario & they are none yours, all
yours. Your face
is a cloud, combed across the sky
like a Passion Play.
                        I see it melt downwind
re-arrange
the form of itself to accommodate
new knowledge.
                 Amy, a woman

will lie naked next to you
& no refusal you can conceive
will possibly work.
She'll take
something of you in her mouth

& you'll stay there.
Some say wings.
Some say solid ground.

AVOWAL/VOICES

I said No because all the past ones never worked
Then I said Yes eyes yes teeth, lips
I said No Ronda, think of yr career, Art, *IT'S*
         yr lover, the time it takes
Then I said Yes corkscrew tunnel & tube
                 yes ethereal fingers twisting
   cock to heart beat

I said No, no more, dinner's cooking, look
    yr crumpling my apron, no, I
Said yes, then I said oh yes, come over here'n
        stand by yr brother, honey
He said Aw, I'm crossin the bridge, yes I'm climbin
Then he said No, don't baby, where you takin us
He said Ah-hanh, twin, I hear you
    breathin in your ear
Then he said no wait, I don't have a coat, I got *No* shoes
    it's cold, wait I. . .

MISTER HARP

Take back the sun   my eyes are sore
    or let me enter yr burnt eyes
Take back the glazed
rocks my knees are stiff
or let me sit in yr lap.
I'll lick wrinkles from yr forehead
(take back the clouds)
    swallow yr salt sweat, take
back the shuddering waves.
Are you a tight harp,
        a clawed hoof
a rain dancer?
        Am I a moist lip
proud wheat,
    a stone
idol?
    Take back the sound
of oars, I'll bite yr guitar
hear with my teeth
    you stroke, I'll bite
Take back the shooting
stars or let my fingers
fly, take
Back take Back the fiery sand.
Let Me Bury My Eyes.

HYMN

I would lay the road with pure honey
    sticking to every side-path foot-tread
each step for you   a sweet coming home.
I would clear the sky each evening at sunset —
    that spot-lit, deep-shadowed, tree-molding
        light.   chew the bay laurel.   inhale
eucalyptus fumes.
               I would eat salad of nasturtium
flowers — hotter even than their leaves. . .

Where can I take you,   into some
        unknown space,   discoverer?
I would open your eyes, be hold
I would have you see me, rosy coal
    down deep in the heart's pit.

Where I went wasn't where I wanted to go.
What I said I wanted wasn't it.
Open my eyes, discoverer.
Open my unknown eyes

CONVERSIONS/WINTER SOLSTICE

The love that knots you unzips its black cape
The love that knots you unzips
its black cape & there's another cape
with buttons   the love that knots
you unbuttons its black cape & there's a
snapped cape, a tied cape, the knotted love
unsnaps, unties
            does not unknot.

The father strips his black shell   there's a son inside
the son strips, a father
      strips, a son

     The longest night sheds its cloak, sheds
its cloak of clouds, a day sneaks out.
A short day dribbles out of a cloudy mouth,
the mouth is black as night.

                    Out of a black
toothless night   a dawn-pink tongue glistens
a long tongue, a tongue drawn to holes
into a dark hole a long tongue probes, is swallowed

in a belly of a black beast
       a white heart pounds
pounds with tiny white fists
                 turning like a star.

RAVING # 16

Dammit   you fit!
no ideal
construction I make
has the power to nestle in
like you do, bird's nest, cradle.
A fact
either proves a theory

or develops its own. My arms
want to shriek out:
     one grabbing
        the other stiffing: Stop!

our stomachs rub together.
those little hairs as I stroke
the planed wood of yr back.
A body
either proves what you have to say

or just goes ahead anyway.
my heart is in my heart.

RAVING # 26, ROTATIONS

Faith-healer puts her hands on rock:
the whole scene sprouts water.

Then the tide of loving pulls her back to the cave lip.
She sits & watches, scratching belly

fear eating her back off, bemused.
          faith-healer puts her
hands on rock, she feels
"rock," the rock stays.

Who dried up the landscape?
I was FLOWIN !
                    His fingers are everywhere
          between my feet, I swallow his eyes like vitamins!
          red & green lights.

I put my hand on the rock.
                    In faith
I   pray   for   RAIN!

JOHN IOZIA

    Except for a few appearances in Gay Sunshine, most notably with "America"—a brilliant take off on Allen Ginsberg—Iozia's work has not appeared much, so I suppose this is something of an introduction. I find that difficult to believe, as I've been privately enjoying the work for several years. His private edition of Everything Reminds Me of Everything Else, *1974, remains one of those rare books of poems I dip in and out of with great enjoyment and to remind myself of how to say something succinctly and well.*
    Epigrammatics are Iozia's strength: he writes a kind of super-distilled and absolutely personally slanted Haiku. And his longer poems—such as "My Favorite Cuban" included here—become the longer version of Haiku—what the Japanese call Tanka. Iozia's voice is that of the gay dandy, the jaded poseur, the over-drugged, overgossiped total camera with a scalpel-like observation and an unnerving tendency toward dreaming and sadness. Baudelaire would have enjoyed these poems. He too lived and communicated from the razor-edge of society. He would have agreed with John Iozia that decadence isn't merely a state of mind—it's the only true state of mind for a poet.

FAG ART

Fag art sucks.
Fag art takes it up the ass.

Fag art will make you go
To the Eagle's Nest Saturday nights,
Put five dollars in the jukebox
And sniff poppers while
Cruising Jack Brusca.

Fag Art will make you
Change your clothes a lot
At Fire Island.

Gay Art will make you play
Inez Foxx 45s at 33rpm
And make you think it's a man
Singing about another man.

Fag Art will make you squander
Your most profound insights
On Vince Aletti's sex life.

Fag Art will drive you to writing
Manifestoes in subway tea rooms.

Fag Art is not only queer at night,
It's queer during the day
When you don't want to think about it.

Fag Art is a wet dream
You'll never be able to explain
If you've got a dick in your mouth.

LONELINESS

Twice a day,
At twelve and four
I walked to the harbor.

The boat came,
People boarded.
Salons and so longs.

Dinner
Then an old Lana Turner movie.

ANOTHER VERSION CONCERNING THAT VIRGIN

We gypsies are packed
And ready to get the car
To motor off to Raleigh.
Lots of to's today.

All the illusions are boxed,
Folded, suitcassed, and organized
For this is the first day of Virgo on speed.

Enter pure virgin, clearly crashing,
Shattering all old crystal myth convention
You irreverent bitch wench.

THE FOURTH OF JULY, 1974   * * *

He wouldn't take me up to Park Avenue
So I didn't invite him to Hudson Street;
**** Independence Day, honey.

JAMES DEAN BLUES

The tightness of downwardly pointed nipple
Darkens whitest skin of his blonde intention
method t-shirt macho nighttime blossoms coolest
Glance from crotch to thigh & troubled eye —
Oh red-nyloned jacket Galahad!
United in tragedy with '47 Mercury or '55 Ford,
Surrendered perfect youth
Somewhere just west of town
Where all lonesome motel pornography
Killed the best & fucked the rest.

CONCERNING TWO INTERIOR DECORATORS

They're gonna get out
An old *Casa Vogue*
And dish.

New season;
short hair,
shaved balls,
Bill Blass suits.

ART NOUVEAU

Dandelion,
babies born,
Innocent
Hard-on
Realized.
    * *
Pyramids
maze,
gather
majesty.

My integrity is defenceless.
And his intuition
Only wants to go to bed . . .

Well, we were always polarized.

OBJECTIVITY

I realized as we
Passed each other
How many insights
You can have
Walking away from something.
         *   *
Something in you
    WET
says no.
         *   *
Marijuana
Is twenty-six
Message units.

MY FAVORITE CUBAN

My favorite Cuban
Isn't yours.

My favorite Cuban
Attended Havana Military Academy
And has eleven names.

My favorite Cuban
Ascended Havana's secret frequencies
And early learned the day from night.

My favorite Cuban
Remembers rebel Communists
Machine-gunning patrons and friends
In the name of the People
At Tropicana and Flamingo.

My favorite Cuban
Was stripped of his gold
By Heroes of the Revolution
As he fled Fatherland and family
Into Floridian exile.

My favorite Cuban
Endured Miami's changes.
It isn't an island
So he didn't stay long.

My favorite Cuban
Went downstream
On the Venezuelan
Nightclub circuit.
He's got an image
Of filthy-rich Caracas.
Someday maybe
He'll share it with you.

My favorite Cuban
has lived in New York awhile now
And everything changed
Since he came.

My favorite Cuban
Named the names,
Focused the lights,
Liberated human potential
And raised the expectations
Of all tribes for all times.

My favorite Cuban
Is part of an original spell
Transforming the alienation
Of original sin to celebration
Of our differences
And I'll always love losing it there.

My favorite Cuban
Conquered infinite controversy
And danced with cultural hostility
Until his heart wept flames.

He's an anthropologist's wet-dream
And a man's man.

My favorite Cuban
Is always brave.
I worship him everywhere
And especially now.

My favorite Cuban
Knows the power in a prayer for two
And the effects of his fire on your ice.
He is always in demand.

      12.05.78

LAST NIGHT AT THE FLAMINGO

There were two thousand queens last night at the Flamingo.
Before the sun came up they dropped a thousand dollars
in drugs on the dance floor.

Eighteen superb mixes got sixty thousand oohs and
Forty thousand aahs last night at the Flamingo.

Two queens got six replays on a pinball machine
As I stared at the Rockola jukebox next to them
Last night at the Flamingo.

Two hundred and twenty-eight egos were destroyed
Last night at the Flamingo.

Forty thousand cigarettes were smoked
Last night at the Flamingo.
Thirty five thousand of them were menthol.
The rest were Mafia.

Seven queens forgot where they were
At least half the evening
Last night at the Flamingo.

Ten thousand plastic cups
Were flung to the floor

As six thousand cups of coffee disappeared
Last night at the Flamingo.

Four thousand sleeping pills were swallowed
In a masturbatory rush of self-administration
Last night at the Flamingo.

Seventeen hysterectomies were performed
Last night at the Flamingo.

I saw one queen checking hemlines
Behind a banquet
Last night at the Flamingo.

Twenty people fell out of the booth
Last night at the Flamingo.

Eight thousand questions were asked
And nine thousand answered
Last night at the Flamingo.

A thousand conversations
Drowned in music
Last night at the Flamingo.

Thirty-seven queens changed their clothes
At least twice last night at the Flamingo.

Five hundred phone numbers
And seven hundred promises
Changed partners
Last night at the Flamingo.

Eight hot records, so new
They're not even on the radio yet
Produced a thousand yawns
Last night at the Flamingo.

Two people fell in love
with each other
Last night at the Flamingo.

The seeds of eight thousand orgasms
In three downtown bath houses
Were planted last night at the Flamingo.

Three hundred-fifty bottles of Ethyl Chloride
Were consumed by six hundred white goddesses
On a honky-tonk safari
Last night at the Flamingo.

At least one person passed out
Last night at the Flamingo.
Unfortunately, I was dancing with him
And didn't get to see who it was.

Fluctuations in the price of life
Caught my eye last night at the Flamingo
And several bids couldn't survive introductions.

On my way home I spotted two queens
Licking the pavement outside the door
Last night at the Flamingo.

When I brought my white pants to the cleaner today,
He asked me if I'd been rolling around with the pigs.
"No," I said, "Last night I was at the Flamingo."
      11.29.78

A TRUE LIKENESS
LESBIAN AND GAY WRITING TODAY

DRAMA

GEORGE WHITMORE

George Whitmore is one of the polymaths of the current generation of gay writers. He is the author of a book of poetry (Getting Gay in New York, *1976), of various short stories ("Black Widow" in* Christopher Street, *"The Guermantes Way" in* Drummer, *etc.), and of the sensational true-life novel,* The Confessions of Danny Slocum, *St. Martins, 1980. Less known are Whitmore's plays:* The Caseworker, *produced by the Playwrights Horizon in 1976, and* The Rights, *put on by the Glines in 1980.*

Two other one acts, revolving around the life of Gertrude Stein, Flight *and* Legacy *were also produced in 1979.* Legacy, *published here, is that rarity—a short, intensely moving, fully realized imaginative leap—in this case into the lives of three lesbian women at the end of one of their lives. All of Whitmore's plays have dealt with gay relationships—in both* The Rights *and* Legacy, *it is the unresolved relationships, those brought forward from an already idealized or half forgotten past into a chaotic, emotionally fraught present. Both plays also deal with the generation gap among gays—and how we can distance or correctly counsel the young. The great woman of* Legacy, *who haunts the play's every moment, has been universally but differently loved by each of the characters on stage. That even the dead can still be unveiled is another of Whitmore's discoveries.*

The Legacy

A Chamber Play for Three Women

The Legacy *(paired with another one-act,* Flight, *and under the general title of* A Life of Gertrude Stein*) premiered on March 23, 1979 at the 18th Street Theatre in New York City. The cast was:*

    Suzanne — Jean West
    Flora   — Bonnie Young
    Alvah   — Sharon Ferry

Characters: Suzanne
              Flora
              Alvah

Place: The parlor of a house in a mountain resort.
Time: A September afternoon, 1934.

>*(Stage right, a chaise lounge; left, an easy chair with a tea table next to it. Upstage, a rusticated archway hung with drapes; beyond that, a hallway.)*
>
>*(At rise, the stage is empty. A pause. A bell rings. SUZANNE crosses the hallway left to right, upstage. A pause. SUZANNE and FLORA appear in the hallway. Their voices are low.)*

SUZANNE: You're soaked. Please give me your sweater. I'll hang it in the kitchen in front of the fire.

FLORA: Thank you. Will she see me?

SUZANNE: *(Taking FLORA's sweater)* You're in the house, aren't you?

FLORA: I wasn't sure.

SUZANNE: And your parcel?

FLORA: No. No. I'll keep it with me. Thank you.

SUZANNE: Very well. Please go in and have a seat.

FLORA: Thank you. Is she well enough to see me?

SUZANNE: Please. Have a seat.

>*(SUZANNE exits left)*
>
>*(FLORA pauses in the archway. She holds a parcel to her chest. It is wrapped with brown paper and string. She takes off her wet knit cap. Looks into the room. Crosses to the chair and sits)*
>
>*(SUZANNE enters from the hallway)*

SUZANNE: Are you warm enough?

FLORA: I'll be fine in a moment. Thank you.

SUZANNE: Your parcel is soaked. Why not put it down?

FLORA: The sun was shining when I left the hotel then half way up the hill the sky turned black and it began to rain.

SUZANNE: Why don't you set it down?

FLORA: Your carpet . . .

SUZANNE: It won't harm the carpet. May I take your cap?

FLORA: Oh . . . Thank you.

> (SUZANNE takes the cap and exits right)
>
> (FLORA sets down the parcel, next to her chair. Folds her hands in her lap)
>
> (After a pause, ALVAH enters left)

FLORA: *(Turning)* Alvah.

ALVAH: I must warn you not to kiss me or embrace me . . .

FLORA: Of course not.

ALVAH: *(Crosses to chaise)* Or to get too close to me at all.

FLORA: Of course.

> (ALVAH sits on the chaise and pulls a rug over her legs)

ALVAH: You're soaking wet. Don't you have an umbrella?

FLORA: It was sunny when I left the hotel, then the cloudburst . . .

ALVAH: You're shivering. Would you like—

FLORA: No. No thank you.

ALVAH: Suzanne is making tea.

FLORA: Oh, I won't be staying but a few minutes.

ALVAH: That will warm you up.

FLORA: I didn't know I would be staying for tea.

ALVAH: We won't have an English tea.

> *(A pause)*

ALVAH: Is that it? *(Gestures to parcel)*

FLORA: It . . .

ALVAH: My legacy.

FLORA: Yes.

ALVAH: As you said in your letter.

FLORA: Yes.

ALVAH: You've changed. A great deal.

FLORA: And you.

ALVAH: Oh yes. My size.

FLORA: Yes.

ALVAH: But your face has changed.

FLORA: Has it?

ALVAH: Oh, yes.

FLORA: You look so very well. I didn't know what to expect. I read so many different things in the papers. But you really do look well.

ALVAH: Thank you. Where are you staying?

FLORA: Oh, The Antlers. That's right—

ALVAH: Are you enjoying your stay?

FLORA: —down your hill. You can see the rooftops from your doorstep.

ALVAH: We came at night.

FLORA: It's a very famous hotel, they tell me.

ALVAH: Oh? I've seen nothing of the countryside. And the windows in my room *(She catches her breath here, as she often does)* are screened by stands of pines.

FLORA: What a shame. It's—

ALVAH: There's nothing to see when I look. But then, I'm always resting and not often at the windows. The pines—hiss at night. Actually do. I lie resting and hear them hiss. They throw off—a fizz.

FLORA: Winter will be here soon. Will you stay?

ALVAH: We haven't been told.

FLORA: The papers said—

ALVAH:	We've told the papers nothing. We've told them a few things, but nothing about staying or going.
FLORA:	Has the climate been beneficial?
ALVAH:	I know one must be in a climate.
FLORA:	Oh, yes.
ALVAH:	*(After a pause)* And rest. At its worst, it's like knives to the chest.
FLORA:	*(After a pause)* I see. Will you be — cured?
ALVAH:	I only mention it because you seem curious. That's the worst of it. I must rest. Then I'll be told if there's a cure for me. Others have been cured.
FLORA:	The papers—
ALVAH:	I read that I'd been cured. I haven't read that I'd died. Yet.
FLORA:	I'm so relieved to see you . . . Everyone in Chicago was . . . Everyone sends her best.
ALVAH:	You see, Suzanne had to keep you waiting.
FLORA:	Of course.
ALVAH:	She has to make her decisions.
FLORA:	Is she your nurse, then?
ALVAH:	Yes. That too.
	(FLORA looks away, at nothing in particular)
FLORA:	The reason I've been coming here every day—
ALVAH:	Please understand. This is the house of a patient.
FLORA:	I do understand. I was just so—
ALVAH:	And everything here is about the patient. Not about the patient's visitors or about the newspapers.
FLORA:	Of course. *(Picks up the parcel)* I only came to deliver this.
ALVAH:	Ah.
FLORA:	And to see you after so many years, of course. I don't want to tire you.

ALVAH:	I've wondered why, if this was your only errand, why then you didn't simply leave the parcel with Suzanne.
FLORA:	Why I wanted to see you and—
ALVAH:	Of course.
FLORA:	And I have a short message. I promised—
ALVAH:	Your parcel and your message. And things to see for yourself.
FLORA:	I promised Mademoiselle.
ALVAH:	Yes?
FLORA:	I would come in person if possible and tell you . . . This is your legacy—
ALVAH:	As you said in your letter.
FLORA:	Before she passed away she asked me to bring it to you if possible and to tell you . . .
ALVAH:	After years of such a great silence there must be much to be said.
FLORA:	That this is your legacy and that you were closest to her heart. Of all of us.
ALVAH:	*(After a pause)* Thank you for coming so far.
FLORA:	So. Here is the parcel. And— *(Standing)* —I have delivered the message.
ALVAH:	Please stay. Please sit down. Suzanne will be bringing tea.
	(FLORA sits)
ALVAH:	*(After a pause)* Would you like to open it for me?
FLORA:	No. I'd rather not. Really.
ALVAH:	Do you know what it is?
FLORA:	Yes. I think so. Yes.
ALVAH:	Well? Aren't you curious?
FLORA:	No.
ALVAH:	You seem a curious person.
FLORA:	I'd rather not.

	(SUZANNE enters carrying a tray with teapot, etc. Sets it down and pours for ALVAH and FLORA)
FLORA:	*(Taking cup from SUZANNE)* Thank you.
ALVAH:	*(Taking cup from SUZANNE)* Thank you.
	(SUZANNE exits. FLORA and ALVAH sip their tea)
ALVAH:	I'm curious myself. But not too curious. Do you girls carry on her work?
FLORA:	Oh, we see each other. Everything — has changed.
ALVAH:	Do you give lessons.
FLORA:	Yes. Do you miss your work?
ALVAH:	Yes.
FLORA:	There's a lovely piece in the Art Institute.
ALVAH:	Yes. We knew I wouldn't be able to work when we decided I would do the tour.
FLORA:	And you must miss your house in France.
ALVAH:	Oh, yes. There are two houses. One in the city, which I miss very much and we've always been there, and one in the country, which has been torn down by now.
FLORA:	Oh, I'm sorry.
ALVAH:	It had to come down. I haven't seen — the spot, yet.
FLORA:	I see.
ALVAH:	I miss a lot of the things. We brought all the things from the house in the country to the city, so things are a jumble there now.
FLORA:	What is your house like?
ALVAH:	Oh, a very ordinary house, with a pavilion for my work.
FLORA:	Is it large.
ALVAH:	The pavilion is large. The house is comparatively small. Still, we have a large, very modern bath and a modern kitchen. The French love the idea of effi-

	ciency, but I had to move heaven and earth to achieve it in our house. Now the bath and kitchen are very impressive, though they don't impress the Americans. *(Beat)* What *will* you do now?
FLORA:	I'm not sure.
ALVAH:	You have money.
FLORA:	I have some money. And I'll give lessons.
ALVAH:	Yes.
FLORA:	It's a great burden — off me.
ALVAH:	Yes. Helping the dying die a long death is a great burden.
FLORA:	And, Alvah, she was so—
ALVAH:	Will you take this? *(Holds out cup and saucer)*
	(FLORA rises and takes the cup, sets it on tray, sits)
ALVAH:	Thank you.
FLORA:	If you get well . . .
ALVAH:	Yes.
FLORA:	Will you return to France, or will you continue your tour? Will you come to Chicago?
ALVAH:	Perhaps. If there is a cure for me.
FLORA:	The girls would be so pleased.
ALVAH:	Yes. But now you can tell them you've seen me . . .
FLORA:	Yes.
ALVAH:	And what's become of me.
FLORA:	*(After a beat)* They would be so pleased to see you and to hear you lecture.
ALVAH:	A suitable pastime for Chicago matrons.
FLORA:	All Chicago—
ALVAH:	Yes.
FLORA:	*(After a pause)* Not all of them are married.
ALVAH:	We'll see.

	(A pause)
ALVAH:	*(Holding out her hands)* Will you bring me my legacy then?
FLORA:	*(Looking down at parcel)* If you like. *(Rises and picks up parcel)* It's terribly wet. I'm afraid I had no raincoat to cover it with.
	(FLORA crosses and gives ALVAH the parcel. ALVAH puts it on her lap)
ALVAH:	*(Tugs at string)* We need a good knife. *(Tug)* No . . .
	(FLORA returns to her chair)
ALVAH:	The string is rotten. *(Breaks the string)* There. *(Looks up)* You know what it is?
FLORA:	Yes.
ALVAH:	*(Drops her hands. Looks down at the parcel)* Well. It's heavy. Sodden.
FLORA:	It was too—
ALVAH:	Yes. *(Begins to unwrap the paper)*
FLORA:	You *were* her favorite. Always.
ALVAH:	The box is—*(Rips off a corner of the box)* Letters. *(Takes out a handful of envelopes)* My . . . *(Looks through the envelopes)* The ink has run on these . . . All . . . Unopened? All my letters?
FLORA:	Yes.
ALVAH:	Unopened?
	(A pause)
FLORA:	At first there was—a torrent of letters. They kept coming. But we were forbidden to write you. And I would ask, why? Then I would ask, what does Alvah say? And she would say nothing. I stopped asking. She must have put them away. I never saw them in the trash. It was an unspoken law that none of us would write and I . . . Then there were fewer, and they were never mentioned. Then fewer. And I wondered about them. I wondered about you. Then, finally, I decided—thought to myself—she

	had nothing to say about you because—she wasn't reading your letters. But was putting them away—somewhere. I never saw them in the trash.
ALVAH:	Everything . . .
FLORA:	And I simply thought to myself—well, Alvah could write *me*. But you . . . And you were—such a disappointment to her. Running away. Not dancing. I don't know. I didn't know. I would say, but Alvah wants to be an artist. She doesn't want to dance. Then, later I would say, have you seen what Alvah has done? In the papers? They're saying the most terrible things about her in the papers. I thought it was terribly amusing. But she . . . So, finally I stopped saying anything at all. All of us wondered—
ALVAH:	What had become of me.
FLORA:	What you had done to . . . Then, over the years, things changed, of course. But I still—
ALVAH:	Everything . . .
FLORA:	You were—
ALVAH:	Yes. Closest to her heart. The tea must be cold.
FLORA:	*(Puts her hand to the teapot)* Yes. It is.
ALVAH:	Will you fetch Suzanne?
FLORA:	*(Rising, picking up teapot)* Of course.
	(FLORA exits with teapot)
	(ALVAH sits quietly with tears rolling down her face)
	(FLORA enters and sits)
	(ALVAH wipes away the tears)
	(A pause)
ALVAH:	You know, I'm not fond of English things. But there is one thing the English have that I'm very fond of. We have two of them in the city now and I might have brought one with me here, but one doesn't . . . One can't find them here in America. They're the padded chintz tea cozies the English have to keep

their tea warm. I've been to England twice and each time my only purchase was a tea cozy. When we learned I would have to stay here Suzanne began housekeeping. One afternoon while I was resting Suzanne went down to the town and returned and said, There are no tea cozies in America. I could have told you that, I said. They have covers for their teapots; that is, not lids, but covers, knit or crocheted, to put over the pot. I know, she said. I found some in the town made by the ladies there. But they had no tea cozies, only the covers. So I came away without one because I knew a towel would do as well. But she won't use the towel, so our tea is cold.

FLORA: *(After a pause)* Perhaps you might read them. Now.

ALVAH: Ah. I know what's in them.

FLORA: But, perhaps as a —

FLORA: No. Everything . . . Would you like to take them with you?

ALVAH: Oh no.

FLORA: Then, perhaps just to the hotel. You might read them there. Then you could —

ALVAH: No. No. I couldn't.

ALVAH: You aren't so curious, then. And what was your legacy?

FLORA: No.

ALVAH: *(After a pause)* There will have to be a great deal of thought about these letters. There's a perfection about them. Unopened. And their being brought here by you. And your message.

FLORA: Alvah. At the end —

ALVAH: No.

FLORA: Her mind was gone.

ALVAH: Please.

FLORA: *(After a pause)* All the beautiful costumes are gone. I packed them away myself. I wrapped each piece in tissue paper and put them away in trunks. According to her instructions. Then I made cases for the trunks. Stitched them up tight. I had a boy put them away in the attic. She wouldn't allow a photograph, a mirror on the wall. All the properties—the fans and headdresses, the finger cymbals . . . were packed away and put up in the attic. The family came and took them away. I would have liked . . .

ALVAH: The Mystery of the Chinese Maiden.

FLORA: Something. A sash. Anything.

ALVAH: Now your duties are over.

FLORA: Yes.

ALVAH: And you'll give lessons. And will you travel?

FLORA: No. Perhaps.

(SUZANNE enters with the teapot and sets it down)

ALVAH: Young girls come to me, and Suzanne turns them away.

(SUZANNE exits)

ALVAH: We won't have them. But there is always, with some man or another, among the many that come and go so often, a young girl, too timid to ask her questions, not like the others. And I look in her eyes, and I turn away. I leave her to Suzanne and talk to the men. If I were to speak to these young girls—I would tell them: Have no masters. But I can't—speak to them. They break my heart. Their eyes with their questions. As yours were. Once. And mine, perhaps. But I talk to the men and Suzanne talks to the young girls. *(Chuckles)* In France I'm called Le Monstre. But not for my discourtesies to young girls.

FLORA: The monster.

ALVAH: Yes. An accolade. A beloved monster. The famous don't fall in France, you see. Their deeds become

	petty. They diminish in life. Rather, they—petrify . . . But then, there's America.
FLORA:	You're very famous here.
ALVAH:	Oh, yes. And this is a great test. But I believe the Americans have been impressed. As they wouldn't be with our plumbing.
FLORA:	*Much* impressed. Now that—
ALVAH:	The French aren't impressed by their objects of worship. And I'm an object of worship in France. Once the French have ascertained—a substance for themselves, they won't be swayed by impressions.
FLORA:	There has been so much written about you here.
ALVAH:	Oh, yes. Jokes and slander. Which are a different matter. Entirely. Oh, yes. So we were surprised and delighted on our tour and would like to go on with it if we can. The Americans don't listen, but they look. In Pittsburgh I went to a roller rink and—the skaters there—I was very, very moved. Then we came here. *(Beat)* Will you come to France if you travel? Now that you're free?
FLORA:	No. I don't know.
ALVAH:	He's in Paris, you know.
FLORA:	Who?
ALVAH:	Our young man. Is it indecent or amusing to speak of him now?
FLORA:	"Our young man?"
ALVAH:	Yes. Remember?
FLORA:	Oh.
ALVAH:	Though he's not young now.
FLORA:	No.
ALVAH:	I think of him as our young man.
FLORA:	He loved you. Not me.
ALVAH:	Oh, he comes and goes. Let's not let him stand between us again.

FLORA:	He sent me a gift, from abroad, once.
ALVAH:	Oh?
FLORA:	A handkerchief. It had a border made of tiny flags. He enclosed a note — of apology.
ALVAH:	I didn't know. And after that?
FLORA:	Nothing.
ALVAH:	I see.

(A pause)

ALVAH:	Do you ever dance?
FLORA:	No. In the evenings sometimes.
ALVAH:	In your rooms.
FLORA:	Yes.
ALVAH:	Young bamboo stirred by a gentle breeze, where no one but the Master sees she passes. Daughter of the Forbidden City, jasmine floating on her sleeves . . .
FLORA:	Forbidden views are those most yearned for, she passes by on dainty feet bearing blossoms. To the Shrine of Buddah, incense enwreathed. Daughter of the Forbidden City . . .
ALVAH:	Ah, what mysteries its precincts hold. What delights her robes enfold.
FLORA:	Holy —
ALVAH:	Holy Nun of the Holy City . . .

(A pause)

FLORA:	She wept for you.
ALVAH:	Will you take the letters?
FLORA:	You were closest to her heart.
ALVAH:	Everything is in the letters.
FLORA:	No.
ALVAH:	What shall I do with them?

FLORA: How should I know?

ALVAH: There will have to be a great deal of thought now about—

FLORA: Near the end she wouldn't eat. I would find her lying in bed in the morning. Like a stick. Awake. She wouldn't sleep. I had to put the food in her mouth and clamp her jaw shut with my hands. Hold her nose. I made her swallow it.

ALVAH: If you had written . . .

FLORA: The last morning I went upstairs. The bed was empty. There was a trail—across the newspapers and clothing on the floor—to the bathroom. Drops. I found her in the bathroom.

ALVAH: My sweet Flora . . .

FLORA: You see, she'd had a second stroke during the night and she'd dragged herself to the bathroom and in the bathroom she had the last, the third stroke.

(ALVAH begins coughing)

FLORA: *(Rising)* What shall I do?

ALVAH: Suz-anne.

(FLORA exits. ALVAH throws the parcel to the floor)

(SUZANNE enters with a glass of opaque liquid and helps ALVAH drink it. FLORA stands by the archway. SUZANNE puts down the empty glass and wipes ALVAH's forehead with a handkerchief, pushes back stray whisps of hair, murmurs some words)

ALVAH: Better. Thank you. Fine. Much better. *(Gets her breath back)*

FLORA: *(After a pause)* Shall I go?

SUZANNE: No.

ALVAH: No. Stay. I'm . . .

(SUZANNE sits on the edge of the chaise and strokes ALVAH's hair)

(FLORA returns to her seat)

FLORA: I've tired you and upset you. I'm so sorry.

ALVAH: No. *(Takes a few deep breaths)*

SUZANNE: No blood has come up.

ALVAH: *(A faint chuckle)* Not like in the novels. This possibility of blood . . . It's very, very dry. That's why I was fooled. They told us others have been fooled, because of the dryness. One thinks of blood, of course. But there's not often any. With me.

FLORA: But — ?

ALVAH: But then you die, you see.

FLORA: I see.

ALVAH: I do want to see America.

SUZANNE: Please.

ALVAH: *(Gestures to parcel)* And all my past is here.

FLORA: *(Stands)* I really must go.

ALVAH: Must you?

FLORA: I'm afraid I must.

ALVAH: Such a great many things happened. Such a great number of people were there. And then they were gone and others came. And so many things were changing. All the time. It's all in the letters. Everything.

FLORA: I really must go. I've tired you and made you ill.

ALVAH: But don't you want to hear?

(FLORA turns to go, pauses)

(The lights fade out)

END

JOSEPH MATHEWSON

Joseph Mathewson's first novel, The Love Tribe *(NAL, 1969) dealt with the breakdown of sexual conventions in the midst of an intense and very druggy late sixties New York City youth commune. His second novel,* Alicia's Trump, Avon 1980, *is a mystery set in Greenwich Village, the Soho Art Scene and various occult sects around the city, starring an attractive, liberated and distinctly individual woman turned detective, Alicia Von Helsing. Despite this, Mathewson sees himself primarily as a dramatist: and that is how he is represented in this anthology: by a short play called* Canned Soup, *a hilarious and quite trenchant comedy of a contemporary lesbian woman, what she has to do, and comes to eventually enjoy doing in order to find a job equal to her capabilities. I attended a reading of this play with Austen Pendleton as Ted Bean, and I'm convinced that he will soon join the ranks of Tartuffe etc. as one of the great comic characters.*

An earlier, full length play, Man Proposing, *premiered at North Western University in 1979, was another complex and gender-role defying comedy. It starred a current sex icon of our times, Harry Reems, who handled the role of the confused, ambitious, bisexual artist who will do — and eventually does — anything to get an exhibit of his works — with surprising elan and aplomb.*

Canned Soup

AT RISE: The office of Theodore (Ted) Bean, director of public relations for Homecooked Soups. Blowups of colorful soup can labels decorate the windowless walls. TED sits at his desk, but only his hands are visible on either side of the morning paper. On the desk are framed photographs of Ted's wife and two children, a telephone, a calendar, a box of cigars and an ash tray. Upstage is a coat closet. Inside its door is a full-length mirror, but the door is closed now.

ROSELLA PHIPPS enters through the only other door, which is at right. She carries a steno pad, a file of resumes and a coffee cup which she sets on the desk. Dressed to make the most of an ample, curvaceous body, Rosella could be in her thirties or a hard-living twenty-five. She is a women of two distinct moods; this one is cloyingly cheerful.

TED
I'll have my coffee now, Rosella.
ROSELLA
I already thought to bring it, Mr. Bean.
  (Without lowering the paper, TED reaches for the cup.)
Next to the telephone. To your left — I mean right.

My left, your right. There.
  (As TED drinks)
Is it O.K.?
TED
Fine.
ROSELLA
Just the way you like it?
TED
Right.
ROSELLA
I want to learn all your little habits.
TED
Two months on the job and already you're remembering I take my coffee black. Congratulations.
ROSELLA
Thank you, Mr. Bean. So how did your teams do over the weekend?
TED
Fourteen to six, eighteen to three, thirty to nothing.
ROSELLA
That's wonderful.
TED
They lost.
  (As TED put down the paper, we see a man in his late thirties or early forties, wearing a starched white shirt and a just-pressed three-piece suit. The walls of his office have been closing in on Ted for some time now; his voice has a certain edginess, but still retains a trace of his gentle Southern boyhood.)
Well — what's today?

ROSELLA

It's Monday, Mr. Bean.

TED

(Leafing through the paper)

Why so it is. Says so on every page. And the calendar agrees. I know it's Monday, Rosella. The question is, what am I doing this Monday?

ROSELLA

How silly of me.

(Reading from her steno pad)

To start with, you're seeing applicants for the position as your assistant.

(Handing him the file of resumes)

Personnel's picked out three.

TED

(Reading)

Fong May Sue. Juanita Perez. Leslie Jordan. Leslie Jordan?

ROSELLA

Yes.

TED

Must be some mistake.

ROSELLA

No. I'm sure.

TED

How does your average male wasp with a name like Leslie Jordan slip past personnel? Hmm? Where's the affirmative action in hiring a guy who might speak English as a native tongue?

ROSELLA

Mr. Bean.

TED

Where's the affirmative action in hiring a guy who might be able to count past ten?

ROSELLA

(Calling off right)

Miss Jordan?

                           TED
Where's the affirmative action —
    (LESLIE JORDAN appears in the doorway. In her early twenties, she wears a beret and a severely tailored pants suit. Her hair is cut boyishly short. To the greatest extent possible, her costume should be the only clue to her gender.)
                         ROSELLA
Here she is now, Mr. Bean.
                           TED
She?
    (Standing)
Of course. Miss Jordan, I'm Ted Bean. Please come in.
    (To Rosella as LESLIE enters)
Anything else for this morning?
                         ROSELLA
    (Reading from her steno pad)
Mrs. Dixon wants to see you as soon as the proof for the new — oh, right — they never taught us how to say cream of asparagus in shorthand — the proof for the new cream of asparagus label is coming back from the printer, and Mrs. Dixon wants to see you, I said that. And then at eleven you're interviewing — this is a real toughie — the Northern New Jersey Association of Hydroponic Farmers.
                           TED
Bravo. That's it?
                         ROSELLA
Yes, Mr. Bean.
                           TED
Fine. You can close the door as you go — unless the lady prefers it open?
    (LESLIE shakes her head. ROSELLA exits, shutting the door.)
Please have a seat, Miss Jordan. Or is it Mrs.?
                         LESLIE
No.
    (While LESLIE sits, TED lights a cigar and remains on his feet, occasionally pacing in back of her.)

TED

Miss Jordan, then. Or how about Ms.? Myself, I grew up in the South, so Ms. always makes me think of what the dark—the black—it was what the cook used to call my mother: Miz Luanne. Still, it's your name. For all I care, you can call yourself Muhammed Ali.

LESLIE

Thank you.

TED

Well?

LESLIE

Yes?

TED

Which is it?

LESLIE

Oh. It's—I like to be Ms. Jordan. Please.

TED

Fine, Leslie. Why?

LESLIE

I beg your pardon?

TED

Why do you like to be Ms.? Or to put it another way, do you prefer Ms. because you feel that any other title would place in some box, bag or category?

LESLIE

Thank you.

TED

What?

LESLIE

That's a very nice way of putting it.

TED

Then why on earth do you want this job?

LESLIE

The work sounds interesting.

TED

Public relations?

LESLIE
Yes. The pay—

TED
Is dandy.

LESLIE
And I gather the fringe benefits—

TED
Can't be beat. But how can any amount of cash or subsidized orthodontics induce you to publicize Homecooked Soup? You wish to remain unboxed, bagged or categorized. And yet you would willingly label yourself as a flack whose day is devoted to pushing processed glop on a careless and criminally undereducated public.

LESLIE
I like your soups.

TED
You can't be serious.

LESLIE
I like everything about them—even—just the way the can feels: round and solid and heavy. You pick one up, you know you've got something.

TED
You've got a heavy can. What about the contents?

LESLIE
I like them.

TED
Which ones?

LESLIE
All the ones I've tried.

TED
Name two.

LESLIE
Split pea with ham and . . .

TED
Don't say chicken vegetable.

LESLIE
Why not?

TED
Were you going to say chicken vegetable?

LESLIE
No.

TED
I want the truth.

LESLIE
What if I was?

TED
If you were to say you like our chicken vegetable soup, I would lose all respect for you. Is that what you were going to say?

LESLIE
No.

TED
But didn't you just tell me you like all our soups?

LESLIE
The ones I've tried. Some more than others.

TED
You've tried the chicken vegetable?

LESLIE
Yes.

TED
Where would you rank it?

LESLIE
Somewhere in the middle.

TED
What's at the bottom?

LESLIE
There isn't any bottom. There are a few standouts, and the rest is all middle.

TED
Even the chicken vegetable?

LESLIE
Yes. What's wrong with the chicken vegetable?

TED

It tastes like shit.

LESLIE

It's given me some very happy times.

TED

Then you don't know what happiness is.

LESLIE

Yes I do. It's knowing something for sure. It's knowing every time I open a can that says split pea with ham, that's what I'll get inside. And all I have to do is mix it up with milk — or even just with water — and heat it, and it's going to taste good and be filling and nutritious. And cars these days, the gas tanks are always exploding. And they'll probably find out fluoride gives you gum cancer. But your soups, Mr. Bean, they are one of the last things in the world you can really count on, what Shakespeare calls an ever-fixed mark that looks on tempests and is not shaken. That's what I like so much about them. That's why I want to work here.

(Standing)
I did want to work here.

TED

Calm down. Leslie. That was just a little test.

(ROSELLA enters.)

ROSELLA

Mr. Bean?

TED

Yes?

ROSELLA

Mrs. Dixon'll see you.

TED

(Stubbing out his cigar)
His master's voice. You'll excuse me?

(As TED exits, ROSELLA crosses to Leslie, who has remained standing. This is the other Rosella, businesslike and somewhat grim.)

ROSELLA
He won't be long. Well look at me.
(Turning Leslie towards her)
Has he made you cry?

LESLIE
No.

ROSELLA
Leslie?

LESLIE
Almost. Rosella, this isn't going to work.

ROSELLA
I say it will.

LESLIE
That man could be violent. He could throw me out.

ROSELLA
It's the chance you take if you want this job. Would you rather stay home and sterilize the apartment?

LESLIE
I just try to keep it clean.

ROSELLA
You have already removed the porcelain from the sink. It's time you got back in the world.

LESLIE
Yes, Rosella.

ROSELLA
Perhaps you'd rather work with strangers again.

LESLIE
No, Rosella.

ROSELLA
Your last experience might have taught you that, fundamentally, there are only two types of men out there — rapists and faggots.

LESLIE
It taught me. I want to work with you. But can't I get the job by being myself?

ROSELLA

If you were any other sort of woman, maybe you could. But a wasp?

LESLIE

They hired you.

ROSELLA

(Placing her hands on her prominent breasts)
I think they liked my smile.

LESLIE

I hate it when you joke like that.

ROSELLA

Leslie, look — they hired me as a secretary. But you, my bashful star, you can be so much more — as long as you have some competitive edge. If I wasn't convinced of that, I would not have arranged this charade. And I tell you it will work. But you've got to do your part.

LESLIE

I'm trying.

(ROSELLA drags LESLIE to the closet and opens the door, showing her the mirror.)

ROSELLA

Just see yourself. Jesus, LESLIE — what was our first lesson?

LESLIE

How a man stands.

ROSELLA

And how does a man stand, Leslie?

(LESLIE throws back her shoulders; ROSELLA rolls her eyes to the heavens, and here begins a section in which ROSELLA coaches LESLIE in standing, sitting and walking like a man. In general, LESLIE continues to err on the side of too great delicacy, while ROSELLA overcompensates in the other direction. The section can be freely improvised, however, to make the most of the performers' comic gifts. It ends:)

ROSELLA

What was that?

LESLIE

The way a man walks?

ROSELLA

That was a lady orangutang with a cork up her ass.

LESLIE

Rosella!

ROSELLA

(Demonstrating)
This is how a man walks.

LESLIE

It's not the way Mr. Bean walks.

ROSELLA

Show me.
(As LESLIE does so)
That's a goose step.

LESLIE

Yes! Rosella — he's so much worse than you said he'd be.

ROSELLA

Details.

LESLIE

That awful cigar — he's a cave man and that's his club.

ROSELLA

You don't observe things, Leslie. All right. I have an advantage. I see what he doodles and throws away. Birds. John James Audubon he's not. But when Mr. Macho doodles, out come our feathered friends. And if he thinks he's alone, I hear him whistle, too: "I'm called Little Buttercup." "Three little maids from school are we." Yes. I tell you, Leslie, the man is not what he seems to be, and you will fascinate him.

LESLIE

Even if you're right — I do observe some things, Rosella.

ROSELLA

Like what?.

LESLIE

Like you. Like a whole different you.

ROSELLA

Explain.

LESLIE

Well it's—you won't be angry?

ROSELLA

Promise.

LESLIE

It's things like:
 (Giggling, a parody of Rosella)
"They never taught us how to say cream of asparagus in shorthand."

ROSELLA

Jesus, Leslie. I have to act like that. The man expects it.

LESLIE

But just supposed I'm hired. He'll have expectations of me, too, won't he? What if I become the thing I tell him I am?

ROSELLA

That's only here. Look at me: When I'm back home, am I all soft and simpery?

LESLIE

No, Rosella. I can't say you are.

ROSELLA

Then not to worry. Come five o'clock, I'll peel that big butch costume off. You'll be my little girl again. Trust me?

LESLIE

Yes.

ROSELLA

He won't be long. You know what to say?

LESLIE

 (Reciting)
Because of people like me, Mr. Bean, labels are less often—less often . . .

ROSELLA

Reliable!

LESLIE
Reliable as guides to contents.

(As LESLIE continues reciting, ROSELLA shuts the closet door.)

You are constrained by an affirmative action hiring policy.

ROSELLA
He's coming.

(Hugging her)
Be strong, Leslie.

LESLIE
Strong and manly.

ROSELLA
You got it.

(THEY kiss as TED enters, studying a sheet of paper. HE notices the women but has reached his desk before the unusual nature of what he has noticed hits him.)

TED
Rosella!

ROSELLA
Phone's ringing.

TED
Come back here.

ROSELLA
Got to get the phone.

TED
Miss Phipps! God damn it!

(ROSELLA exits, shutting the door.)

LESLIE
Can we . . .

TED
I'm waiting.

LESLIE
(Sitting)
Can we continue with the interview?

TED
Do you seriously think, Ms. — what the hell —
    (Searching for her resume, then finding it)
— Ms. Jordan, that after the nauseating scene I have just witnessed, there is any chance I'd hire you?

LESLIE
When you know the truth.

TED
The truth is, you were kissing Rosella Phipps.

LESLIE
Mr. Bean, I was trying to tell you why it is I like your soups so much. You open a can of oyster stew, what you get inside is oyster stew. The same with turkey noodle. You open a can —

TED
I get the point.

LESLIE
The point about soup. But these days, Mr. Bean, fewer and fewer people resemble cans of soup. You see?

TED
No.

LESLIE
Because of — well — people like me, labels are less often reliable as guides to contents. You read my label, Mr. Bean, what does it say?

TED
Young woman of irregular tastes.

LESLIE
But what if you opened me up?

TED
I don't suppose you'd want a man to do that.

LESLIE
You're right. I'm not that sort of guy.

TED
Ms. Jordan —
    (As LESLIE shakes her head)
Mr. Jordan?

LESLIE
Leslie's fine. Now can we go on with the interview?

TED
Do you mean to sit there in that absurd little hat, in that travesty of masculine attire, and tell me that you are a man?

LESLIE
Not only a man, Mr. Bean, but the kind of man you want.

TED
Go on.

LESLIE
Because, on the one hand, you would like to work with a man, but on the other, you are constrained by an affirmative action hiring policy weighted in favor of women and even less desirable minorities. This is all correct?

TED
For the sake of argument.

LESLIE
You took me for a woman. So did your personnel department. Hire me and you satisfy them and yourself.

TED
Let's back up a second. Why do you think I'd rather work with a man?

LESLIE
You believe a woman's place is using your soups, not publicizing them. At least that's Rosella's impression.

TED
And you and Rosella?

LESLIE
We live together?

TED
Do you indeed? Well — that could be trouble.

LESLIE
If I get this job, Mr. Bean, I'm sure I can keep our private relation separate from our professional.

TED
Even when you hear the talk?

LESLIE
What talk?

TED
There's a lot of Rosella to talk about — huh? I mean, those knockers.

LESLIE
Very impressive.

TED
Impressive?

LESLIE
Foxy.

TED
And that kind of a twitch when she walks.

LESLIE
For sure.

TED
This is not disturbing you?

LESLIE
No.

TED
Just a little man talk.

LESLIE
The old locker room spirit — right?

TED
Right.

LESLIE
Which reminds me, Mr. Bean, Rosella tells me you're a sports fan.

TED
You, too?

LESLIE
Damn straight. You see the Jets yesterday?

TED
Wouldn't have missed 'em.

LESLIE

What a team: two and six this season, so I wasn't expecting much.

TED

You get much?

LESLIE

You saw the game?

TED

You get much from Rosella? You know what makes her scream? Has she taught you that little trick that really drives her wild—the one with two fingers and an ice cube? Well, what is this? I have great difficulty believing that blush ever saw the inside of a locker room, Mr. Jordan.

LESLIE

Are you suggesting that I am not a real man?

TED

Show and tell time, Leslie.

LESLIE

You surprise me.

TED

If I was that good at drag, I think I'd watch the innuendoes.

LESLIE

Statistically speaking, Mr. Bean, men who are into female apparel are more often than not exclusively heterosexual.

TED

But you are what I would describe as extremely sensitive, Leslie. The lightest reference to twat—

(As LESLIE jumps)

—there!—and you're all to pieces. Are real men ever so sensitive?

LESLIE

Very few. But the possibility still exists. And if you don't believe it exists, I don't care if you do believe I'm a man, because I wouldn't want to work for you anyhow.

(Standing)

So just forget it. And thank you for your time.

TED

Leslie.

LESLIE

What?

TED

Calm down.

LESLIE

That was just another of your little tests? Oh, dear — I'm sorry.

TED

Don't be. It's refreshing to find someone who's truly fond of canned soups and still has any finer feelings left. I'd almost forgotten the combination's possible. Sit down, won't you?

(As LESLIE sits)

Rosella's right, you see. I would indeed rather work with a man, not because of a preference for men, but because I worship women.

LESLIE

And you don't think women should work?

TED

I don't think women should work *here*. God — anywhere — just not here.

LESLIE

But why?

TED

You have a color television?

LESLIE

Yes.

TED

Then you know how sometimes the color goes, so you fiddle around with the aerial and it generally comes right back. Well that's what happened to me about the time I got moved into this job: the color just drained right out of my life, and I couldn't find any aerial to fiddle with. First thing I thought was, the trouble might be here in me, that I had allowed myself to get locked into this corporation that shuffles you around without a lot of previous consultation — and pays you damn well for going without a murmur. So I thought it might be that, or maybe the kids.

(Showing Leslie the photographs)

That's little Helen and this is Freddy. They are in secondary schools costing respectively four thousand and three thousand six hundred dollars a year, and the Lord knows what their college tuitions'll be like. And this is my wife, big Helen. She has impeccable taste—married me, didn't she?—but it all costs money. So for a while there I thought I might be seeing things in black and white because of the necessity of bringing in an awful lot of cash for people who don't always grasp what you have to go through to get it. I figured I'd feel the same in any job. But then I began to realize that there is something about this job in particular, that this job is a constant, daily reminder of the magic that's all but dead in the world, and what we do here is part of the process that killed it. It's hard enough on a man. I would prefer not to subject a woman to this brutalizing atmosphere.

LESLIE
But you hired Rosella.

TED
If the woman's already brutalized, it doesn't matter so much. Christ—sorry. Forgot you're living with her.

LESLIE
Those awful things you said about Rosella—you had to be sure I'm a man. Isn't that why you said them? You and Rosella . . .

TED
I haven't laid a finger on her.

LESLIE
What about the others? The other men here?

TED
You know man talk, Leslie. It doesn't necessarily mean anything.

LESLIE
But you believe it?

TED
Let me put it this way. There are only two basic kinds of woman in the world, the good ones, the goddesses—and the rest. I could be one hundred percent diametrically wrong about Rosella, but somehow I just can't see her as a goddess, can you?

(As LESLIE stands and heads for the door)
Leslie, wait. Where are you going?

LESLIE
You think I could work here now—work with Rosella—knowing what all you men are saying?

TED
You wouldn't be working *with* Rosella. You'd be working *over* her. Makes all the difference. If you really care about that girl, you could do her a big favor, shape her up, keep her from being so — free with herself. Of course, if I'm right about Rosella, her kind of woman only understands one thing, which is brute domination. And now I think about it, you just may not have it in you to treat some cunt —

(As LESLIE reacts)

— there! — you're sensitive. And that is something to be treasured. Maybe it's better you don't work here. Men and women, it coarsens us all. Good luck, Leslie.

(TED appears to loose himself in his work. When LESLIE speaks again, after a pause, there is a new note in her voice. It is not yet self-assured, but aimed in that direction.)

LESLIE
What would I be doing?

TED
Hmm?

LESLIE
If I got the job, what would I be doing?

TED
Sharing some of the load with me.

(Finding a paper on his desk)

Here, for instance: publicity on a new line we're testing. God — it even makes the chicken vegetable look good: Start the day the Homecooked way.

LESLIE
Soup for breakfast?

TED
It wasn't my idea.

LESLIE
That's too bad. I think it's marvelous.

TED
Seriously?

LESLIE
(Returning to the desk)

I told you, Mr. Bean, I love your soups. Why so negative?

TED

Because, sitting in this office, I have come to understand the profound effect canned soup has had on the war between — on the way men and women relate. But as to this job . . .

LESLIE

(Sitting)
Tell me about the war.

TED

The war. All right. The way I've come to see it, there used to be a balance between the sexes — tense, but still a balance. Man went out to hunt and kill and bring home the bloody carcass. And woman forgave him for killing. She hallowed the dead thing and turned it into the stuff of life.

LESLIE

By cooking?

TED

Exactly. And even though the killing was necessary, somehow the function of forgiveness always seemed the more important. Man came increasingly to resent this fact, which is why he took so much away from woman — financial power, political power. He even travestied woman at the soup pot as witch at the caldron and burned her. But what he could never take is her essential power, because it's spiritual. Man has bloody hands and only woman can clean them. That is her gift. Nothing can strip it from her, but she can give it away — as she has. And in return for what? A mess of pottage. Convenience. Canned soup. We don't need a priestess in the kitchen — just a can opener. But men do still get dirty, don't they, Leslie? And now there's no one to make us clean again. Is it any wonder I loathe this job?

LESLIE

But the way you talk about it — it hasn't coarsened you.

TED

You're surprisingly easy to talk to. These thoughts go round in my head. I need someone to share them with. Thank you, Leslie.

LESLIE

Thank you, Mr. Bean.

TED

(Touching her hand)
Ted.

                    LESLIE
Ted.

                    TED
        (Abruptly withdrawing his hand)
I'm sorry.

                    LESLIE
It's fine.

                    TED
You seem so real. Is it hard to do?

                    LESLIE
Not with practice.

                    TED
And when you're dressed this way, you feel like a woman, too?

                    LESLIE
How is that supposed to be?

                    TED
Light, I'd think, and open—wonderfully open.

                    LESLIE
The opposite, Ted. Quite the opposite.

                    TED
Then why do it?

                    LESLIE
If it's what you're born for, it's hard to stop doing. But you've thought about it yourself—dressing up?

                    TED
I've speculated.

                    LESLIE
Go on.

                    TED
Well, the image I get—I realize you're the one with all the practical experience.

                    LESLIE
I said, go on.

                    TED
The image I keep getting is the first day of fall, when it's still warm

but the air is clear and the sky is that deep forever blue you never see in summer. And I'm running on a beach, not so people notice. I'm something they take for granted, like one of those birds — sanderlings, are they? — the little brown ones that dart right down to the tide.

LESLIE
You have an image like that, and you've never — experimented?

TED
With dressing up? Not really. Just for shows at school — and in church. I used to be an acolyte — you know? — long red cassock, lovely white surplice. Whenever I had them on, I remember, I did feel a very deep sense of peace. But now when I try to go back to church, I can never stay through till the end, which is the whole point — isn't it? — the blessing. The hymns make me cry. People look at me strangely. I have to leave.

(LESLIE takes off her beret and hands it to Ted.)

LESLIE
Try this.

TED
What?

LESLIE
People look at you strangely because they think you're a man. Women are allowed to cry — almost expected to.

TED
Try it here?
(As LESLIE nods)
I can't.

LESLIE
Why not?

TED
Rosella could walk in any second.

LESLIE
Who's the boss? Look, Ted, if this was a locker room and you and me were teammates, we'd change clothes together, suit up. O.K.? So what is an office but the locker room for the big corporate game — right?

TED
Right.

LESLIE
And who is the captain of this particular team if not Mr. Theodore (Ted) Bean — right?

TED
Right.

LESLIE
And can't the captain wear any goddamn thing he goddamn well pleases?

TED
Goddamn right.

LESLIE
So try the hat on, Ted.

TED
(Picking up the phone and dialing a single number)
Rosella? No disturbances for the next five minutes.

(TED hangs up, stands and, taking the beret, crosses to the closet, which He opens. He puts the beret on, examines himself in the mirror inside the closet door, then turns to Leslie.)
Well?

LESLIE
It's a start. Take off your jacket, Ted.

(Standing as He does so)
Good. A few well-chosen accessories, you could cry your eyes out and nobody'd look at you twice.

TED
I wouldn't have to worry what hymn they were going to play — even — "The Day Is Past and Gone." You know it?

LESLIE
No.

TED
(Singing)
"The day is past and gone."

LESLIE
Let's see you without the tie.

(TED pulls his tie out from under his vest, unknots and removes it. During the next few lines, LESLIE knots the tie loosely around her neck while TED, with little tucks and adjustments, gets into the spirit of his new costume.)

TED

People don't all know the same things any more, do they? That's one of the reasons why the hymn is so personally meaningful. It's by Sullivan, Sir Arthur Sullivan, so of course it reminds me of the operettas with Gilbert and the days when I used to do that sort of thing, at school. I went to a private boys school. We took all the parts ourselves.

LESLIE

You were one of the three little maids?

TED

I wasn't good enough for leads.

LESLIE

Just a chorine, eh?

TED

I liked being in the chorus for the same reason I liked being at the school. You see? We all read the same books and ate the same really horrible fried chicken and watched the same football games together. And what have we got today in the way of common, binding experiences? Pro ball? Television?

LESLIE

Homecooked Soups. Yes. You don't appreciate it, Ted. But we could be at war. The economy could go down the tubes. Everything we thought was good and true and dependable could just disintegrate. And your soups would still be exactly the same, everywhere, Maine to California. That means something. And if I am going to work here—

TED

The job is yours if you want it.

LESLIE

I said *if* I am going to work here, you have got to learn to take a more positive attitude.

TED

I will.

LESLIE

You'll have to learn to live in the present, too, not in the past and gone.

TED

I'm sorry. They were happy days.

LESLIE

Which are over. This is the here and now. And if we are going to work together in the here and now — if you are going to be my captain, Ted — I don't want you rooting for the other team.

TED

You see I can change.

LESLIE

There's more to it than buying your first pair of panty hose. The change has got to be in here. You have got to care about those soups. You have got to care about the whole soup lifestyle. Canned soup, Ted: self-contained nutrition, the one perfect food for spaceship earth. And so simple. You don't need anyone to fix it for you. A couple of seconds in the microwave and there it is, piping hot, ready to eat. And you don't need anyone to eat it with. In fact, if all a guy has got is some broad he can't really count on — or a broad like this big Helen of yours, who all you can count on is, she'll spend you into the poor house — face it man, if that's all we've got, we're better off alone. We can give more time to the company. Sell more soup. Canned soup: the food of self-reliance — hell, Ted, the existential food of the future. That's what we've got to get out there and push.

TED

We?

LESLIE

Yes.

TED

Then you'll take the job?

LESLIE

If you can shape up.

TED

With you here I can.

LESLIE

Ted —

(Shaking hands)
—it's a deal.

TED
What a blessing.
(Removing the beret and returning it)
God—the weight you can take off my back.
(Picking up the phone and dialing a single number)
Rosella? Will you step in here a minute?
(Hanging up)
She'll be so happy.

LESLIE
Will she indeed?

TED
Not at first, perhaps. I suppose she's not accustomed to being kept on a short leash. But in time I'm sure she'll be grateful you care enough to take a firm hand with her. Firm and manly—eh, Leslie? That's the ticket.

(As ROSELLA enters, carrying her steno pad, TED puts on his jacket.)

Ah, Rosella.

ROSELLA
Mr. Bean.

TED
Sorry I snapped like that. You'll accept my apology?

ROSELLA
Yes, sir.

TED
Thank you. Now, have the hydroponic farmers arrived?

ROSELLA
They just got in.

TED
(To Leslie)
You'll excuse me? I have to do an interview for "Soup's On." My tie?

(Startled, LESLIE removes the tie and gives it to TED, who reties it and stuffs it under his vest. ROSELLA eyes this exchange with wonder and suspicion.)

Thanks. "Soup's On" is our house organ, Leslie — and after this next issue, your baby, all yours.

ROSELLA

Miss Perez and Miss Fong are still out there.

TED

Do they talk English?

ROSELLA

Yes.

TED

Then tell 'em Leslie's got the job, Rosella. Isn't that grand?

(Whistling "The Day Is Past and Gone," TED exits.)

ROSELLA

What the hell is going on here?

LESLIE

That is what I would like to know.

ROSELLA

What did you have to do to get this job?

LESLIE

Just grow up. What do you have to do to stay here? The old ice cube routine? The little trick with two fingers that makes you scream?

ROSELLA

What was that man telling you? Lies! Lies about me — and you believed them?

LESLIE

Whatever it was, Rosella, it wasn't all lies.

ROSELLA

Meaning?

LESLIE

If we are going to work together — I should say, if you are going to work for me — if you are going to be my secretary — I don't even know how good you are.

ROSELLA

Damn good.

(LESLIE sits in Ted's chair.)

LESLIE

I'm tired of taking so much on faith. Happiness is knowing things for sure.

ROSELLA

What is this, Leslie?

LESLIE

I'd like some proof, Rosella, some hard evidence. You've got your steno pad?

ROSELLA

Of course.

LESLIE

Would you like to sit?

ROSELLA

All right.

(As ROSELLA sits, LESLIE swings her feet up onto the desk.)

LESLIE

O.K. Take a letter . . . cunt.

(Blackout and curtain.)

THE EDITOR

Felice Picano's poetry, essays, short stories, interviews, book and drama reviews, and excerpted novels have appeared in *Mouth of the Dragon, Gay Sunshine, Fag Rag, Poetry Now, Island Fire, Orgasms of Light, Gaysweek Arts and Letters, Gay Community News, Christopher Street, Mandate, Blueboy, Drummer, The London Gay News, German Esquire, Little Casear, The Islander, New Dawn*, etc.

His four novels, *Smart as the Devil*, 1975, *Eyes*, 1976, *The Mesmerist*, 1977, and *The Lure*, 1979, have been published in England, France, Germany, Spain, Portugal, Argentina, Brazil, Australia, the U.S. and Japan; several were best-sellers and Literary Guild selections. His book of poetry, *The Deformity Lover*, 1978 is now in its third printing. Short stories have appeared in a half dozen anthologies in the U.S. and England.

Picano plans to have his fifth novel, *Late in the Season* published by Delacorte in 1981. A novella, *An Asian Minor: the True Story of Ganymede as Told by Himself*," will also appear in 1981. He is currently putting together a book of gay themed short stories, *Gay Tragic Romances*, a new book of poetry, *Window Elegies and other Poems*, and is beginning another novel.

Lest all of this suggest ambition, or worse, some kind of puritan work ethic, Picano wishes to assure his readers he is merely trying to keep out of trouble and off the streets: a not completely successfully realized goal at this time—as many will testify.